Shadow and Reality

What was it like to be a Christian in the first three hundred years after the life of Christ? What vision inspired the Christians of that era? What message does primitive Christianity have for modern man?

In this book, Herbert Musurillo provides the answers. From the writings of the primitive fathers, he has selected those passages that illuminate their world and their beliefs. The translations are his own—in clear and modern English that renders faithfully the thought and style of men who saw the world as a shadow cast by the reality of heaven.

Here, the early Christians speak for themselves. And so do the pagans who witnessed the spread of this "foreign sect" throughout the Roman Empire. With Professor Musurillo as guide, the reader finds the world of the primitive church come alive—an experience not soon forgotten.

Other MENTOR-OMEGA Books
of Related Interest

THE DEAD SEA SCROLLS AND PRIMITIVE CHRISTIANITY
by Jean Danielou

A Jesuit Professor at the Catholic Institute of Paris
demonstrates the relationship between the facts revealed in the ancient scrolls and the traditional view
of Christian faith. (#MP405—60¢)

DAILY LIFE IN THE TIME OF JESUS
by Henri Daniel-Rops

A comprehensive study of the land and people, political, economic, scientific, and cultural currents, as they
existed in Palestine during the time of Jesus. Translated by Patrick O'Brian. (#MQ570—95¢)

THE LOVE OF LEARNING AND THE DESIRE FOR GOD
by Jean Leclerq, O.S.B.

A study of the manuscripts of the medieval monas-
teries reveals their role in preserving the culture of
the past. By a distinguished scholar and Benedictine
monk. (#MT432—75¢)

VARIETIES OF MYSTIC EXPERIENCE *by Elmer O'Brien*

This is an anthology and interpretation of the key
writings of the major mystics—from Plotinus and
Origen through John of the Cross and Fenelon.
(#MT631—75¢)

The Fathers
of the
Primitive Church

by HERBERT MUSURILLO, S.J.

A MENTOR-OMEGA BOOK

Published by

THE NEW AMERICAN LIBRARY, New York and Toronto
THE NEW ENGLISH LIBRARY Limited, London

From twenty centuries of literature
and scholarship, Mentor-Omega Books
present a treasury of Catholic thought
for the modern reader.

TO JAMES H. REID, S.J.

Imprimi Potest:
John J. McGinty, S.J.
Provincial

Nihil Obstat:
Edward J. Montano, S.T.D.
Censor Librorum

Imprimatur:
Terence J. Cooke, D.D., V.G.

Copyright © 1966 by Herbert Musurillo

FIRST PRINTING, MARCH, 1966

Library of Congress Catalog Card Number 65-22036

MENTOR TRADEMARK REG. U.S. PAT. OFF. AND FOREIGN COUNTRIES
REGISTERED TRADEMARK—MARCA REGISTRADA
HECHO EN CHICAGO, U.S.A.

MENTOR-OMEGA BOOKS are published *in the United States*
by The New American Library, Inc.
1301 Avenue of the Americas, New York, New York 10019,
in Canada by The New American Library of Canada Limited
295 King Street East, Toronto 2, Ontario,
in the United Kingdom by The New English Library Limited,
Barnard's Inn, Holborn, London, E.C. 1, England

PRINTED IN THE UNITED STATES OF AMERICA

PREFACE

The following Introduction and selections from the writings of the Fathers of the primitive Church are intended to be a stimulating sampling of the wonderful riches and vast resources of the early Christian period. The texts span the period from Clement of Rome (A.D. 90) to Athanasius and the first ecumenical Council of Nicaea (325). The general tone that seems to characterize the theology of the Church in the pre-Nicene period is represented by Origen and the Alexandrian school, who regarded the obscurity of our present faith as the shadow for the divine reality which will be revealed to us. Athanasius, the great giant of the Arian controversy, was truly the last Father to think within the mold of the pre-Nicene Church, and he formed the link with the golden age of fourth-century theology.

I have tried to introduce the student to the best texts and the most interesting sources, always in my own translations, and without theological preoccupation. The panorama is indeed too vast for a single volume, and of necessity I have had to be selective. All throughout, the focus is on the themes that bind Christians rather than the dogmas that divide them. But as Ignatius of Antioch wrote in Section 2 of his letter to bishop Polycarp: "You cannot cure every wound with the same bandage. . . . The season bids you to reach unto God, just as pilots look for the winds and the storm-tossed sailor seeks the harbor. . . . But the prize is immortality and eternal life. Of this you are certain." For the shadows of this world, however dark, surely lead us to the reality that is to come.

CONTENTS

Preface   v

Introduction   11

1. Clement of Rome
   First Epistle   49

2. *The Didache*   57

3. *The Epistle of Barnabas*   63

4. *The Second Epistle of Clement to the Corinthians*   67

5. Ignatius of Antioch   72
   Ignatius to the Ephesians   74
   Ignatius to the Trallians   75
   Ignatius to the Romans   75
   Ignatius to the Smyrnaeans   76
   Ignatius to Bishop Polycarp of Smyrna   77
   Polycarp to the Philippians   78
   The Martyrdom of Bishop Polycarp   80

6. *The Shepherd of Hermas*   88

7. The Pagan Reaction
   The Palatine Graffito   102
   The Christians of Bithynia and Pliny   103
   Pliny's Letter to Emperor Trajan   105
   Trajan's Reply   107
   Lucian of Samosata   107
   The Story of Peregrinus   109

8. Inscriptions from the Roman Catacombs   111
   The Magic Square   114

9. The Age of the Apologists and Gnosticism   117
   The Gospel of Thomas   120
   "A Hymn of the Naassenes"—from Hippolytus'
       Refutation of all Heresies   122

vii

The Secret Book of John   122
The Odes of Solomon   125
The Gospel of Truth   129
"Light Serene"   131
St. Justin the Martyr   132
The First Apology of St. Justin   133
The Dialogue with Trypho of St. Justin   134

10. Irenaeus of Lyons   136
    Against Heresies   137

11. Melito of Sardis   142
    On the Pasch   144

12. *The Address to Diognetus*   146

13. The African Church
    The Acts of the Scillitan Martyrs   150
    Tertullian   152
    On Flight in Time of Persecution   155
    On the Flesh of Christ   156
    Against Praxeas   157
    On the Prayer   158
    The Adornment of Women   158
    Apologia for Christianity   159
    The Passion of Saints Perpetua and Felicitas   161

14. Minucius Felix: *Octavius*   173

15. Hippolytus of Rome   183
    The Apostolic Tradition   184

16. Clement of Alexandria   188
    From the *Paedagogus*—"Hymn to the Savior"   189
    Paedagogus   190
    Exhortation to the Pagans   191
    Tapestries   191
    Who Is the Rich Man Who Is Saved?   192

17. Origen of Alexandria   194
    From *First Principles*—On Man's Free Will   199
    From *On Prayer*—Man's Will and God's
       Foreknowledge   200

From *Against Celsus*—The Power of Christian
  Virtue   201
From *Homilies on Leviticus*—The Allegorical
  Interpretation of Scripture   202
First Principles   202
From *Homilies on Numbers*—Origen on the
  Atonement   203
From *Commentaries on the Song of Songs*—The
  Love of the Mystic for Jesus   204
*Origen's Discussion with Heraclides and His Fel-
  low Bishops on the Father, the Son, and the
  Soul*   205

18. Methodius of Olympus   212
    From the *Symposium*—"Thecla's Hymn"   214

19. Cyprian and the Decian Persecution
    St. Cyprian of Carthage   220
    On the Unity of the Church   221
    A Document from the Decian Persecution   225
    The Martyrdom of St. Cyprian   226

20. Arnobius: *Against the Pagans*   229

21. Lactantius   234
    The Divine Institutes   237
    On the Deaths of the Persecutors   241

22. The Triumph of Constantine   243

23. Athanasius of Alexandria   244
    On the Incarnation of the Word   246
    Excerpts from *On Virginity*   249
    The *Life of Antony*   250

24. Christian Epitaphs
    The Abercius Inscription   260
    The Epitaph of Pectorius   262
    A Christian Curse-Inscription from Tanagra   263

Selected Bibliography   266

Index   269

INTRODUCTION

The story of the primitive Church begins with the mystery of the empty tomb. Theologically (Augustine, *On John* 9–10), the Church had been born from the heart of the Crucified as the blood and water poured from His spear-pierced side. But surely, as Paul wrote to the community at Corinth, "If Christ has not been raised, then our preaching is in vain and your faith is in vain" (I Cor. 15.14). For this event no other explanation has ever been put forward that would completely satisfy either the facts or the feelings of Christianity, save that of the announcement of the Good News: "He is risen as He said." [1]

After Christ's earthly life and the series of theophanies that followed it, the saddened band of disciples could only wait for the enlightenment of the Comforter who was to come. Hence the preternatural phenomena of Pentecost once again underlined the special mission of the disciples as "apostles," that is, as legates sent forth to men. Luke's vivid account in the Acts of the Apostles (2.1–42) comes from a generation later, but it surely enshrines a precious and traditional historical core. The phenomena of the shaken house, the rushing wind and the flames, the ecstatic speech with which those assembled in the upper room gave tongue to their experience, moved even those who had come to the Holy City for the feast. The word was quickly passed: the followers of the crucified Galilean had seen visions and dreamed dreams (Acts 2.17; Joel 2.28), and were designated to enroll all men under the name of Jesus, that is, of the Savior.

[1] For the earlier rationalist theories of the Resurrection, see C. Guignebert, *Jesus* (tr. by S. H. Hooke, New York: University Books, Inc., 1956), pp. 490 ff.; a sounder approach was reflected in E. Hoskyns and N. Davey, *The Riddle of the New Testament* (London: Faber & Faber, Ltd., 1947). For a summary of the problems on the life of Jesus from Schweitzer to Bultmann and Bornkamm, see Hugh Anderson, *Jesus and Christian Origins: A Commentary on Modern Viewpoints* (New York: Oxford University Press, 1964).

The Apostolic Kerygma

Even at this early stage, before the more formal organization of later years, we hear of the "church, the apostles, and the elders" (Acts 15.6), corresponding loosely to the political structure of the Hellenistic communities; there was no clear blueprint, worked out in every detail, of how the Church would proceed from day to day now that the Master was gone. And yet we learn that there were two focal points in the growth of the early communities (Acts 2.42): the apostolic preaching of the Good News and the communion in the breaking of bread. Thus, apart from almsgiving and works of mercy, the entire spiritual activity of the first Christians centered about the catechesis and the liturgy. We know that in the days of Paul's missionary activity, the liturgical synaxis culminated, after the communal meal, in the narrative of the Lord's final, Messianic banquet (I Cor. 12.23–26) and the sacramental sharing of the body and blood of the Lord. But attendance at these mysteries was restricted to those who had been enlightened and baptized. On the other hand, there was the apostolic kerygma, which in its most primitive form consisted of a brief account of Jesus' life, works, and death as the suffering Servant of Iahweh in the spirit of Isaiah, the promised Messiah (Acts 2.22 ff.; 3.12 ff.; 4.24 ff.). These impassioned instructions, which often concluded with an ecstatic manifestation of the Spirit, provide glimpses of the essence of the evangelion, the proclamation of the Good News. The evangelion similarly complemented the practice of Jesus Himself, who would visit the synagogues and after the reading of a passage from the prophets declare, "Today this scripture has been fulfilled in your ears" (Luke 4.18 ff.). Narrative-fulfillment, the outpouring of the Spirit, the immersion of baptism, and the sharing in the Lord's mysteries constituted the regular pattern of Christian life during these early days under the guidance of the apostles and their chosen assistants, the elders.

The most controversy among historians has centered about the crucial time from the death of Jesus until the publication of the Synoptic Gospels. During this period the apostles, under Peter, met at Jerusalem (Acts 15.9 ff.) to determine the policy of the Church with regard to Gentiles, and their course of action was confirmed by the subsequent preaching of Paul, Barnabas, and Timothy throughout the communities of Asia Minor and Greece. This break with the synagogue, signalized by the martyrdom of the deacon Stephen (Acts 7), was one of the chief points of difference between early Christianity and the Essenian community of Qumran. For the Church, as founded by Jesus upon the Rock, was always in essence universalist: it never suffered from the ingrown, ghetto atmosphere of the congregation we have come to know from the Dead Sea Scrolls. Surely the apocalyptic vision of the covenanters, their preoccupation with the symbolic war between the children of light and the offspring of Belial, had a clear affinity with the imagery of the Johannine gospel and the book of Revelation.[2] An examination of their biblical exegesis and their austere, celibate lives (not uncommon among Jewish monastic communities, as for example in Egypt) may shed some light on the origins of early Christian monasticism and the Gnostic repugnance for marriage as the work of the wicked Aeons. There were, indeed, a number of textual parallels between the Gospels and the Essene documents; and it was only natural that many of the first Christian writers, especially those of Jewish descent, should have drawn upon the same stream of apocalyptic, mystical, and ascetical Judaism that nourished the covenanters of Qumran. But many scholars, in the enthusiasm of the discovery, have perhaps exaggerated the dependence of Christianity upon Qumran. Obviously the environment that created the one and the other was the same, but one cannot pass from a reading of the Essenian documents to those of primitive Christianity without noticing a profound difference. We are at once in an entirely new world, since clearly the Essenes were too sheltered in their remote, unworldly enclave to envision the redemption and the conquest of the world by the sign of the Spirit and the power of the name of Jesus. It would therefore seem unjustified to attribute to this tiny and remote sect the origin of much of Chris-

---

[2] For a discussion of the relevance of the Scrolls for early Christianity, see, for example, A. Dupont-Sommer, *The Essene Writings from Qumran* (tr. by G. Vermes, Oxford: Blackwell, 1961), especially, pp. 368–78; Dupont-Sommer represents the most extreme position, suggesting that Jesus showed a "perfect agreement with the fundamental doctrines and spirituality of the sect," p. 377. For a more moderate view, see Jean Daniélou, *The Dead Sea Scrolls and Primitive Christianity* (tr. by S. Attanasio, Baltimore: Helicon Press, Inc., 1958; Mentor Omega Book, 1962). As Daniélou concludes, "This momentous discovery provides us with the setting in which Christianity was born . . . and certainly it helps us to see wherein the unique and distinctive character of Christianity lies," p. 128.

tianity's "organization, rites, doctrines, 'patterns of thought,' and its mystical and ethical ideals." [3]

Between the Council of Jerusalem and the spread of the four Gospels different tales soon took form: Logia, or sayings; healing tales; parables; accounts of the Lord's passion and death. The neophytes were eager to learn of "Jesus of Nazareth, a man attested to you by God with mighty works and wonders and signs which God did through him in your midst, as you yourselves know—this Jesus, delivered up according to the definite plan and foreknowledge of God" (Acts 2.22–23). Hence it was that the first need of the Christian community was for men skilled in writing a narrative in Greek of the Lord's words and works. Even the earliest Gospels, Mark and Matthew, display a highly sophisticated narrative technique, which had affinities with Hellenistic biography and miracle story and the Hebrew midrash. And yet the Gospel is itself a unique form: it is an announcement of prophecy fulfillment, and biographical elements are subordinated to the eschatological message. Thus the Gospels are the complement of Christ's own preaching as reflected in the eighteenth and following verses of Chapter 4 in Luke, where Jesus, after reading a passage from Isaiah in the temple, comments: "Today this Scripture has been fulfilled." Luke and Acts, however, more closely approximate history in the Hellenistic manner. They emphasize an "orderly account," and the scrutiny of the sources that the neophyte Theophilus "may know the truth concerning the things" he had already heard from the oral catechesis (Luke 1.3–4). The three Synoptics, as they are called, are closer because of their methods and use of common source materials. The Gospel of John, however, remains quite removed from the spirit of the other three by virtue of its intense religious unity and highly artistic selection of details. John's work emerged from a Christian community that appreciated the force of symbolism and allegory; his book is primarily a book of signs, set down as a witness to the truth of Jesus' mission as the Logos, or the Word of God (John 20.30). As the series of "signs" unfolds, the theme of John's prologue and the first Johannine epistle becomes apparent: the story of Jesus is a struggle between the Light and the prince of Darkness, and the children of Light are ranged in mortal combat against the sons of wickedness. Thus the narrative of events takes on a further, symbolic dimension that is

---

[3] Dupont-Sommer, *op. cit.*, p. 373.

realized especially in the healing of the man born blind (John 9.13 ff.), the raising of the dead Lazarus (John 11.17 ff.), culminating in the Pharisaic plot against Jesus' life. The Darkness breeds hatred and malice: the Light brings simplicity and love. "Men loved the darkness rather than light" (John 3.19); but those who by faith have accepted the light have passed from death to life (John 5.24). The Fourth Gospel's subtle mysticism and its stress upon the link between sign and intellectual assent reveal a kinship with the contemporary Jewish scholar, Philo of Alexandria, and anticipate the apologetic and allegorical tendencies of Origen and the Alexandrian school.

Since the nineteen-twenties scholars under the influence of Martin Dibelius and Rudolf Bultmann have striven to analyze the Gospel narratives in terms of certain Jewish-Hellenistic literary forms, or genres, which were claimed to be the relics of the evolving oral catechesis, reflecting the concrete religious experience, the so-called *Sitz im Leben* of the Christian community. Some of the early categories which Dibelius invoked were the parable; the paradigm, or illustrative tale; the legend; the passion story; Bultmann and his disciples discovered still further divisions. To the scholar who approaches the problem from the viewpoint of pagan classical and Hellenistic literature, the parallels are perhaps not impressive; and whatever be the final judgment on the success of the form-critical school, it must be admitted that such analysis derives largely from a scrutiny of the Gospels themselves, and the "form" remains a postulate of the preliterary Christian catechesis rather than a genre or form in the traditional sense. In any case, no analytical method can lose sight of the fact that the catechesis and the liturgy were the two great foci of the religious energy and dynamism of the primitive Church, and it is within this context that we are to mark the origin and development of all early Christian creativity. Hence the method of form-criticism, as inaugurated by Dibelius, Bultmann, and their followers, is pursued in highly different ways by Scripture scholars. In the long run, despite the many years of analysis and scrutiny, the Gospels have not yet delivered up their mystery. For there is really little evidence of contemporary form-development aside from the actual Gospels themselves, and to say that what we find therein is very much like the stories found in the later satirist Lucian, the Talmud, or the pre-Christian healing stories from the medical shrine at Epidaurus, is no satisfactory explanation.[4] The analytic approach of English scholars like G. Kilpatrick and C. H. Dodd,[5] which attempts to support the historical substance behind the Scriptural narrative in terms of biblical preoccupations of the early Christian community, would seem much more fruitful. For to conclude, as Bultmann does,[6] that Christianity is based on little more than a Gnostic redemption myth is not only to go beyond the evidence, it is perhaps to undermine the foundations of Christian belief. Thus the problem of the "form" in early Christian literature goes far beyond the requirements of literary analysis and enters into the domain of historical criticism.

As the Church spread from Palestine through Asia Minor, Greece, and Italy, a new form of instruction developed: the epistle sent out to distant communities and destined to be read in one or more churches. In fact, we derive our most detailed knowledge of the worship and practice of the churches during this earliest period before the Apostolic Fathers from the Pauline epistles. Moreover, the laws of the Christian catechesis are operative in Paul, in the handing down of an oral tradition, not only about the Church's teaching, but also about the events of Jesus' life. This process of transmission has much in common with the rabbinical Halakha—with the result that the oral preservation of truth was perhaps far more rigid than the form critics would seem to suggest.[7] From Paul, however, came the first account of the Last Supper and the apparitions of the risen Christ, antedating even the Gospels, since it appears in the first epistle to the Corinthians (11.23–34; 15.1–8). Paul

---

[4] See M. Dibelius, *A Fresh Approach to the New Testament and Early Christian Literature* (tr. by B. L. Woolf, London: Ivor Nicholson & Watson, Ltd., 1936); for a more moderate approach, see Anderson, *op. cit.*, pp. 32 ff.

[5] See G. D. Kilpatrick, *The Origins of the Gospel According to St. Matthew* (London: Oxford University Press, 1946); C. H. Dodd, *The Apostolic Preaching and Its Developments* (London: Hodder & Stoughton, Ltd., 1936). See also K. Stendahl, *The School of St. Matthew* (Uppsala: Univ. Nytestamentlige Seminar, Acta, 20, 1954). One of the solid contributions of the present century is Matthew Black, *An Aramaic Approach to the Gospels and Acts* (2nd ed.; London: Oxford University Press, 1954).

[6] See, for example, R. K. Bultmann, *Primitive Christianity in Its Contemporary Setting* (tr. by R. H. Fuller, New York: Meridian Books, 1956), pp. 196 ff. For a criticism see Anderson, *op. cit.*, pp. 37–38.

[7] See especially B. Gerhardsson, *Memory and Manuscript* (Lund: C. W. K. Gleerup Publishers, 1961), and R. P. C. Hanson, *Tradition in the Early Church* (London: Cambridge University Press, 1962).

prefaced his narrative with the words "what I also received"; and again, "I received from the Lord what I also delivered to you." Here are no traces of the popular tale that circulated until it was embellished with vivid detail.

From Paul came our earliest historical portrait of the assemblies of the early Church; he spoke of the tendency to drunkenness at the agape and the petty squabbling (I Cor. 11.18–21), the disorder among Christians vying to be heard as they spoke, or at least thought they spoke, in tongues (I Cor. 14.26; 14.10–12). By this time Christians met separately, away from the synagogue, in a private meeting place or in a house (see Philemon 2). Paul mentioned the apostles, prophets, bishops, or presbyters ("elders"), deacons and deaconesses in the organization of the various churches; however, Ignatius of Antioch would point out that presbyters were of a lower order, distinct from the bishops or "overseers" of the community.

The Johannine book of Revelation, or the Apocalypse, was written as an open letter to the seven oldest churches of Asia Minor. Composed by John while he was in exile on the island of Patmos (Apoc. 1.9), it was to be delivered to the seven "angels" or bishops of Ephesus, Smyrna, Pergamum, Thyatira, Sardis, Philadelphia, and Laodicea, and for each bishop there was a special message. But the author himself called the book a prophecy (1.3), a revelation which will "show his servants what must soon take place." In tone and treatment it recalls the Jewish eschatology of the book of Daniel, and the late apocalyptic literature of *Enoch* and *Jubilees*. The solemnity of the heavenly scenes in the throne room of the Lamb and the frequent hymns (5.9 ff., 7.15 ff., 11.17 ff., 15.3 ff., 18.2 ff., 19.1 ff.) suggest the atmosphere of a Jewish liturgical service. To further complicate matters, strata of different periods of time were evidently combined in the final text of Revelation, which was intended at least in part as an anti-Roman polemic. The author's ecstatic visions are transformed into a highly complex and obscure symbolic texture that allows of many interpretations. Clearest, however, is the prophecy of the Church's triumph over the Roman Empire, symbolized as the harlot seated among the seven hills, "with whom the kings of the earth have committed fornication" (17.2). Unfortunately, the book throws very little light upon the organization of the early Church. Indeed, a mysterious fusion of prose poetry and Hellenistic allegory, the book of Revelation must have been difficult even for the early Christians to comprehend. It was a charism that was soon destined to pass away.

The Church Spreads

Thus structured under the apostles and their appointed
bishops, the Christian communities spread and flourished:
from Palestine (Jerusalem, Caesarea, Damascus, Sidon, etc.)
to Antioch in Syria, where the faithful were first called
Christians; [8] Tarsus, Lystra, Iconium, Perga grew up in
Asia Minor, with a heavy concentration of churches around
Ephesus, Miletus, Smyrna. In Greece there were Philippi,
Thessalonike, Athens, Aegina, Corinth; Salamis and Paphus
on the island of Cyprus; Cyrene and Alexandria in Africa;
in Italy there were communities at Pozzuoli and Rome. [9]
The second Christian century would see the rise of churches
at Vienne and Lyon in Gaul, and other cities in Germany,
Yugoslavia, around Carthage in North Africa, and even as
far as Pontus on the Black Sea. [10] As Tertullian would soon
shout triumphantly, "We are but of yesterday and we have
filled the world!" (*Hesterni sumus, sed vestra omnia imple-
vimus.*)

[8] See the twenty-sixth verse in the eleventh chapter of Acts.
The name probably originated from the popular (and sometimes
even derisive) labeling of the disciples of a particular philosopher
or school; compare Herodians (Matt. 22.16), Caesarians, etc.

[9] For a map of the first-century communities, see F. van der Meer
and C. Mohrmann, *Atlas of the Early Christian World* (tr. by M. F.
Hedlund and H. H. Rowley, London: Thomas Nelson & Sons, 1958),
p. 1.

[10] St. Peter's founding of the Church in Rome and his subsequent
role with regard to the whole Church have been sharply reexamined
by O. Cullmann, *Peter, Disciple, Apostle, Martyr: A Historical and
Theological Essay* (tr. by Floyd V. Filson, London: Student Christian
Movement Press, Ltd., 1953). His thesis that Peter was the leader
of the entire Church only at Jerusalem (see pp. 228 ff.) does not
explain the later patristic evidence—for example, the epistle of
Clement of Rome to the Corinthians (which Cullmann passes over),
Irenaeus, Cyprian. At no point in the early Church, even where
the evidence is admittedly scanty, is there any hint that the action
of the Roman Church was in the nature of a *usurpation* or an
unnatural development. Surely this early agreement is more striking than the silence upon which, for the most part, Cullmann bases
his case. For a discussion of Cullmann's thesis, see Otto Karrer,
Peter and the Church: An Examination of Cullmann's Thesis (tr.
by R. Walls, New York: Herder & Herder, Inc., 1963).

Roman Opposition

But the spread of the new Palestinian sect began to arouse the suspicion of the Roman authorities, who had always been quick to check the formation of political or religious clubs (*collegia*) that did not have the sanction of the official government. They not only felt that these new cults tended to undermine Roman morals, they feared that mutiny and rebellion could get an easy footing through the protected secrecy of of groups that met under the pretext of divine worship. For some time, too, as Suetonius and Dio Cassius suggest, there was public confusion about the relationship between the Christians and Jews. Indeed, the Christians as a group might well have avoided annoyance if they had formally claimed the privileges for their own customs and cult practices that the Jews had possessed at least since the time of Julius Caesar. Despite the discrimination from which the Jews suffered, especially in large cities like Alexandria, and the misunderstanding that was their usual lot in Italy, their religious freedom had been assured in Roman law. Why the early Church did not fight for the same privileges is one of the legal mysteries of primitive Christianity, and the consequences were to perdure for many centuries, even after the Constantinian victory at the Mulvian Bridge.

As it was, the difficulties were irreconcilable. The good Christian had been told to expect persecution, and in fact welcomed it as a test of his loyalty to the crucified Savior. And the loyal Roman official, especially under emperors who were intent on preserving the old Roman morality and traditions (such as Claudius, Trajan, Hadrian, Aurelius and Decius), had but one recourse: to crush this new Oriental sect which was gaining ever-increasing numbers of proselytes. They had various means: the illegality of private clubs or associations not approved of by the authorities; the principle of respect to the images of the emperor and his family, which if not adhered to was punishable under the law of treason; and, lastly, the general power Roman officials enjoyed of coercion, that is, of compelling Roman citizens or subjects to keep the peace, if necessary by imprisonment, exile, or flogging. An example is the famous letter of Pliny, proconsul of Bithynia, to the emperor Trajan, which relates how the Christians were suspected of breaking various laws, and as a test were asked to sacrifice before the images of the emperor and the gods. But not until the edict of Decius (249–50) was Christianity as such declared illegal and subject to the penalties of *lèse-majesté*. If before the reign of Decius we may not speak of a persecution of Christianity in the strict sense, this does not mean that the Christians might not often have been used as scapegoats, as they were under the reign of Nero, when they were publicly executed in cruel and sadistic ways to divert the attention of the populace from the suspicion that it was the emperor himself who was behind the burning of Rome. In spite of this, Tacitus (*Annales* 15.44) sharply suggests that the Christians were rightly punished, "for hatred of the human race," even though the penalties inflicted by Nero were excessive. About this time, according to the tradition, Peter and Paul were also executed in Rome. "It was Nero," according to Eusebius (*Ecclesiastical History* 2.25.5), "who began to put the apostles to death. The tradition is that Paul was beheaded in Rome and that Peter was crucified during Nero's reign; and this story is supported by the fact that their graves still have the names of Peter and Paul." And citing Dionysius, bishop of Corinth, Eusebius reports: "In our own city of Corinth both also founded our community and instructed us; similarly they preached together in Italy and suffered martyrdom together at the same time" (Eusebius, *Eccles. Hist.* 2.25.8).

Because of Rome's geographical position, all the great teachers of the mid-second century visited there at one time or another. The Gnostics Valentinus and Marcion preached their illuminationist doctrines, Justin established a school there and taught Tatian the Syrian (who would later adopt Gnosticism) and Irenaeus; Hermas, the author of *The Shepherd*, was a kinsman of Pope Pius (d. about 154); and Polycarp visited Rome shortly before his martyrdom. It was in Rome that the pagan doctor Galen resided under Marcus Aurelius, and perhaps here he penned his striking eulogy of the Christians who "preserved unbroken chastity throughout their entire lives." [11] In the Arabic version of Galen's *Summaries of Plato's Dialogues* (about A.D. 180), we read: [12]

For their contempt of death and its sequel is patent to us every day, and likewise their restraint in cohabitation.

[11] See Philip Carrington, *The Early Christian Church* (2 vols.; London: Cambridge University Press, 1957), ii, p. 257.

[12] R. Walzer (ed.), *Plato Arabus* (London: Warburg Institute, 1949), I, p. 99; see also R. Walzer, *Galen on Jews and Christians* (London: Oxford University Press, 1949).

For they include not only men but also women who refrain from cohabiting all through their lives; and they also number individuals who, in self-discipline and self-control in matters of food and drink, and in their pursuit of justice, have attained a pitch not inferior to that of genuine philosophers.

The influence of the Roman Church during this period, as Bishop Carrington suggests [13] derived not only from its being founded by Peter and Paul, but also from its central position, and its "solidity, conservatism, hospitality and generosity." [14] Thus its theology naturally gained stability and also its leadership of the Church as a whole.

The Christian Martyrs

The martyr literature of the second and third centuries offers a vivid portrait of the trials Christianity suffered at the hands of zealous government officials. In addition to the Julian law of treason, the ordinary police power allowed local magistrates to suppress all breaches of public order, even by violent means, especially when dealing with the class called *humiliores* (those without office or property), or inhabitants within the empire who were not full Roman citizens. Even when a Roman citizen was convicted of a capital crime (e.g. treason), which allowed the penalty of death by decapitation, normally the penalty would not be exacted and the guilty person would be sent into exile. So it was under Domitian, when the consul Flavius Clemens was executed for "atheism," whereas his wife Domitilla was banished to a deserted island (Dio Cassius *Roman History* 67.14); these were among the first Christians from the ranks of Roman nobility to be thus punished, and their names have been associated with tombs in the Catacomb of Domitilla, outside of Rome. For the ordinary "humble" Christian, who did not enjoy full Roman citizenship, the penalties for his crimes were painful and degrading. He had no chance for exile; he might be nailed to a cross, burned in an oven or over a slow fire, or finally exposed to the beasts of the amphitheater without the necessary weapons or knowledge to subdue them. The execution of the Christians condemned

---

[13] Carrington, *op. cit.,* p. 316.
[14] *Ibid.,* p. 88, with the list of Roman bishops from Linus on p. 71.

to the amphitheater also supplied added spectacles when the stock of gladiators ran out. Gibbon was unfair in accusing the ancient martyr acts of exaggeration; [15] but it must be admitted that, granted the general cruelty of the times, the conscientious Roman governors used only those means which would, they thought, reduce this new religion to submission, destroy its bishops or leaders, and terrify the general masses of believers. But they underestimated the vigor and pertinacity of the men and women whose glory it was to suffer persecution for the Name.

While the general body of believers were undergoing these ordeals from without, there were other forces at work within the Church itself. The first period of development belongs to the Apostolic Fathers: out of this time came the famous epistle of Clement of Rome, which attempted to settle the schism that arose at Corinth; the *Didache*, or *Teaching of the Apostles*, an important document for our knowledge of early liturgy and practice; the fascinating series of dream sequences called *The Shepherd* of Hermas; and the seven authentic letters of Ignatius of Antioch, composed while he was on his way to be martyred by the beasts of Rome under the emperor Trajan. Other documents considered as belonging to this period are the *Epistle of Barnabas* and an apologia for Christianity known as the *Address to Diognetus*, which may, however, be a compilation of much later date. Even at this early date the documents provide glimpses of the spirit and doctrine of the later Church, its hierarchy, liturgy, and austere moral code.

The middle of the second century inaugurated a period of great turmoil as well as dogmatic growth. The so-called Apologists, Justin, Tatian, Athenagoras, and others, mark the beginning of Christian polemic—an attempt to present the case for Christianity to the Jewish and Gentile world. In form many of these documents are open letters, ostensibly addressed to Roman magistrates; in practice they served as well to enlighten and encourage the faithful themselves. Justin's work epitomizes the orderly doctrine and apologetic of this early school and preserves for us some precious fragments of the primitive Greek Liturgy.

---

15 E. Gibbon, *The Decline and Fall of the Roman Empire* (2 vols.; New York: Modern Library, Inc., 1932), I, 467 ff.

Gnosticism

But the Church's interpenetration with the world led to more serious crises. About the middle of the second century, during the reign of Hadrian, the great Gnostic teachers flourished in Egypt, Syria, Pontus, and Rome. The more important writers were Basilides, Marcion, Valentinus, and Bardaisan, and their name is taken from the "secret doctrine" which they claimed to have directly from the Lord as an esoteric key to the Scriptures and tradition of the Church at large. Among their pretensions normally were long lists of genealogies, to explain the emanations of Christ, the angels, men, and devils, and the rise of evil in the universe. They anticipated Manichaeism by postulating two ultimate principles, one Good, the other Evil. Marcion and his group rejected the Old Testament and the "God of the Jews," and of the New he retained merely the Gospel of Luke, omitting the chapters on the childhood of Jesus. The stranger God of the New Testament, according to Marcion, sent His Son with merely an appearance of a body, to live in Galilee without birth, infancy, or baptism. The different branches of Gnosticism preached widely divergent doctrines, and there is admittedly little which unites them. But for the most part they taught a redemption by illumination, which is the privilege of the perfect and is an intuition of the destruction of the forces of the evil Aeons by the Son of God. In general they counseled against marriage, but it was common knowledge that the private lives of many of the early Gnostic theologians was not above suspicion.

Our main sources for the orthodox reaction against Gnosticism are the works of Irenaeus and Hippolytus; but there are references to their influence as late as Methodius of Olympus (A.D. 290) and even St. John Chrysostom, especially in his work *On Chastity* (about A.D. 390). But with the discovery in 1945/46 of thirteen Gnostic codices from the third or fourth century, written in Coptic and found near the village of Nag Hammadi in Egypt, we have been able to form a clearer idea of their doctrine and teaching, at least of the Egyptian sect, which seems to have been heavily Valentinian. Among the contents of the Jung Codex is the famous *Gospel of Truth*, which has now become a prime object in the study of second-century Gnosticism. The Syrian Gnostics seem to have been the first to use vernacular songs and hymns in connection with their liturgy and devotions, and those which we have preserved have a haunting, mystical beauty. The apocryphal *Acts of John* and *Acts of Thomas* contain several moving pieces; Hippolytus preserved a Gnostic hymn in his *Philosophumena*. The Syriac *Psalms of Solomon*, composed in imitation of the Hebrew psalter, but with a specifically Christian thematic background, may reflect traces of Gnostic belief. In any case, their profound reflective vision of Christ and the Virgin, the love that binds the members and the Head, gives these hymns a high place in the literature of the early Church.

Further Development of the Church

The proconsul Pliny wrote to the emperor Trajan (*Epistle* 10.96) that the Christians of Bithynia were wont "to meet before dawn to sing a hymn to Christ as to a god." Developing out of the Hebrew psalmody, the Christian hymn seems to have originated in the East, perhaps in imitation of the Gnostic psalms; found later in the West, it was used to add variety and devotion to the liturgical services. But the Christian hymn developed slowly, largely because of the authority of the biblical psalms and canticles. Ancient hymns are found at the end of Clement of Alexandria's *Paedagogus* and toward the close of Methodius of Olympus' *Symposium on Chastity*. The Byzantine hymn "Light Serene," used today in the Oriental liturgy, can be traced back perhaps to the middle of the second century; and a third-century Oxyrhynchus papyrus (P. Oxy. 1786) contains the words and music of a lovely doxology that is probably of Alexandrian origin. The popular hymn was one of the chief dogmatic vehicles of the primitive Church, and the songs of Arius and the Gnostics would find their rebuttal in the Trinitarian hymns of Alexandria and of Latin-speaking Europe. Only the fourth century would see the rise of the great Christian poets, the Syriac Ephraem of Nisibis, Prudentius of Saragossa, Paulinus of Nola, and Ambrose of Milan. Thus was inaugurated a great poetic, liturgical tradition which was shared in common by both East and West, but tended to be brushed aside in the heat of the dogmatic controversies that would later divide the Christian churches.

In the earliest days of the Church, all literature that was not intended for liturgical use was composed for one purpose: the defense or explanation of the faith for the instruction of the Christian or the information of their pagan or (less often) Jewish adversaries. The martyr acts, to begin with, arose from the practice of the Roman courts scattered throughout the empire. Roman notaries regularly preserved accurate court records of trials, and copies of these could usually be obtained by the parties involved. Some of these accounts of which copies were made remained comparatively unembellished, as for instance the *Acts of the Scillitan Martyrs* (A.D. 180); others like the *Martyrdom of Polycarp*, the *Martyrdom of Pionius*, and the *Acts of Apollonius*, were embellished for apologetic aims. Many of the accounts we possess were first collected by the historian Eusebius in the third century. The *Acts of St. Cyprian* are considered to be very close to the court record; but the more narrative, apocalyptic *Passion of Saints Perpetua and Felicitas*, emanating from Tertullian's circle about the first decade of the third century, would seem to have had the further purpose of glorifying the Montanist doctrine of the "spiritual man," who was independent of the established Church and followed the direct revelation of the Spirit. In these early acts, chronicles, and lives of saints (such as Athanasius' *Life of Antony*) the line between history and edifying fiction is sometimes very thin. However, the purely fictional biography is a fourth-century creation—such as, for example, St. Jerome's *Life of Paul the Hermit*—where the aim of edification and witness was felt to be of far greater value than the ascertainment of historical fact. Therefore, granted that the historian's task in studying the documents of the primitive period, before the Peace of the Church, may be a difficult one, still it is not impossible, and the general skepticism of Gibbon and of others is far too naïve to explain the growth of the Christian phenomenon. Even the Church historian Eusebius may not always have understood the evolution of Christianity in the centuries that preceded his own observations; and yet he managed to preserve a wealth of factual documents that allow the patient scholar to reconstruct the Christian story with a vividness that Eusebius himself did not perhaps grasp.

Sextus Julius Africanus (d. after A.D. 240) wrote the first Christian chronicle of world history; but his work was far surpassed by Eusebius of Caesarea, who was suspected of semi-Arianism after he had taken the oath of allegiance at Nicaea. Eusebius' *Chronicles* are preserved only in Armenian and remain a valuable source: his incomparable *Ecclesiastical History*, dealing with the Church from its beginnings to the victory of Constantine, is an invaluable witness, despite his lack of historical technique or analytic power. Eusebius' apologetic preoccupations made it impossible for him to recognize the struggle and growth of the Church in the world; but he at least made an attempt to bridge an enormous gap of knowledge by the preservation of ancient data and documents which would otherwise have been buried in oblivion. Even so, as a historian he was not completely uncritical, and the true evaluation of his achievement is yet to be established. Actually, in the present account I have attempted to dispense with the structure of Eusebius and allow the sources to speak for themselves.

Even before the fall of Jerusalem under the Roman invasion by Vespasian and his son Titus in A.D. 70, Christianity had begun to move westward through Asia Minor and Greece, now building upon remnants of Hellenistic Jewish communities, now striking out afresh under the inspiration of the Pauline vision. Greek became the dominant language of the Church; and the books that had been accepted into the Septuagint version of the Old Testament constituted the Christian canon. It was unfortunate, in many ways, that the Jewish communities abandoned this widely spread Greek bible and, under the pressure of disputation with the Christians, adopted only those books which were represented in the Hebrew, losing as a result many of the beautiful later books (some of which had been translated from the Hebrew) such as, for example, the Wisdom of Sirach, or Ecclesiasticus. But the migration out of Palestine was accelerated by the self-styled messiah, Bar Kokba's revolt,[16] which was finally crushed by Hadrian's legions, and the refounding of Jerusalem as a Roman city in A.D. 135. After this time the Jewish Christians submerged their identity in a now predominantly Gentile Church.

Christian Monasticism

Around the middle of the third century the so-called anchoretic (from the Greek *anachoreō*, to withdraw) movement began, as a new interpretation of the implication of

[16] In a cave used as a hideout by the rebels at Wadi Murabba'at, Jordan, were found a cache of documents connected with the uprising. In one of the letters, the leader calls himself "Simon Ben-Kosebah, prince of Israel." See F. M. Cross, *The Ancient Library of Qumran* (New York: Doubleday & Co., Inc., 1961), p. 18 for the discovery and the literature.

Jesus' message. As early as 162 the pagan doctor Galen had remarked on the Christians' extraordinary practice of chastity. And we know from the struggle with the Gnostics, this was not because of disdain for marriage or the notion that it was positively sinful, but rather from an exalted ideal of the way to Christian perfection. The ascetical movement received added impulse from the life and teaching of Origen of Alexandria, who, becoming a eunuch for the kingdom of heaven, showed how austerity and piety could best serve the interests of the Church in his severe devotion to the Scriptures and the work of the theological schools at Alexandria and Caesarea in Palestine. Eusebius, in his biography of Origen, given in the sixth book of his *Ecclesiastical History,* may well have exaggerated Origen's asceticism: but it must be confessed that the picture of the austere scholar denying himself to search the Scriptures had a deep influence upon later ascetical thought.

The pattern becomes clearer when we consider the effects of the painstaking investigation carried out under Decius in 249 to 250. Under pain of capital penalties all Romans had to obtain a *libellus* testifying that they had offered sacrifice and libation to the gods; and even the great bishop Cyprian of Carthage thought it prudent to flee to the hills to escape the temptation. For even those who had purchased documents of identity without performing the sacrifices were labeled *libellatici* and classed with those who had in fact denied the faith. Dionysius, bishop of Alexandria, tells us (in Eusebius' sixth book) that many good Christians sought to avoid the dilemma by running off to the caves and fertile oases of the Nile Valley. This had in fact been the regular practice of criminals and tax delinquents from the earliest days of the Roman administration. Their *anachorēsis,* or "retreat," hardly resulted from pious motives, and the native Egyptian knew the desert and its ways so well that no Roman legionary could find him. In any case, the pattern of escape had been laid down, and the Nile Valley had long been known as the settling place for groups of pious ascetics, both Jewish and Egyptian, some of whom followed the same sort of covenant as the Essenians of the Dead Sea. Thus many factors combined to make the Egyptian desert a fertile place for the blossoming monastic movement; and here all the older religious symbols, the battle against the darkness and the spirits of iniquity, the martyrdom of the flesh, being in the world but not of it, took new root and created a wholly new psychological milieu.

Not until about the year 270 do we hear of men and even women going off to the Egyptian desert for purely ascetical reasons, although from the *Symposium* of Methodius of Olympus (about 290) we infer that communities of ascetics had existed in the cities for some time before that. The first historical figure whom we can identify is the Copt, St. Antony, from Coma in the Nile Valley, and we owe the account of his life to a work that came out of Alexandria under the name of Athanasius. Whether or not it was indeed written by the controversial anti-Arian bishop, it does show Alexandria's orthodox position, which was that traditional Trinitarian views were supposed to be supported by authentic asceticism and mysticism, and subordinated to the legitimate hierarchy. The influence of the *Life of Antony*, especially in the Latin version (used especially for this edition) can hardly be estimated: monastic centers flourished throughout Italy, Gaul, England, and Ireland, in imitation of the great desert Fathers—even when the climate, customs, and religious environment seemed unfavorable. Composed in Alexandria about the year 356–7, the *Life* was translated into Latin only a few years afterward. Along with Origen's life and writings, it perhaps did more to establish the ascetic movement in and outside of Egypt than any other document in the history of the early Church.

St. Antony of Egypt

The *Life* was written in the form of a letter and addressed to the monks outside of Egypt who had requested from the Alexandrian bishop accurate details about the life of the sainted anchoret. The resulting moving portrait of the holy man, surrounded by the demons of the desert, relieving the afflicted, discoursing against the Arian heretics, and struggling with the vibrant drives of his own body, would remain an important symbol for many centuries to come. And, we are told in Section 47, "when the persecution had ended . . . Antony returned to his solitary hut and there became a *daily martyr in conscience,** continually fighting the battle of the faith." Thus, once the struggle against a hostile administration had ended in the Constantinian Peace, the next great religious movement came about: the growth of great monastic foundations, under St. Basil and Gregory of Nyssa in the East, and Cassiodorus, Benedict, Jerome, and Augustine in

* My italics.

the West. But all the roots of this religious phenomenon went back deeply into the second century, and the source of the vows and rules of the later Orders can be found in the intense religious fervor of the men and women who withdrew to the desert to confound the world and its demons and to be alone with Christ. Eventually, the ascetics grouped about one great leader, such as Antony, for advice and direction; and, later, rules were drawn up (as with Basil, Pachomius, and Augustine) for economical direction and purposeful achievement. In time, the strength of the monastic community would discomfit the established hierarchy in the capitals and cities throughout the empire, but this problem was not envisaged by the founder-bishops, Basil, Augustine, Ambrose, and the rest.

The Church and Hellenism

Those who, like Harnack, accuse the Fathers of Hellenizing Christianity have little sympathy for the magnitude of the task which lay before them: the dissemination of the implications of Christ's message for all men, and the meaning of His life and death. It is easy to speak of Hellenization; and yet it was precisely the questioning spirit of the Greco-Roman mind that challenged the principles of the Gospel and attempted to extract from the Bible a coherent dogmatic structure.

The spirit of the Apostolic Fathers was one of preservation, of holding fast to the *paradosis*, the transmitted truth. The Apologists, however, especially Justin the Martyr, attempted for the first time to "prove" the doctrines of Christianity in the systematic manner of the schools, and to defend Christian monotheism much as the enlightened Jews of Alexandria, on the testimony of the Scriptures, had commended their own received doctrines. Justin stressed the rational approach to the Christian notion of God as infinite and eternal; he preserved precious testimony of the sacramental liturgy of his day; but his concept of the Trinity and the work of the Atonement still awaited clarification by Irenaeus and the Alexandrian school.

Irenaeus of Lyons was the first of a long line of biblical theologians which would include Hippolytus, Origen, and the Cappadocians in the East, and Ambrose, Augustine, and Jerome in the West. Faced with the evolving Syrian and Egyptian Gnosticism, he presented a rational structure for the *paradosis* and supported it by the Scriptures, as taught by the legitimate hierarchy that traced its origin to the Apostles. In the Quartodeciman controversy (on the establishment of the date of Easter), Irenaeus interceded with Pope Eleutherius (about 174–89) to allow the Asiatic Christians to celebrate the death of the Lord on the first day of the Jewish Passover, 14th Nisan, a custom that went back apparently to apostolic times, whereas in the majority of churches, including Rome, the Lord's death was always commemorated on the Friday before Easter Sunday.[17] Although he conceded the stability and orthodoxy of the Church of Rome and agreed that it was necessary for all other churches to follow its lead in most cases, when it came to long-standing custom, as with the date of Good Friday, Irenaeus pleaded the cause of the minority and urged that it be allowed to retain its ancient practice. The controversy is now a dead one, but it is historically instructive as a blueprint for the amicable relationships among the various Christian churches, especially coming from a theologian of the loyalty and competence of Irenaeus.

Irenaeus also inaugurated Atonement theology. Christ the true Logos (whom the Gnostics had misunderstood), the divine Son, recapitulated in the flesh the entire race of mankind insofar as He came as the second Adam to restore the state of friendship with God and represented in Himself humanity's ultimate perfection to be attained by the restoration of the divine image in man. Although there are in Irenaeus' work traces of the Devil's Ransom theory,[18] he presented us with an authentic system of redemption: man's rebellion was restored by the total obedience of the Lord's Servant in a life which culminated in a sacrificial death. Jesus completed the incorporation of all men in God by leaving within the Church the memorial of His Passion and the doctrinal as well as sacramental means by which man may become united with God. Irenaeus thus laid the foundation for a complete biblical theology firmly founded upon the

---

[17] See the discussion in Carrington, *op. cit.*, pp. 374–91. For the problems confronting the Eastern churches at the present time on establishing a date for Easter, see Timothy Ware, *The Orthodox Church* (Baltimore: Penguin Books, 1963), pp. 304–10. A fixed calendar date for Easter would be a desideratum for all churches that follow the Gregorian or New style calendar.

[18] According to this theory, the Devil was tricked into thinking that Christ was a mere man; therefore Christ's death humiliated him and forced him to relinquish his hold upon mankind. The Devil is both paid the ransom for mankind and tricked at the same time.

meaning of Christ's Atonement and recapitulation as preserved within the liturgical life of the Church.

Much the same view of the Atonement was adopted by Methodius of Olympus in Lycia (about A.D. 290). Methodius was primarily a moral and ascetic teacher, dedicated to an intense revival of Stoic virtues within the framework of Christian chastity. His chief work, the *Symposium*, which was dedicated to a group of consecrated women of Lycia, is a glorification of chastity as the fulfillment of the Platonic Eros. For Methodius, Christ's passion was a mystic ecstasy in which He brought forth the Church; the Church, as Virgin Mother, continues to bring forth sons to Christ, the Archvirgin, nursing them with the milk of her grace and doctrine. Redemption for Methodius was a restoration of man's moral fortitude by the second Adam. Christ by His life and death, by His very assumption of the same clay from which Adam was made, restored to man the power to persevere in chastity—for this is the sign that man has regained the gifts lost in Paradise—but this is to be perfected by adhesion to the liturgy and the salutary doctrines of Mother Church. Methodius, though trained in Platonism and in the school of Origenist theology, revolted against both; and he adapted the Irenaean redemption theology for his own ascetical ends. The result is a curious mélange with overtones of an earlier subordinationism; and into this broad ascetical structure Methodius fully incorporated the theory of Christ's final return and thousand-year reign on earth.

Primitive Christian Eschatology

St. Paul's picture of Christ's final coming in the First Epistle to the Thessalonians was developed and, indeed, exaggerated by many of the early Fathers, especially the so-called Chiliasts, or those who believed that Jesus would come and, after raising the dead, reign over the just for a period of a thousand years. After this period, the good would be separated from the evil and the latter consigned to the torments of hell. Still others, who followed Origen and his disciples (among them, St. Gregory of Nyssa), maintained that even the damned would be restored at the end of many aeons, when God's justice would have been finally satisfied. The small group that held to the thousand-years reign included Irenaeus, Methodius of Olympus, Justin, Lactantius, Commodianus the Latin poet, and others. Of them all, Lactantius had the best description.[19] After Christ will have come down to earth, preceded by a cloud of fire and a legion of angels, the Devil will be bound and cast into a dungeon, and Christ will gather the just into a holy City. Here,

> Honey will drip from the stones and springs of wine and milk will gush forth. All wild beasts will be tame: the wolf will walk innocently with the sheep, the calf will feed with the lion, the dove will share with the hawk, and the serpent will lose his venom.

This will be the first resurrection. But at the end of the millennium, the beast will once more be unchained, and as the just are hidden underground, fire and brimstone will rain on earth, while the wicked will be allowed to fight and destroy themselves with the Devil gleefully in their midst. After this,

> There will be an earthquake; the mountains will be riven and the valleys sucked down into the Abyss; and the bodies of all the dead will be collected into a place called Polyandrion, the land of many men.

God will clothe the just in angelic shapes (this is in the Origenist tradition) and deliver the wicked to a fire of perpetual torment. Lactantius brought pagan and Christian eschatology together in violent confusion; but his picture would inspire poets and artists for many centuries, even when the doctrine of the Last Things had been purified and presented in a colder, more philosophic form.

The Early Liturgy

Despite the famous controversy on the date of Easter, the liturgy itself occasioned no serious quarrel among the various churches. A study of the texts preserved by the *Didache* and the works of Clement of Rome, Justin, Hippolytus, and others reveals that the *eucharistia* remained substantially the same: a prayer of thanksgiving to God for the wondrous

---

[19] H. Blakeney (ed.), *Lactantius' Epitome of the Divine Institutes* (London: S.P.C.K. House, 1950). The *Epitome* was written to a certain Pentadius after A.D. 314. Its version of the two resurrections is easier to follow than in Lactantius' larger work, *Divine Institutes*.

favors granted to the human race, culminating in the account of the life and death of Jesus and the narration of the Last Supper. This prayer the fathers (e.g. Methodius) called the *anamnēsis,* or memorial of the Passion, which commemorated both the death of Jesus and His memorial supper at the same time. Nothing in the Church was more conservative than the sacramental ritual and the eucharistic liturgies, and the fourth-century anaphoras, as they were called, found in the *Prayerbook of Bishop Serapion,* the papyrus from Dêr Balyzeh, and the liturgy of St. Ambrose of Milan, all contain the elements already present in the second-century formulas. The genealogical line from the Apostolic Fathers to the modern Christian liturgies of East or West, in no matter what language, stands out clearly: the Liturgy commemorates the Lord's final supper with His apostles and the act whereby He showed, in the bread and wine of the Jewish passover meal, His broken body and His blood to be shed upon the cross of Calvary.

In many ways the early Church liturgy resembled the synagogue service: as in the synagogue, there was the cantillation of the Scriptures, psalmody, prayers, instruction, and hymns.[20] The very form of the anaphora or Eucharistic prayer proper was "thanksgiving by narrative," that is, by an account of the great works of God toward His people. Although fore-Mass (as it is called) kept closest to the synagogue, it too began to show divergences as early as the second century, when Christian hymns were introduced, especially in the East; and the influence of Syriac poetic forms had a marked influence upon the homily and the didactic hymn. There are several hymnlike passages in the controverted *On the Pasch* attributed to Melito of Sardis, and the balanced, isocolonic arrangement of many of the sentences foreshadows the later Syriac *memrâ,* or poetic sermon with lines of counted syllables. The subject of Melito's sermon, moreover, would seem to be related to the Passover haggadah,[21] save that the preacher now explained the Exodus story in terms of its Christian fulfillment. At this early date

---

[20] In Egon Wellesz (ed.), *The New Oxford Dictionary of Music* (London and New York: Oxford University Press, 1957) see Carl H. Kraeling's "Music in the Bible," I, pp. 283–312 and Eric Werner's "The Music of Post-Biblical Judaism," I, pp. 313–35.

[21] See F. L. Cross, *The Early Christian Fathers* (London: Gerald Duckworth & Co., Ltd., 1960), pp. 103–9, and Michel Testuz, *Papyrus Bodmer XIII: Méliton de Sardes: Homélie sur la Pâque* (Cologny-Genève: Bibliothèque Bodmer, 1960), pp. 17 ff., with the literature there cited.

we find the essence of the Christian kerygma: the Lord's death achieved our escape from bondage to sin just as the slaying of the Passover lamb was the divine means of ensuring the salvation of the Jews in Egypt. The sermon of Melito once again underlines the liturgical setting of early Christian doctrine, as well as its fundamental pattern of shadow-fulfillment, type and reality.

Indeed, the organic development of patristic theology can only be understood when seen as closely related to the growth of the liturgy. So many of our extant documents followed from the instructions that were delivered at the baptismal synaxis or during the liturgy itself, after the reading of the sacred texts. Melito's homily is a good example of the way in which the instruction bridged the gap between sacred history and symbolic fulfillment. For if the fore-Mass with its psalms and readings stressed the old law, the eucharistic prayer was the final revelation of the new, a mystery which only the illuminati could witness, only those who had crossed the Red Sea by the saving waters of baptism and had risen mystically with Jesus. Just as all the Church's sacramental rites have their center in the liturgy, so it may be said that all of patristic theology developed out of, or in close connection with, the primitive eucharistic banquet, the supreme act of worship of the Christian community. That theology should grow and deepen in the course of centuries, with the pressures of heterodoxy on the one hand and sheer thirst for knowledge on the other, was only to be expected. That theologians of East and West, Catholic and non-Catholic, Jewish and Christian, should so sharply disagree in later years on facts and interpretation is not surprising. Yet in times such as these it is important that the call of the simple Christian kerygma should once again be heeded by all men of goodwill.

The Problem of Religious History

Theology for the Apostolic Fathers was still unself-conscious and unreflective; it began formally with the Apologists —with Justin, Aristides, Athenagoras, and Quadratus—forced as they were to present the Christian kerygma within the context of a Greco-Roman rationality, that is, to defend and prove its doctrine, and by so doing to explicate what had been largely an undifferentiated *paradosis*. The process was taken further by Irenaeus and Hippolytus, by the Africans

Tertullian, Minucius, and Cyprian, and found its culmination in the vast projects of the Alexandrian catechetical school. Irenaeus transformed Atonement theology into a philosophy of history: the manifestation of the Logos achieves the restoration of the cycle, and God's plan for the human race proceeds from the new beginning accomplished by the new Adam. Hippolytus adapted Philo's allegorical mode of interpreting the Old Testament to the union of Christ and the Church, and he turned the story of the chosen people into the wedding of God and the human soul. St. Ambrose surely drew heavily on the works of Hippolytus for his exposition of the psalms and the Song of Songs; Origen, if not directly influenced, was attracted to the same approach and technique in his *Commentary on the Song of Songs*. He derived his view of the history of salvation from both Irenaeus and Hippolytus, focusing his entire method of exegesis on the tension between the shadow of the Jewish past and the image and reality of the Christian epiphany that would come. Methodius of Olympus shared the same view of religious history: the past is Shadow, the Christian present is the Image, and the Hereafter is the Reality that will be revealed to us. Thus the core of Alexandrian theology consisted of the technique of Philonian allegory fused with Irenaeus' eschatological vision of human history. This structure would become convenient for instructing catechumens, especially in the form commended by Augustine and Gregory of Nyssa, and put into practice by Cyril of Jerusalem at the end of the fourth century, by the poet Commodianus, and the African apologist Lactantius.[22]

In any case, sacred history was always an important element of theological controversy, and from the third century we find Irenaeus, Methodius, and Augustine on the one hand, and Origen and his followers on the other, presenting divergent views on the actual nature of the Fall of man. Irenaeus' and, indeed, the predominant view, was that man's Fall was a historical event which took place as described in the book of Genesis and that the entire purpose of redemption was the restoration of the divine image lost, or at least besmirched, by Adam's rebellious act. Origen, however, saw the book of Genesis as largely allegorical, and he interpreted

---

[22] The method of catechesis that taught the meaning of sacred history is outlined in my article, "History and Symbol: A Study of Form in Early Christian Literature," *Theological Studies* 18 (1957), pp. 357–86; see also "Symbolism and Kerygmatic Theology," in *The Encounter with God: Aspects of Modern Theology* (New York: The Macmillan Co., 1962), pp. 107–37.

the insertion of the human soul into a human body as the
effect of "being brutalized through folly," that is by being deceived into sin through the Devil's wiles. Redemption to
Origen meant the restoration of the near-angelic state that
man possessed before the Fall and achievement of the divine
likeness to which he was destined. Origen thought that the
human body is irrational and bestial and that it interferes
with the comprehension of the Scriptures and a mystical
union with the Logos; hence in the final Resurrection, man
will receive not his own body but a new "pneumatic" structure which will be perfect and spherical, a suitable instrument
for the operation of the spiritual senses. Thus, Origen's concept of man's nature and the Fall is intimately connected
with his explanation of asceticism and mysticism, and with
his doctrine about Heaven and the Last Things.

After the crisis of Gnosticism, the most important theological controversies in the Church revolved about the Trinity
and the Incarnation. Philo of Alexandria had taught the
existence of a created Logos, which hovered between the
Godhead and men.[23] The various Gnostic sects preached
different, fantastic series of emanations, which would bridge
the gap between God and creation, between infinite Good and
created malice and impurity.[24] The Neoplatonists were developing their own theory of a four-stage process of emana-
tion. The reality of the world proceeds outward as ripples on
the sea: first there is the One, the source of all things; next
Mind, or Nous, which operates by intuition and possesses all
the divine ideas; then comes the world Soul, which appre-
hends all things discursively and, in its successive thinking,
originates Time and Space. The last principle in the divine
hierarchy is Nature, which operates by a kind of imaginative
dreaming, and the result of the dream is the physical, sensual world. Plotinus' work, the Enneads, edited about A.D.
270 by his disciple Porphyry (a devout anti-Christian, dis-
liked by many a Church Father), contains the fullest explanation of this theory, which had a considerable influence upon
some of the later patristic explanations of the divine processions.[25]

23 See H. A. Wolfson, *The Philosophy of the Church Fathers*
(Cambridge: Harvard University Press, 1956), I, 177–78, 365–67, with
the literature there cited.

24 *Ibid.*, pp. 495 ff.

25 *Ibid.*, pp. 202–4, with the sources cited.

Trinitarian Theology

The roots of Trinitarian doctrine go back to the ancient formulas of blessings found in the early Christian letters and to the various baptismal formulas. There were many different kinds of blessing, in the name of Jesus and of God the Father; and testimony to the unity of God was often coupled with a statement of belief in the divinity of Jesus and the divinity of the Spirit. The formation of the Creed, for example, involved the fusion of the Christological formula, as it is called,[26] and the Trinitarian one as seen in the *Apostolic Tradition* of Hippolytus. Thus the Creed of Nicaea is used as the test of orthodox faith, especially with the addition of the crucial word *homoöusios,* "of the same substance" (as the Father). The formula of greeting, of blessing, and of baptismal initiation had become, unfortunately from some points of view, a dogmatic weapon to ensure uniformity of belief. Through the genius and insight of Athanasius, the two controversial words, *homoöusios* (of the same substance) and *homoiousios* (of like substance) were later both considered acceptable as designations of the Son and the Father. The post-Nicene victory of the Athanasian party and the ultimate predominance of Cappadocian theology (that is, as preached by Basil and his brother Gregory of Nyssa, and Gregory of Nazianzus)—all this established Trinitarian doctrine for many centuries.

But the doctrine of Nicaea was itself the result of forces operative in East and West even in the days of Justin and Irenaeus. The two writers who exercised the greatest influence upon pre-Nicene thought were Tertullian and Origen. Tertullian brought his sharp intellect to bear on the problem of how three could be designated one, that is, how Father, Son, and Spirit could rightfully be called God. He truly created a new Christian vocabulary to express the intricacies of the doctrine.[27] The persons of the Trinity share in a single substratum, substance, and power; yet each has an individual property or note, and are distinct in "grade," in "form," in *"species"* (i.e. Latin *species*, in their "manifestation"). Ter-

[26] See the vast bibliography in J. Quasten, *Initiation aux Pères de l'Eglise* (tr. by J. Laporte, Paris: Newman Press, 1955), I, 34–36.

[27] See especially René Braun, *"Deus Christianorum," Recherches sur le Vocabulaire Doctrinal de Tertullien* (Paris: Editions du Cerf, 1962), pp. 555 ff.

tullian at once denied the heresy of the Monarchians, who
accepted but one Father, who appeared now as Son and Spirit;
on the other hand he firmly opposed those who accused the
Christians of being "tritheists," that is, believers in a triad
of gods.[28] Though the three persons—Tertullian spoke of the
"first," "second," and "third"—share a common substratum,
they differ in "property," "form," "person," that is, in role and
function and not merely in name. And although the terms
"person" and "substance" do not convey all the subtlety of
fourth-century theology, they nevertheless indicate the path
that Latin doctrine would take.[29]

The Insight of Origen

Origen, with his clear distinction between persons, saw the
problem rather as that of the divine unity. His work still
shows traces of the second-century subordinationism of
Justin, whose stress on the distinction between Father and
Son resulted in their relationship being conceived as that of
superior to subject, king to regent, substance to image. The
famous transcript of Origen's *Dialogue with Heracleides* was
probably the source of some of his influence over the theology of Egypt and the Middle East. The terminology is
striking: Origen spoke of "three gods" and approved of
Heracleides' expression, "one power" (*dynamis*). In this
dogmatic discussion, however, Origen spoke clearly of the
share of the three persons in the one *ousía*, or substance;
hence they are *homoöusios*, "of the same substance." They
are distinct *hypostaseis*, or "things," and hence, from this
point of view, three individuals or real individual species; [30]
they are one, however, in unity of thought, in identity of will,
and in their common harmony (*symphonia*). Adapting the
Aristotelian terminology for his analysis of the Trinity,
Origen seemed to suggest that the analogy is taken from the
relationship between genus and species; but it is only an
analogous use of terms in a case that is quite unique. In any

---

28 *Ibid.*, pp. 156–57.

29 See Wolfson, *op. cit*, pp. 325 ff. on the origin and use of the
word *persona*; and cf. Braun, *op. cit.*, p. 238. For the development
of the doctrine through St. Hilary of Poitiers, see P. Galtier, *Saint
Hilaire de Poitiers, le premier docteur de l'église latine* (Paris: Beau-
chesne, 1960).

30 For a discussion of the analogy, see Wolfson, *op. cit.*, p. 321
and also Braun, *op. cit.*, pp. 178 ff.

case, Origen's use of the term *homoöusios* and his analysis of substance and person were most important in the growth of the doctrine until Athanasius' day. By then the terminology had hardened and all traces of subordinationism had been purified; after Athanasius the way lay open for further speculations by Gregory of Nyssa and Nazianzus on the nature of the processions, the relations, and the problem of "circumincession," that is, the mutual presence of the three persons of the Trinity founded on their unity of substance, intelligence, and will. But the outlines of the doctrine had already been laid down by the middle of the fourth century —and for this achievement we are largely indebted to the work of Tertullian and Origen.

The Nature of Jesus: Christology

Progression from the Christological to the Trinitarian formula in the sacramental liturgies was only natural once Christianity spread beyond the area of Semitic influence.[31] A similar process was at work in the controversies that arose over the nature of Jesus. Once the Gnostic fantasies had been successfully repressed—Jesus was truly God's Son, born under the Law with a body that truly suffered—the immediate problem arose as to how a man could be called God or Son of God and how such irreconcilable opposites could be united. The earliest writers called the humanity of the Word a garment, covering, or a house or temple in which God dwells (Tertullian, Hippolytus, Clement of Alexandria, Athanasius). Once more it was Tertullian who was the first to explain the nature of the union between the two natures or substances in Christ: Jesus' "double state was not confused but united in one person, God and the man Jesus" (*Against Praxeas* 27.11).[32] Origen, too, though not so clear as Tertullian, spoke of the composite Christ, whose humanity was the "veil" behind which the divinity was hidden; and the Word used the human nature as an "instrument" by which to communicate the divine message.[33] Origen for the first time used the Greek term

---

31 See, for example, O. Cullmann, *Earliest Christian Confessions* (tr. by J. K. S. Reid, London: Lutterworth Press, 1949).
32 See Braun, *op. cit.*, p. 314.
33 See Marguerite Harl, *Origène la fonction révélatrice du Verbe Incarné* (Patristica Sorbonensia 2, Paris: Editions du Seuil, 1958), pp. 205 ff.

"God-man," and taught that in Jesus opposite predicates could be mutually shared because "Jesus' soul and body became one being with the Divine Logos" (*Against Celsus* 2.9). Hence "the Son of God can be said to have died because of the reference to that nature which admitted death" (*First Principles* 2.6.3). Origen was evidently responsible for the precise Greek theological terminology which would become the tool of the fourth- and fifth-century councils.

Origen's work still signified a period of painful transition, and the clear Christological doctrine would not emerge until after the semi-Arian conflicts and, indeed, after the council of Chalcedon. But Origen fired all of the Greek-speaking world with the love of the divine Logos, subtly uniting his theology with a devout mysticism. His personal asceticism, which was singularly devoted to the penetration of the Christian mysteries, and his fasting and prayer, which Eusebius described and which were intended to shed light on the meaning of the Scriptures, all gave a vital stimulus both to monasticism and to the study of academic theology. Even if Origen's methods were crude and his use of Scripture arbitrary in the extreme, his teaching of the allegorical sense would have a profound impact on exegesis even to the present day. In fact, in all areas of theological studies Origen's influence was greater than any other Church Father's with the exception of St. Augustine.[34]

Athanasius

By comparison, Athanasius was a much duller writer—but far more sober, precise, and orthodox. His method of teaching aimed at clarity without complexity; indeed, his sermons and pastoral letters showed that he envisaged a wide and sometimes illiterate audience. Athanasius was at heart a monk and only the fortunes of the Alexandrian Church kept him from living in the eremitic settlements along the Nile. His defense of the orthodox position of Nicaea was ultimately a practical one; for his asceticism and his Atonement theology were intimately united with what he taught on the nature of the Word. The redemption in Athanasius' work is one both of reconciliation and union, of restoration of the divine image by union with Jesus the son of Mary. Trinitarian theology

[34] For a less favorable view of Origen, see Hans von Campenhausen, *Die griechischen Kirchenväter* (2nd ed.; Stuttgart: Herder & Co., 1956), pp. 43 ff., and the English version, *The Fathers of the Greek Church* (tr. by S. Godman, New York: Pantheon Books, Inc., 1959), pp. 40 ff.

and Christology become one: for if Christ had not been the substantial image of the Father, Athanasius taught, he could not have formed the divine image in anyone. As he fought against those who denied the divinity of the Holy Spirit, Athanasius taught that the Spirit too was truly God, proceeding from the Father through the Son. The sacraments were the Church's precise means for effecting our union with Jesus and for restoring the divine image in the souls of men.

The Egyptian monks were some of Athanasius' staunchest allies against the Arians and the other foes who besieged his spiritual rule of the Alexandrian patriarchate. The Coptic works on virginity and the Greek treatise on the same subject (if authentic) breathe a poetic fervor; and the enthusiasm engendered by the masterful *Life of Antony*, especially in the Latin version in which it circulated in the West, had a profound effect upon monastic life throughout the Mediterranean world. It made clear that evangelical perfection as practiced by the monk or consecrated virgin would lead more securely to a union with the Logos and a restoration of the divine image in man; thence would come an illumination of the mind, larger control over the rebellious flesh, power over the demons and the evil forces of this world. Athanasius' tragic life furnishes deep insight into the growth of Church doctrine and practice, and the cry "Athanasius against the world!" became a battle cry for many who would follow in his path.

The Theology of the African Church

Alexandrian theology must not be confused with the theology of the African Church, which is represented chiefly by Tertullian, Minucius Felix, Cyprian, Arnobius, and Lactantius. Two important martyr acts emerged from Africa, the *Acts of the Martyrs of Scilli* and the *Passion of Saints Perpetua and Felicitas*; and an important Latin version of the Bible circulated in the African Church before the publication of Jerome's Vulgate. Minucius Felix, Arnobius, and Lactantius were generally more conservative in their adoption of a specifically Christian style; Tertullian, on the other hand, did not hesitate to create his own theological vocabulary or to adapt traditional Latin terms to Christian usage. Cyprian was the first to use the Bible liberally throughout his writings, in the manner of the Semitic commentators, and by the time of

St. Hilary of Poitiers the process of Christianization within the Latin language was complete.[35]

The Latin West had its own problems. But, despite the visits of Marcion, Valentinus, and others, to Rome, it was relatively untouched by Gnosticism. Without the advantage of the Egyptian desert, the Nile valley and its melancholy oases, the monastic movement was slower in developing. The Latin Church, too, engaged less in dogmatic speculation— Rome had always had a reputation for conservatism—and the liturgy and hymonody of the West had less of the ecstasy and poetry of the East. Though different in style, Minucius Felix and Tertullian both represented the austere legalism of the West. Both were lawyers; Roman law and a Stoic philosophy had been their early training ground. Minucius' work, in fact, presents a certain patrician Christianity whose greatest asset is the purity of its philosophy and moral code; Christology and liturgy seem secondary considerations in the conversion of the pagan Caecilius at the close of the charming Ciceronian dialogue.

For these reasons, the *Octavius*, written perhaps in the first quarter of the third century, reflects none of the dogmatic crises that had been shaking the churches of the East. The author resembles Arnobius and Lactantius in this respect. Even within the shadow of Constantine's victory, their approach was still apologetic and polemic. They were still fighting the opposition of Roman society and officialdom, whose approval meant far more to them than it did to the Fathers of the East. The ridiculing of pagan rites, which forms so large a part of Arnobius' work, had already been dealt with, more copiously and subtly, by Clement of Alexandria. Indeed, the East had long since broken with pagan poetry and, to an extent, with its philosophers, whereas the Latin churches retained a tendency to show greater respect for the traditional poets and writers of Rome. The influence of Cicero, for example, upon Minucius, Arnobius, and Lactantius, was quite striking and deep-seated; and it would grow with Ambrose, Augustine, and Jerome. The Latin writers sometimes give the impression that the saint of the West was built upon the Stoic foundations of Cicero—a situation which caused Jerome, for instance, to have grave scruples. In the East, the pagan prototype for the earlier Fathers had been, in part, Socrates, until his influence was dispelled by the

---

[35] See Christine Mohrmann, *Liturgical Latin: Its Origins and Character* (Washington: Catholic University of America Press, 1958), pp. 47 ff.

scholarly austerity of men like Origen and Athanasius and the later Basil, Gregory of Nyssa, and Chrysostom)—all dedicated churchmen with monastic sympathies, dedicated to the study of the Scriptures and keen for theological controversy.

Tertullian (about 155–after 220) was an early exception to the general tendency of the West, and his theological and moral achievements were not to be surpassed until the conversion of Augustine. Tertullian's prodigious, wide-ranging mind touched all fields and included ecclesiology and the sacraments, morals, liturgy, and asceticism, in addition to his contribution in the area of Trinitarian speculation. Minucius Felix's range was surprisingly meager by comparison, and hence it is hard to believe (as St. Jerome suggested) that he came after Tertullian and even knew something of his work. The work of Cyprian, the gentle, prudent bishop of Carthage (200/210–58), is also comparatively meager as a theological source. A busy and efficient administrator, a scrupulous ecclesiastic, Cyprian wrote letters that present a vivid portrait of the Church of Carthage in the mid-third century. At the same time his work reflects traditional attitudes on penitential discipline and the forgiveness of sins, the Eucharist, and religious asceticism. Dominant are the legalistic controversies over heretical baptism—Cyprian disagreed with Rome for denying the validity of the sacrament as conferred by heretics —and the problem of the lapsed and the *libellatici*, or those who had purchased certificates of pagan sacrifice. Cyprian was another Roman lawyer; and these controversies impelled him to formulate a theory of the Church and its ministry. This theory has given rise to one of the most exciting controversies of recent years, centering on the little tract, *On the Unity of the Church.* Of particular concern has been the authenticity of the passage, rejected by some editors, which links the authority of Rome with the "primacy (*primatus*) given to Peter." Both the "primacy" passage and its alternate (which stresses rather the collegiate authority of all the bishops) depend on equally weighty manuscript evidence. The priority of the alternative versions is disputed, but the theory that both texts go back to Cyprian himself seems, when all is said, the conclusion best suited to the evidence.

Constantine: the Peace of the Church

Arnobius, who flourished under the persecution of Diocletian (304/5), was Lactantius' teacher, and surely the two together offer an instructive insight into the evolution of the African Church during the period of transition. It was in 317 that the emperor Constantine summoned Lactantius to Gaul to act as tutor for his oldest son, Crispus. Arnobius' only work, *Against the Pagans*, is a fervent protestation of faith by a devout pedant as yet not completely at home in Christianity. His use of pagan sources is fascinating and prodigious; but his notions of God and the Trinity, the purpose of the Church, and the destiny of the human soul were confused and hardly in line with traditional Christian belief. Nonetheless his apologetic approach to the proof of Christ's messianic mission from the prophecies and miracles would become standard in the theological schools for many centuries.

Lactantius was the greatest stylist of the early Latin church, and it is instructive to see the wit, venom, and withering irony of a Cicero or a Juvenal totally converted to demolishing the pagan stronghold. Like his tutor Arnobius, his ideas of Christianity were sometimes grotesque, as, for example, his view that there are but two persons in the Trinity (the Son being subordinate to the Father), since a third person, generated by the Father, had revolted from authority and had become the Devil. His is perhaps the most vivid and poetic picture of the return of Jesus at the end of time for a thousand-years' reign. But Lactantius was on firmest ground in his treatise *On the Deaths of the Persecutors*. Here his rhetoric finds a stimulating target—the cruelty and sadism of the emperors—and his writing often has the value of contemporary witness, although it is not the sole historical source. For by this time Constantine had seen the vision which foreboded divine victory and had crushed the forces of Maxentius at the Milvian Bridge in the year 312. Shortly after, the Senate had erected the great triumphal arch that represented the Unconquered Sun as Constantine's patron deity, but ascribed his victory, as one of justice, to an unnamed divine power and to his own greatness of soul. At a conference at Milan in 313, Licinius and Constantine came to an agreement regarding the freedom of worship of the Christian Church, the restitution of property, and the exemption from public burdens. Unlike Licinius, Constantine, though as yet unbaptized, was effectively a Christian from the time of the great victory of 312 and used every opportunity to make the Church an effective partner in his establishment of an undivided rule.

Between the years 313 and 321 Constantine attempted to settle the schism that arose in Africa under Donatus, who had been elected bishop of Carthage by a fanatical and dissident group. Calling upon the bishop of Rome, Miltiades, to preside at the synod of Arles, Constantine thought he could suppress the Donatists by law; ultimately he had to abandon the attempt as a failure. More successful, however, was his role in the Arian controversy. The first ecumenical council at Nicaea was one of the most important in Church history, and yet its records, or *acta*, were never preserved, and we must piece together information from sometimes unreliable sources. Constantine was no theologian; his only aim was harmony within the empire. After letters to Arius and to bishop Alexander of Alexandria failed to end the controversy, the emperor summoned a council at Nicaea to which bishops all over the empire might come at state expense. On May 20, 325, some two or three hundred bishops, representing Rome, Alexandria, Carthage, Antioch, Caesarea, and other sees, gathered in Bithynia. St. Athanasius accompanied his bishop to Nicaea, but his role there seems to have been purely secondary. Of the priests and bishops present, the majority, we are told, sided with the bishop of Alexandria in condemning the doctrine of Arius, and the famous Creed of Nicaea, which may have been based on an older Palestinian formula, was drawn up by Bishop Hosius of Cordova and approved by the other Fathers at the council. The *homoöusios* formula, which went back to Origen, was ultimately accepted, and when Arius and his group would not assent to the Creed, the emperor declared that they would be exiled. Arius fled to Palestine and, with the help of sympathetic followers, circulated his doctrine through popular sermons and songs. Later, in a personal interview with Constantine, he assured the emperor that he would accept the Nicaean formula, and Athanasius (successor to Bishop Alexander in 328) was ordered to reconcile all Arians who wished to make their peace. Athanasius' tactic was to delay, and though Arius was finally reinstated at the synod of Tyre in 335, he died mysteriously in the following year before he could be formally reconciled. Athanasius was then banished from his see to Treves, where he remained until after Constantine's death in 337. It was the first of his many exiles from Alexandria. In 355, the emperor Constantius convoked a synod at Milan and the council, controlled by Athanasius' enemies, once more deposed him. This time, after a series of hairbreadth escapes, Athanasius took refuge with the Fathers of the Egyptian desert, and it was to this period (355–62) that we owe some of his greatest works, including the *Life of Antony* (if it is indeed from his hand) and its most influential Latin translation. Athanasius enjoyed comparative peace under the emperors Jovian (363–64) and Valentinian (364–75). In 365 he was exiled again under Valens for about four months. But, recalled in the winter of 366, the aged bishop was finally allowed to end his days in peace. He died on May 2, 373, closing a truly unbelievable chapter in the history of the primitive Church.

The great pagan statue of Victoria still had to be removed from the Senate house, but at Constantine's death the battle of Christianity had already been fought and won. The glory of the victory was somewhat dulled by the sordid fighting which surrounded his final years. When he was dying, in 337, Constantine summoned the Arian Bishop Eusebius of Nicomedia to administer the sacrament of baptism, and the first great Christian emperor was baptized only on his death-bed. It was an irony that would have pleased Gibbon. In any case, by this time, the great bark of Peter was fully launched and on its way: all the major doctrines had been discussed and elucidated and all the seeds of controversy had been sown, to flourish and occupy the theologians for many centuries. For the miracle of Christian growth can best be detected and studied in the first writers who spoke, however imperfectly, of the primitive kerygma and subjected its message to the scrutiny of reason and argument.

When they did this, they were merely following the command of Jesus to go and teach and make disciples of all the nations. The goal of theology can only be the explication of the Christian message through all ages and climes. Like the stout mustard tree of the Gospels, theology must grow and flourish, spreading its branches to the four winds. But just as a tree withers without light and air, so too it will die if it is cut off from its primitive roots. And this is the value of the study of the Fathers. The dialogue that began in the primitive Church over the meaning of Jesus' life and doctrine is still with us today. Despite the grave crises that have ravaged a once healthy and united Christendom, the dialogue remains, and the terms, the tone, and the object of our discourse are still what they were many centuries ago. Indeed, we can only understand the tragic cleavage of Christianity by studying the history of the organism when it was whole and flourishing.

Such is the goal of any study of the Fathers of the primitive Church. From understanding may be bred sympathy and love. Let us recall the great labors endured by the Founder of Christianity and His apostles to establish a community—a family, rather, which would be washed, purified in His name and sealed by His blood. Let us recall, too, that the dialogue in which we are engaged is one in which finite minds collaborate in seeking a single goal—the Godhead hidden in the darkness, and the reality of which all else (in the words of Origen) is somehow shadow.

1

CLEMENT OF ROME

One of the most precious of all the early Christian documents, aside from the New Testament, is the Letter of the Church of Rome to the Church of Corinth, assigned with good probability to the time of Pope Clement, bishop of Rome from A.D. 88 to 97. It has come down to us not only in two Greek manuscripts, but also in a Latin, Syriac, and Coptic version. After an opening in which he apologizes for not taking action earlier, Clement attempts to settle "the strife, friction, and schisms" which were afflicting the community at Corinth (46, 54). It is not clear how the problem arose; but Clement mentions jealousy and envy as the causes (3.2), and stresses the importance of obedience to the elders (57). The discussion of the need for order in religious ceremonial (40) suggests a possible area of conflict; St. Paul (in I Cor. 14.23–40) had stressed the importance of order especially with regard to the preaching of prophets and others gifted with "tongues," or the charism of ecstatic speech. Like Paul (in I Cor. 12.25), Clement emphasized the damage that schisms can do to the body of the Church, and one has the impression that many of the old conflicts within the community still persisted until the early second century.

Clement reveals a very moving style full of reminiscences of the Old Testament (especially in the OT Greek version); he was familiar with the principal letters of St. Paul as well as the epistle to the Hebrews; as for the Gospel story, he merely referred to what "the Lord said." What is interesting about the letter—apart from the doctrinal element—is that even at this early date the Church of Rome displayed concern for a community which was an old Pauline foundation. The unity between the two churches is clear, although Clement was diplomatic in his handling of the local crisis. In Sections 5 to 6 we have the earliest testimony to the martyrdom of Peter and Paul at Rome; Section 20 presents the argument from the order of the world to the existence of a Supreme Being; Section 25 tells the story of the phoenix as a symbol of immortality; and Sections 59.4–61.3 contain a solemn prayer of thanksgiving which probably recalls an early liturgical anaphora. The Roman messenger, Fortunatus (65.1) was also mentioned at the close of Paul's first Corinthian letter, but the name may merely be coincidence.[1]

Irenaeus tells us that Clement was the fourth bishop of Rome, but Tertullian states that he was consecrated by St. Peter himself. In any case, both Origen and Eusebius identified him as the companion of Paul mentioned in Philippians (4.3). A vast body of apocryphal literature grew up about his name, and he was wrongly identified as the Roman consul, T. Flavius Clemens, who had been condemned by Domitian for conversion to the new beliefs.[2]

First Epistle*

The church of God that dwells in Rome to the church of God at Corinth, to the elect who have been sanctified by the will of God through Jesus Christ our Lord, may the grace and peace of God almighty be fulfilled in you through Christ Jesus.

1   We realize that we have been delayed in turning our mind to the problems that are being discussed among you, beloved friends, because of the sudden and repeated misfortunes and calamities that we have suffered, and also to the wicked and sacrilegious quarrel (so foreign and out of keeping with God's elect), which a handful of headstrong, stubborn men have kindled to such a de-

---

[1] For a bibliography on Clement, see B. Altaner, *Patrology* (tr. by Hilda C. Graef, New York: Herder & Herder, Inc., 1960), pp. 99–102.

[2] The body of pseudo-Clementine literature includes the famous *Homilies* that stress the Judaic character of Christianity, and the novelistic *Recognitions* (or "Discovery of Identities"), which has Clement traveling from Rome to the East to hear about the new Redeemer; there he met St. Peter and accompanied him on his missionary journeys. Again, though more orthodox than the *Homilies,* the *Recognitions* reflects a Syrian or Palestinian branch of Christianity with a strongly Jewish background. Both works seem to stem from a second-century source, though the final version is much later.

* For the text, see Kirsopp Lake (ed.), *The Apostolic Fathers* (Cambridge: Harvard University Press, 1959), I, 8 ff.

gree of madness that your good name, so respected and famous among men, has come to be greatly slandered. Anyone who has stayed with you has experienced the high quality and steadfastness of your faith. Everyone has marveled at the serious and gentle piety you have displayed in Christ, spread abroad the generous character of your hospitality, and praised your secure and perfect sense of awareness. For in everything you acted without respect of persons, walking in the laws of God, obedient to your superiors and paying due respect to the elders among you. On your young people you enjoined modest and sober thoughts, and on the women you urged the accomplishment of all things with a pious, blameless, and holy conscience, showing their husbands due affection, and you taught them to remain under the discipline of authority, to live in self-control and to manage their homes with responsibility.

You were all humble, and in no way arrogant, pre- 2 ferring to be obedient rather than to give orders, happier to give than to receive, content with the things Christ has given us, attentive to His words, which you had laid up carefully in your hearts, and keeping His sufferings before your eyes. In this way a profound, rich peace was granted to all, you had an insatiable desire to do good, and the fullness of the Holy Spirit was poured forth on all of you. Full as you were of holy intentions, you stretched forth your hands towards almighty God, begging him to be merciful on your indeliberate sins. Night and day there was a contest among you on behalf of all the faithful, that the number of the elect might be saved through mercy and conscience.

You had a sincerity and an innocence, without malice towards one another. You loathed the thought of any friction or schism. You grieved for the transgressions of your neighbors, and made their sins your own. You were uninhibited in every act of kindness, and prompt for every good deed. Adorned with a most excellent and sober way of life, you performed all things in the fear of the Lord. And the precepts and commandments of the Lord were inscribed upon the tablets of your heart.

Thus you had all glory and reason for praise, when that 3 which was written was fulfilled: My beloved ate and drank, he grew thick and waxed fat and kicked [Deut. 32.15]. Hence there was jealousy and envy, strife, conflict, persecution, disorder, war, and captivity. Thus the worthless were roused against those in honor, the foolish against the prudent, youth against the elders. This is the reason why justice and peace have abandoned us, for each one has given up the fear of God and has allowed his faith to grow dim; nor do men walk in laws of his commandments, nor live the life that befits Christ, but each one follows the desires of a wicked heart, taking on that wicked and malicious envy through which death came into the world.

[So at last, after an opening accolade of praise, did Clement get down to the psychological roots of the trouble in Corinth: jealousy and envy. In Sections 4 to 5 he noted that these were the sources of the greatest sins of the Old Testament, and the reasons for the persecution and deaths of the early martyrs, including Peter and Paul, and all the rest who "gave us the noblest example because of jealousy, suffering tortures and indignities in our midst" (6.1). Clement, then, wanted to remind the Corinthians of the noble truths of the faith into which they had been baptized, and to underline the importance of humility and obedience in Christianity. He began with the source of truth and repentance—the death of Jesus.]

7   Dearly beloved, we are writing this to you as a reminder to ourselves as much as an admonition to you; for we too are in the same arena, facing the same sort of contest. Hence let us do away with all silly, foolish preoccupations and come to that which is the glorious and venerable norm of all our teaching, and see what is good, pleasant, and acceptable in the sight of Him who made us. Let us fix our attention on the blood of Christ and realize how precious it is to the Father, since it was poured out for our salvation, bringing the grace of repentance to all the world. Let us go down through all the generations and see that time and time again the Master has offered the opportunity for penance to all who were willing to turn to Him. . . .

[So was repentance also needed now, and humility. Clement enumerated the examples of the saints, of David, and the humility of the Son of Man Himself, especially in His fulfillment of the Servant Song, or Chapter 53 of Isaiah (16). Then Clement turned (19) to a consideration of God as the source of peace and harmony in the universe, urging that He be a source of inspiration to the dissenters in Corinth.]

It is by his control that the heavens are moved and 20 they obey Him in peace. Both the day and the night follow the course that He has laid down, without hindrance to each other. The sun and the moon and the choirs of stars glide around in their appointed courses in harmony according to His command without the slightest divergence. By His will the earth becomes fruitful and in due season brings forth food in abundance for man and beast and all living creatures on it, without conflict, and without diverging from any of his decrees. These same decisions structure the unsearchable depths of the abysses and the incomprehensible boundaries of the lower world. The chasm of the boundless sea was gathered by his act into its receptacles, and does not transgress the barriers that are appointed for it; it acts just as He has commanded it, for He said: "Hitherto shalt thou come, but no further, and thy waves will break within thee" [Job 38.11]. The ocean, impassable to man, and the continents beyond it are ruled by the same decrees of the Master. The seasons of spring, summer, autumn, and winter, succeed one another in harmony. The stations of the winds fulfill their function at the proper times without any hindrance. And the perennial springs, created for man's health and pleasure, supply their life-giving breasts to mankind without fail, and the tiniest of animals come together in harmony and peace. The great Creator and Master of the universe has decreed that all these things should exist in peace and concord, out of his benevolence for all, and more especially for us who have taken refuge in His mercies through Jesus Christ our Lord—to whom be glory and majesty forever and ever. Amen.

[In a series of transitional paragraphs (21–23) Clement again used Scripture to stress the importance of virtue and repentance. Those who seek peace must pursue it without guile and hypocrisy. "Foolish men," he said, "compare yourselves to a plant. Take the vine, for example: first it sheds its leaves; then comes the blossom, then the leaf, and then the flower. After that comes the green grape, and then the ripe bunch. Look: in so short a time the fruit of the tree becomes ripe" (23.4). The world foreshadows the truth of the resurrection of the body (24); and Clement told the strange story of the phoenix bird of Arabia, which produces offspring out of its own decaying flesh (25). So too is resurrection promised in the Scriptures (26); but for this we Christians ought to cleave to God in fear and in avoidance of sin (28–30). Christians must imitate the faith of the patriarchs of old (31–32). We must follow the will of our Creator without delay (33), in order to share in the rewards promised by the Master (34–36).

[After these general paragraphs, the papal letter gets down to more specific details. In Sections 37 to 38 Clement compares the Church to an army, in which not everyone can be prefects, tribunes, or centurions; but, just as in an army, all must be obedient to the commands of the generals. The Church is also like a body (37.5), and the head cannot operate without the smallest members: "all work together, and all are subject to one authority for the preservation of the entire body" (*ibid.*). Hence it follows that the weak must be cared for by the strong, the poor by the rich, seeing that we have everything from the Lord (38). Those who act otherwise Clement called "senseless, stupid, foolish, and uneducated men" (39.1), and, adapting the words of Job, warned that they shall not be delivered from evil.

[In Section 40 Clement seems to come closer to the source of the friction: the fact that the Master "has commanded us to offer sacrifice and services, but it should not be done at random and in a disorderly way, but at fixed times and hours" (40.1). He reminds them that all have special duties, the "high priest," the "priests," "Levites," and last of all the common people (40.5). Those who act contrary to God's will "will incur the penalty of death" (41.3). The apostles are the source of this hierarchic structure (42); and it is already foreshadowed in the work of Moses (43). Clement goes further: he chides the Corinthians for removing from office bishops who were appointed by the apostles themselves (44). They are exhorted to change their ways by various arguments and examples (45–48). Clement finally urges them to love, after the example of Paul's famous panegyric (I Cor. 13), and urges them to seek forgiveness for their sins (49–54).

[Clement urged that those who were responsible for the conflict at Corinth should depart in order that the community might have peace (54.2). They should, at any rate, "submit to the elders and receive penitential correction, bending the knee of the heart" (57.1). After protesting that "we shall be innocent of this sin" (59.2), Clement embarked on a long excerpt from what seems to be a primitive liturgical prayer (59.2–3).]

59.2   And we shall be innocent of this sin, and we shall ask with sincere prayer and supplication that the Creator of the universe may protect unharmed the number of the elect

that has been counted in all the world through his beloved
Child Christ Jesus, through whom He has called us from
darkness to light, from ignorance to a knowledge of the
glory of his name—and to hope in your name, the
source of all creation, opening the eyes of the heart to
know you, who alone are the most high among the
highest, remaining ever holy among the holy, humbling the
pride of the arrogant, destroying the machinations of the
pagan, humbling the proud and raising up the humble,
bringing both wealth and poverty, bringing death and
life. For you alone are the benefactor of spirits and the
God of all flesh, who look into the abysses, see into the
works of mankind, are assistance to those in danger, the
Savior of those in despair, the Creator and Overseer of
every spirit. The nations of the earth you have multiplied
and have chosen from all men those that love you through
your beloved Child, Christ Jesus; and through Him you
have taught us, sanctified, and honored us.

Be our help and protection, Master, we beseech you.
Save those of us who are in distress, have mercy on the
humble, lift up those who are fallen, turn to those in
need, cure the sick, restore those of your flock that have
gone astray, feed the hungry, release those of us who
are in prison, raise up the weak, encourage those in despair. Let all the pagans know that you alone are God,
that Christ Jesus is your Child, and we are your people and
the sheep of your pasture.

For by your operations you have revealed the eternal 60
structure of the universe: you, Lord, did create the world.
You, who are faithful in all generations, righteous in
your judgments, wonderful in power and majesty, wise in
creation and prudent in your establishment of all being,
benevolent amid the visible world and kindly to all who
trust in you, merciful and compassionate, forgive us our
sins, iniquities, transgressions, and shortcomings. Do not
take account of every sin your servants and handmaids
commit, but purify us with the cleansing action of your
truth, direct our footsteps that we may walk in purity of
heart and accomplish those things that are good and
pleasing in your sight and in the sight of our rulers.

Yes, Lord, let your face shine upon us in peace for our
good, that we may be protected by your mighty hand, and
deliver us from those who hate us without cause. Grant
us peace and harmony, and to all who live on the earth,
just as you granted it to our forefathers who called upon
you in purity with faith and truth, and grant that we may

be obedient to your all-powerful and glorious name, and also to our rulers and superiors on earth.

61   Master, you have given the power of government to them through your magnificent and ineffable might, that we may know the glory and the honor that you have given them, that we may be submissive to them in perfect obedience to your will. Grant them health, Lord, peace, harmony, and stability, so that they may administer the authority you have given them without blame. For you, heavenly Master, have given the sons of men, glory, honor, and authority over all things on earth. Direct their counsel, Lord, in accordance with what is right and pleasing in your sight, that they might administer the power you have given them with piety in peace and gentleness, and thus find favor in your eyes. You who alone have the power to accomplish these and even greater goods for us, we sing your praises through the high priest and the champion of our souls, Christ Jesus, through whom be glory and majesty to you, both now and for all generations, forever and ever. Amen.

[After bringing this liturgical prayer to a close, Clement succinctly summarized the purpose of the letter: to touch on "every topic of faith and repentance and authentic love," reminding them of their obligation to live in harmony. They are men who have kept the faith and have scrutinized the "sayings" of God's revelation (62). Hence they must cease from conflict (63); and for this Clement has sent aged and prudent men to be "delegates between you and us" (63.3).

Clement then closed with a liturgical blessing (64), mentioned the names of the messengers by way of authentication —Claudius Ephebus, Valerius Bito, and Fortunatus—and concluded. The Coptic version adds the subscription "the epistle of the Romans to the Corinthians," but other manuscripts identify it as the letter of Clement.]

2

THE DIDACHE

This invaluable short Greek work, which comes from the first half of the second century, was discovered at Constantinople in 1875 and published eight years later by Philotheos Bryennios, the Greek metropolitan of Nicomedia.[1] Enshrining as it does the earliest liturgical prescriptions outside of the New Testament, and incorporating obviously earlier doctrinal material, the *Teaching* or the *Didache* (as it is called from its Greek title) remains one of the most important discoveries of the past century. It falls into four parts: (A) the doctrine of the Two Ways, the way of life and the way of death (1–6), which some scholars think is a revision of an earlier Jewish document; (B) prescriptions on the liturgy (7–10), and in particular, baptism, fasting, prayer, and the Eucharist; (C) a canonical section, which deals with principles and practice of Church discipline, the respect due to the hierarchy, to prophets and traveling preachers (11–15); and finally (D) a stirring exhortation to sobriety and watchfulness, with reference to the end of the world and the Last Things (16).

The atmosphere conveyed by the *Didache* is difficult to explain, as well as to locate within a definite geographic and historical setting. The Eucharistic prayers are intensely eschatological and are largely unparalleled. The Lord's Prayer should be recited three times a day; Christians should fast on Wednesdays and Fridays; and before baptism, both minister and the subject should fast. The tone of the Two Ways (recalling the *Epistle of Barnabas*) as well as the final

---

[1] The manuscript is now codex 54 in the Library of the Greek Patriarch of Jerusalem, Hashemite Kingdom of Jordan. There are also small Greek fragments from the fourth century, two Latin manuscripts, Coptic, Ethiopic, and Georgian versions. See F. L. Cross, *The Early Christian Fathers* (London: Gerald Duckworth & Co., Ltd., 1960), pp. 8–13, with the bibliography.

exhortation (16) suggests a very primitive Christian community, located perhaps in Syria or Asia Minor. Recent British scholars have suggested that the *Didache* was not so much an actual description of church life as an imaginative reconstruction made by a later skillful writer, who pieced together various early fragments possibly as late as the third century. Sections 1 to 6 of the *Didache,* which contain the doctrine of the Two Ways, have also been found in an eleventh-century manuscript in Munich, in a free Latin version, ending with its own conclusion and doxology. Goodspeed has put forward the view, [2] which seems quite plausible, that this section (called the *Doctrina*) at least in its Greek form was the earliest nucleus of the later *Didache,* that it was a short instruction intended for Jewish proselytes and was later revised for Christian usage. Indeed, some, like J. P. Audet (who would date the *Didache* as early as A.D. 60), have seen in this primitive section some echoes of the Essenian *Manual of Discipline* found among the Dead Sea Scrolls. In any case, the early section of our work, which is contained in the Latin document called the *Doctrina,* qualifies as the earliest Christian document of the post-apostolic period.

The Didache[*]

The Lord's instruction to pagans through the twelve apostles.

1   There are two ways, the Way of Life and the Way of Death, and there is a vast difference between them. The Way of Life is: first, you shall love God who created you, and secondly your neighbor as yourself. And do not do to another anything that you would not have done to yourself. Now the message of these words is this: Bless those that curse you, and pray for your enemies, and fast for those who persecute you. If you love those who love you, what merit will you have? Do not even pagans do this? Love those who hate you, and you will have no enemy.

Refrain from sensual and bodily desires.

---

[2] See E. J. Goodspeed, *The Apostolic Fathers: An American Translation* (New York: Harper & Brothers, 1950), pp. 1 ff.; see also his article in the *Anglican Theological Review* 37 (1945), 228–47.

[*] For the text, see Kirsopp Lake, *The Apostolic Fathers* (Cambridge: Harvard University Press, 1959).

If a person should slap you on the right cheek, offer him the other one, and you will be perfect.

If anyone tries to force you to walk one mile, go two with him.

If someone should steal your cloak, give him your inner garment as well.

If someone should steal from you what is yours, do not demand it back, for you cannot. Give to everyone who asks and do not refuse, for it is the Father's will that all should be given of the gifts that are His. Blessed is the man who gives in accordance with the precept, for he is innocent. Woe to him who receives, for if a person receive because he is indigent, he will be innocent, but he who receives when he is not in need will be judged as to why he received and for what purpose; he will be put in prison and tried for what he has done, and he will not be released until he has paid the last penny. This is the meaning of the words: Let your gift sweat in your hands until you know to whom you should give it.

[The author went on to warn the Christian against murder, perjury, jealousy, and all the grave sins, and urged patience and humility (2–3); he should "daily seek the presence of the faithful" (4.2), be stern in reproving sons and daughters, and be kind to slaves and handmaids (4.9–11). He must hate all hypocrisy and "in the church admit your transgressions" and not "pray with an evil conscience" (4.14). Then he spoke of the Way of Death.]

And this is the Way of Death. First, it is evil and 5 accursed, involving murder, adultery, lust, fornication, theft, idolatry, black magic, charms, robbery, false witness, hypocrisy, duplicity, fraud, vanity, maliciousness, stubbornness, covetousness, foul speech, jealousy, arrogance, haughtiness, boastfulness. Here are the persecutors of the good, haters of truth, lovers of lies, those who are ignorant of the reward of goodness, those who do not adhere to the good or to righteous judgment, who stay awake not for good but for evil purposes, who are strangers to meekness and long-suffering, in love with trivial things, always seeking a return, unmerciful to the poor, uncaring of the oppressed, ignorant of their Creator, murderers of children, corrupters of the creatures of God, who turn away the indigent, crush the afflicted, are defenders of the rich and unjust judges of the poor, totally sinful. My children, may you be delivered from such as these! . . .

7   With regard to baptism: you are to baptize in this way. After first repeating all these words, baptize (in running water) in the name of the Father and of the Son and of the Holy Spirit. And if you have no running water, baptize in any other water, and if you cannot find cold water, use warm. If neither is available, pour the water on the head three times in the name of the Father and of the Son and of the Holy Spirit. And before the baptism, the person baptizing and the one to be baptized should fast, together with any others who are able. Indeed, the person to be baptized should have been fasting one or two days previously.

8   Your fasting is not to coincide with that of the hypocrites, who fast on Monday and Thursday; you are to fast on Wednesday and Friday. And do not pray as the hypocrites do, but in the way the Lord commanded us in the Gospel, as follows: "Our Father who art in heaven, hallowed be thy name. Thy kingdom come, thy will be done on earth as it is in heaven. Give us this day our daily bread, and forgive us our debt as we also forgive our debtors. And lead us not into temptation, but deliver us from the Evil One, for thine is the power and glory forever." Say this prayer three times a day.

9   With regard to the Eucharist, this is the way you should celebrate it. First of all with regard to the cup: "We give thanks to thee, our Father, for the holy vine of thy Child David, which thou didst make known to us through Jesus thy Child. To thee be glory forever."

On the morsel of bread: "We thank thee, our Father, for the life and knowledge thou has made known to us through thy Child Jesus. To thee be glory forever. As this bread was scattered on the mountains and yet was gathered and made one, so too may thy Church be gathered together from the corners of the world into thy kingdom, for thine is the glory and power through Christ Jesus forever."

No one however should partake or drink of Eucharist except those that have been baptized in the name of the Lord. This is what our Lord meant by the words, "Give not that which is holy to dogs."

10   And after you are filled, make your thanksgiving thus. Holy Father, we thank thee for thy holy name, which thou hast made to dwell within our hearts, and for the knowledge, faith, and immortality, which thou has revealed to

us through thy Child Jesus. To thee be glory forever.

Almighty Lord, thou didst create all things for the sake of thy name: thou gavest food and drink to men for their pleasure, that they might thank thee; but thou has blest us with spiritual food and drink and with eternal life through thy Child.

We thank thee above all because thou art mighty; to thee be glory forever.

Lord, remember thy community, to deliver it from all evil, and perfect it in the love of thee, and gather it in from the four winds, once it has been made holy, into thy kingdom, which thou hast prepared for it. For thine is the power and glory forever.

Let your favor come, and may this world pass away. Hosanna to the God of David!"

Let anyone come who is holy; and, if he is not, he should repent.

Maran atha! amen [Come, Lord! So be it!].

As for the prophets, allow them to celebrate the Eucharist as much as they please.

[In the following numbers, the author discussed the reception of traveling prophets and teachers, with rules for determining which ones truly "speak in the Spirit," since this must have been a disturbing problem in these early days. Offerings of firstfruits should be given them in payment (11–13). Section 14 seems out of place, since it concerns the celebration of the Lord's day.]

On the Lord's day you should assemble, break bread, 14 and celebrate the Eucharist, but first having confessed your transgressions, in order that your sacrifice may be untainted. No one who has had a quarrel with a fellow Christian should join your assembly until they have made up, so that your sacrifice may not be defiled. For this is what the Lord meant when He said: At every place and time offer me a clean sacrifice, for I am a great king, says the Lord, and my name is wonderful among the heathen [Mal. 1.11, 14].

[Section 15 urges the appointment of bishops and deacons who are worthy men, truthful, and not lovers of money. They should be respected, along with "prophets and teachers." The author urged all to "act as you have it in the Gospel of our Lord," and concluded with a long warning of the end of the world.]

16   Be watchful over your life. Your lamps are not to go
out, and you must not remain unprepared, but ready, for
you do not know the time when our Lord is going to
come.

Often gather together to seek the things that are of
profit to your souls. For the entire period of your faith
will be of no use to you unless you are found perfect
at the last moment.

Indeed, on the last days false prophets and corrupters
will be multiplied; sheep will be changed into wolves, and
love will turn to hate. And as license increases, men will
hate and persecute and betray one another. And then the
world-deceiver will come as the Son of God, and he will
perform signs and wonders; the world will be delivered
into his hands, and he will commit such outrages as
have never been since the world began.

Then all created mankind will pass into a trial of fire,
and many will be scandalized and will perish. But those
who persevere in their faith will be saved by the curse
itself.

Then will appear the signs of truth: the first sign, an
opening in the heavens; the second, a trumpet blast; the
third, the resurrection of those who are dead, but not of
all, but just as it was said, The Lord will come and all
his holy ones with Him. Then the world will see the
Lord coming upon the clouds of heaven.

3

THE EPISTLE OF BARNABAS

This strange and undoubtedly primitive document was counted as part of Scripture by Clement of Alexandria, Origen, and many other Christians, especially of the Church of Egypt, and occurs immediately after the Apocalypse in the Codex Sinaiticus, a Greek manuscript of the fourth century, discovered by Tischendorf in 1859 in the convent of St. Catherine on Mount Sinai.[1] The so-called appendix of the epistle, Sections 18 to 21, covers the doctrine of the Two Ways much as we find it in the *Didache* (or the *Teaching of the Twelve Apostles*), but probably does not belong to the earliest edition of the letter and is omitted in the Latin version found in a manuscript from the tenth century in the Library in Leningrad.[2] The author seems to have been a convert from paganism, and stressed throughout that the Jews had misunderstood the Old Testament, which had now been fulfilled in Jesus, and the new dispensation in a spiritual manner. Apparent references to the rebuilding of the temple area under Hadrian and other indications seem to point to a date shortly after A.D. 130. The attack on the Jewish interpretation of the Old Testament became a commonplace in later Christian literature and recurs, for example, in the writings of Methodius of Olympus and St. John Chrysostom.[3]

[1] Since purchased from Russia by Great Britain and now in the British Museum.

[2] In the State Public Library (formerly the Imperial Public Library of St. Petersburg), as codex Q. v. 1.39.

[3] See B. Altaner, *Patrology* (tr. by Hilda Graef, New York: Herder & Herder, Inc., 1960), pp. 80–82.

The Epistle of Barnabas*

My greetings, sons and daughters, in the name of the Lord who has loved us, in peace.

Great and abundant have been the ordinances of God in your regard, and I rejoice most exceedingly over your blessed and glorious spirits, seeing that you have received so connatural a grace as the gift of the Spirit. . . .

[The author spoke of the abolition of the Jewish sacrifices and the Jewish fast (2–3), and warned them that the prophecy of Daniel (7.24) concerning the ten kingdoms was at hand; they must live in the fear of God, in order that the Wicked One may have no access (4.9). He then expounded the scapegoat theory of Christ's Atonement (in accordance with I Pet. 2.22–5 and Acts 8.32) in the spirit of the Servant Songs of Deutero-Isaiah.]

5   It was for this reason that the Lord endured surrendering his body to corruption, that we might be purified by the remission of our sins—that is, by the sprinkling of his blood. For what is written about Him partly concerns Israel and partly ourselves; and this is what it says: He was wounded for our transgressions and bruised for our sins. By his stripes we were healed. He was led like a sheep to slaughter and was dumb like the lamb before its shearer [Isa. 53.5, 7].

Surely should we give thanks to the Lord exceedingly, for He has made known to us the meaning of the past, given us understanding of the present, and we are not ignorant about what is to come. And the Scripture says: Not unjustly are the nets spread for the birds [Prov. 1.17]. And this means that when a person knows the way of justice and yet keeps to the way of darkness he will justly perish.

Consider further, my brethren, that the Lord endured suffering for our sakes, although He was the Lord of all the world and the one to whom God said at the beginning of the world: "Let us make man unto our image and likeness." How then could He endure to suffer at the hands of mortals? Listen. The prophets who received

* For the text, see T. Klauser (Bonn: Hanstein, 1940), and also Kirsopp Lake, *The Apostolic Fathers* (2 vols.; London: W. Heinemann, 1912), I, pp. 335 ff.

their grace from Him uttered prophecies about Him; and thus He endured it, to annihilate death, to reveal the resurrection from the dead (and this was why He had to be revealed in the flesh), to the end that He might fulfill the promises made to our forefathers, and that He himself might prepare this new people for himself and show while on earth that He himself will be the Judge after he has raised the dead.

Finally, he went about preaching, instructing Israel, and performing such signs and wonders; and He loved them intensely. But when he was about to choose his own apostles and those who would preach his Gospel (utterly sinful and lawless as they were), then indeed did He show himself to be the Son of God, in showing that He had not come to call the righteous but the sinners. For if he had not come in the flesh, how could men have been saved by looking to Him? For they cannot look straight into the rays of the sun, even though it is the work of his hands and doomed to destruction. So it was then that the Son of God came in the flesh, that He might fill out the total of the sins of those men who had persecuted his own prophets unto death. And hence it was for this reason that He suffered. For God says that the chastisement of his flesh came from them: When they strike their own shepherd then will the sheep of the flock perish [cf. Zech. 13.6–7]. And He was willing to suffer this way, for it was necessary that He should suffer on a tree. . . .

[Now that Barnabas had demonstrated the main reason for Christ's mission, he warmed to his theme: all the rites and rituals of the old law are fulfilled in the new (8–12), e.g., circumcision, the food laws, sacrifices. But despite his somewhat harsh treatment of the Jews who rejected the prophecies, he emphasized that both Jews and Christians, indeed, all men, are meant to be the heirs of the promises of the old law as renewed in the promises of Jesus (13–14). He then continued with his discussion of the passing of the old dispensation in Sabbath-day observance (15), and the Temple, for now the new spiritual temple of the Lord had been erected (16). A short paragraph ends the first part: "So much for that" (17).

[The so-called appendix (18–21) is different in style and seems to have been added later, being derived from the older *Teaching of the Twelve Apostles*. The author went into great detail on what practices constitute walking in the

Way of Light, e.g., avoiding fornication, adultery, sodomy, abortion, and infanticide (19). The outline of the Way of the Black One, as it is called, briefly goes over the same area from the opposite vantage point, and the spirited exhortation concludes (21).]

21.

3–9 The day is at hand when all things shall be destroyed together with the Evil One: The Lord and his reward are at hand [Isa. 40.10]. Again and again I must ask you to be good lawgivers to one another, and remain to each other faithful counselors, putting off all hypocrisy. And may God, the Lord of the entire universe, grant you wisdom, understanding, vision, knowledge of his commandments, and patience. And let God be your teacher, and search out what the Lord requires of you, and make sure that you will be found loyal on the Judgment Day. And if there is any remembrance of what is good, bear me in mind while you meditate on these things, so that my eagerness and my vigilance might bring you some profit—I beg this of you as a favor. While you are still in this fair vessel, do not fail in any of these things, but zealously pursue them, and fulfill every precept as it deserves. This was the reason why I was most eager to write you as well as I could, to bring you joy. Children of love and peace, may you win salvation. The Lord of glory and all grace be with your spirit.

[And so this very moving second part, which is extant only in the Greek manuscripts and not in the ancient third-century Latin version, concludes; though not part of the original letter attributed to Barnabas, it exhibits the primitive beauty of the documents of the early second century, and the spirit of its final passage is that of the Johannine Gospel: "Children of Love and peace, may you win salvation."]

4

THE SECOND EPISTLE OF CLEMENT TO THE CORINTHIANS

The so-called *Second Epistle* is not an epistle but a homily, delivered during the Liturgy (19), and thus it is perhaps the earliest Christian sermon preserved aside from the documents of the New Testament.[1] No firm evidence connects it with Clement of Rome, but we do find it in the two Greek manuscripts which contain the *First Epistle* of Clement, as well as in a Syriac version. An author of the Syrian compilation called the *Apostolic Canons* (from about 400) and the Arabic writer Abu'l Barakat of the fourteenth century spoke of the work as belonging to the New Testament. There are three current theories that explain its origin. Since it was attributed to Pope Clement, some scholars like A. von Harnack have suggested a Roman origin;[2] others like J. B. Lightfoot suggested Corinth itself, pointing to the imagery from the games in Section 7; J. R. Harris and B. H. Streeter put forward the view that it is an Alexandrian homily, and this might be supported by the author's curious quotation from the lost second-century Gnostic work, the *Gospel of the Egyptians* in Section 12. On the whole, it would seem best to assume that the work was originally a homily delivered at Corinth, and the reference to the personal sinful-

[1] See J. Quasten, *Initiation aux Pères de l'Eglise* (tr. by J. Laporte, Westminster, Md.: Newman Press, 1955), I, 64–70.

[2] A view now sustained by E. J. Goodspeed, *The Apostolic Fathers: An American Translation* (New York: Harper & Brothers, 1950), pp. 83–84. He presumed the *Epistle* to be a lost letter of Pope Soter's (166–74), sent to Corinth and acknowledged by Eusebius *Eccles. Hist.* 4.23.11. But this seems to ignore the very personal tone of the homily and the immediacy of the preacher's message in Sections 18 to 20.

ness of the preacher (or "reader," as he calls himself) and the "recompense" (19) calls to mind an itinerant teacher, who has come to the city at the time of the Isthmian games to preach repentance in the spirit of the *Shepherd* of Hermas. He is not one of the elders himself (17.3), for he urges his hearers to pay attention to them after they have gone back to their homes. Indeed, his use of the *Gospel of the Egyptians* might indicate that his own origins were Egyptian, but of this we cannot be sure.[3] The preacher presents an austere doctrine of repentance, probably allowing but one reconciliation after postbaptismal sin (cf. Secs. 8 and 17); but although the work may bear traces of latent Encratism (as perhaps in Sec. 12, in which there is the instruction that there be "neither male nor female," and the citing of the *Gospel of the Egyptians*), it is mainly a pleasing, primitive homily of the period of the Antonines.

The Homily*

1   Brothers, as for Jesus Christ, we should think of him as God, the Judge of the living and the dead; and we must not think lightly for our salvation. For if we think but little of him, we may hope to obtain but little. And those who listen as though it were to insignificant things commit sin; and we sin as well if we are unaware from what we were called, by whom, and to what goal, and what sufferings Christ Jesus endured for our sakes. What return then can we make to him, what fruit can we show him that will be worthy of what He has given us? How many blessings do we owe him? For it was light that He gave us, calling us sons as a father, saving us as we were

[3] It should be recalled that this Greek gospel is not identical with the Coptic gospel of the Egyptians discovered among the Nag Hammadi papyri. Clement of Alexandria quoted the same passage as our preacher. The context appears to be a discussion between Salome and Jesus; when Salome asks the Lord, "How long will death reign?" Jesus replies, "So long as you women bear children." As our preacher paraphrases it, the Lord's kingdom will appear when "the two shall be one . . . and the male with the female as neither male nor female" (12.2). On the *Gospel of the Egyptians*, see M. R. James, *The Apocryphal New Testament* (New York: Oxford University Press, 1924), pp. 10–12, and especially W. Schneemelcher (ed.) in E. Hennecke, *New Testament Apocrypha* (tr. by R. McL. Wilson, Philadelphia: Westminster Press, 1963), I, 166–78.

* See T. Schaefer (Bonn: Hanstein, 1941).

perishing. . . . He called us when we were not, and He willed that out of nothing we should come to be.

[Our obligations to Christ are supported by the Old Testament (2–3), and in the New Testament we are urged to show our good deeds under penalty of condemnation (4). Hence we must give up the sinful world, and live in it as lambs among wolves (5), for our baptism has separated us from Mammon, from adultery, avarice, and deceit; we cannot be on good terms with this life and the Hereafter (6).]

Let us then, my brothers, enter into the contest. There 7 is, we know, a contest close at hand, and many people are arriving by ship [4] for these corruptible games; but not all will win the crown, only those who have struggled hard and done well in the contest. So too we ought to run a straight path in our immortal contest: we too ought to come by ship in great numbers and compete for the crown. And even though we cannot all be crowned, at least let us come close to the victory. . . .

While we are on earth, then, we must repent. We are 8 like clay in the craftsman's hand. If a potter is working on a dish and it goes out of shape in his hands or cracks, he molds it all over again. But if he has gone so far as to put it into his heated oven, there is nothing he can do for it. So it is with us: while we are still in the world, we ought heartily repent of all the evil deeds we have committed in the flesh, so that while we still have time to repent we might be saved by the Lord. For once we have left the world, we can no longer make our confession [5] or repent in the Hereafter. And so, my brothers, if we do the Father's will, keep the Lord's commandments, and keep our flesh pure, we shall obtain everlasting life. The Lord says in the Gospel: If you have not guarded what is small, who will give you what is great? For I say to you, he who is faithful in a very little, is faithful also in much [Luke 16.10]. This then is what He means: keep your

[4] The place where the homily was preached during the Liturgy (see Sec. 17), must have been close to the site of international games; hence Corinth has been reasonably suggested.

[5] "*Exomologesis,*" the public confession of grievous faults, most probably in the presence of the elders, for the purpose of reconciliation after baptism.

flesh pure and your baptismal seal unstained, that we may receive life everlasting.

[Do not say, the author exhorted them, that the flesh will not rise again; as the Lord came in both flesh and spirit, so too will those who are faithful receive their reward also in the flesh (9). Beware of the pleasures of the present life (10); avoid doubt and double-mindedness. As the vine ripens from desolateness and green grapes, so too will the faithful receive God's promises (11). By doing the Father's will, we shall belong to the Church that existed before the ages; for the Church was of the spirit, but was made manifest in Christ; the Church is the body of Christ (14). The preacher then urged all to prayer, penance, and almsgiving (15–16); they should not only hearken to the elders while they are present at the Liturgy, but remember to remain righteous when they return to their homes (17). After warning them again of the Judgment, the preacher admitted his own faults.]

18   Therefore let us join the number of those who give thanks, those who have served God—not those wicked men who are condemned. Indeed, I myself am totally sinful: far from escaping temptation, I am still within the devil's strategems, eager though I am to pursue righteousness; how I would love to come close to it, in fear of the judgment to come!

19   And so, my brothers and sisters, following the God of truth, I am reading you an appeal to give heed to what has been written; thus you might save yourselves and the one who does the reading before you. For as my recompense I beg you to repent with all your hearts, and to give yourselves salvation and life. . . .

20   It ought not to trouble your minds to see the wicked with wealth and the servants of God in difficult straits. We must then have faith, my brothers and sisters. We are engaging in the contest of the living God; and we are being trained by the present life to win the crown in the life to come. No good man has ever won his reward at once; he must always wait for it. Indeed, if God rewarded the just right away, we would immediately become involved in a business transaction, not religion. We would give the impression of being good, when what we would be after would be personal profit, and not piety. This is the reason why God's judgment punishes a spirit

that is unjust and loads it with chains.[6]

To the one, invisible God, the Father of truth, who sent us the Savior, the prince of immortality, through whom He has shown us the truth and heavenly life—to Him be glory forever. Amen.

[6] Some commentators, e.g. Harnack, take this as referring to the chaining or inhibiting of Satan; he is the "spirit that is unjust." Indeed, the entire sentence seems to be out of context, and some of the passage may have been lost.

5

IGNATIUS OF ANTIOCH

Despite some persistent controversies about dates, Ignatius was apparently the third bishop of Antioch after St. Peter and died sometime at the close of the reign of the emperor Trajan (98–117). His seven letters were all composed in the course of his final journey across Asia—until the time when he finally embarked on a voyage to Rome under guard, having been sent by the Roman authorities of Antioch to suffer martyrdom at Rome. The legal details of his arrest and enforced journey are unfortunately not well-known, but the letters in the so-called Middle Version present a moving portrait of an aged bishop going bravely to his death in imitation of his Master. From Antioch he proceeded by land stages or perhaps by sea to the coast of Cilicia, then to the city of Philadelphia (mod. Alaşehir) in ancient Lydia and to Sardes, and finally to the coastal sea of Smyrna (mod. Izmir). At Smyrna Ignatius was met by Bishop Polycarp and many ecclesiastical delegates from the communities of nearby Ephesus, Tralles, and Magnesia. Comfortably installed at Smyrna, though still under the watchful eye of the Roman guard, Ignatius composed his epistles for Ephesus, Tralles, and Magnesia, and also one for the community in Rome, with the help of Burrus, a deacon from Ephesus. From Smyrna he finally traveled to the tiny town of Troas on the Hellespont, there to embark for Rome. According to a later tradition, he sailed from Troas to Philippi in Macedon. But before leaving the coast he dispatched letters to the communities of Philadelphia, Smyrna, and to bishop Polycarp.[1]

[1] For discussion and bibliography, see Virginia Corwin, *St. Ignatius and Christianity in Antioch* (New Haven: Yale University Press, 1960); cf. also my article, "Ignatius of Antioch: Gnostic or Essene? A Note on Recent Work," *Theological Studies* 22 (1961), 103–10, with the sources there cited.

Although four distinct recensions of St. Ignatius' letters exist, most scholars in principle accept the authenticity of the so-called Middle Greek Version. A much longer or interpolated version of the letters seems to have emanated from a late fourth-century heretical circle; a Latin version from the hand of Robert Grosseteste (about 1250) contained four new letters of a highly suspicious character; a Syriac version consisted of only three abbreviated letters; and finally the Middle Version in Greek contains the seven letters mentioned by Eusebius in A.D. 326 and is generally agreed to be the original Ignatian collection.

The authentic collection discloses a deeply mystical, Pauline Christianity, full of the spirit of imminent martyrdom and abandonment of this world. The imagery of the letters reveals some Gnostic influence, and this aspect of Ignatius' theology has aroused wide controversy. Ignatius envisioned Jesus and God as one, for Jesus is the Word, the Logos, who breaks the ineffable silence of the Godhead. The Redeemer has come from the Father to unite men to Him, and Ignatius believes this union is achieved in the highest degree by the martyr's death, by becoming "the pure bread of Christ," ground by the teeth of the beasts in the amphitheater; Ignatius' poetic passion transformed this brutal form of execution into a symbol of great sanctity. It was by men of his character that the early Church was formed and molded.

Yet Ignatius' mysticism is firmly rooted in a profound vision of the concrete structure of the Church. Throughout the "catholic" Church (*Smyrnaeans* 8.2) the hallmark of unity is love, and this union has been revealed by Jesus as the union of the Godhead. Thus, to preserve the union, all who have been baptized must remain subject, in love, to their hierarchy, their bishops, priests, and deacons (*Magnesians* 6.1); and for harmony to be preserved, all heretics and their followers must be excluded from the Church and from the banquet of love, the agape. The union of love is fostered by eating of the "medicine of immortality," the "antidote against death" (*Ephesians* 20.2), which the Savior has left us. And within this harmony, the community at Rome, "presiding in Italy," is "preeminent in love" (*Romans*, Introd.).

The attempts of some recent scholars to cast doubt on the authenticity of the Ignatian corpus, even in the form preserved in the Middle Version, have not been successful. It is true that the exact dates of Ignatius' bishopric, and whether he was the second or third bishop after St. Peter, are still not known, though the theology of the letters can be reconciled with a date late in the reign of emperor Trajan or even early

Hadrian. Controversy regarding the ultimate meaning of Ignatius' message may also still go on, but the letters must be accepted as an important witness to the mystery of early Christianity.

Ignatius to the Ephesians*

[Ignatius urged the community at Ephesus to avoid the Gnostic heresies which were rampant in the area at that time and to be submissive to their bishop. As he approached his martyrdom he urged them to pray for all men "that they may find God" (10).]

18   My spirit is an offering to the Cross—an offense to those who have no faith, but to us salvation and eternal life. Where now is your philosopher, where now your debater? Where is the pride of those who are called wise? Our Lord, Jesus the Christ, was conceived by Mary in God's dispensation from the seed of David and from the Holy Spirit; and He was born and was baptized, that He might cleanse the waters by his suffering.

19   The Prince of this world had no knowledge of Mary's virginity and her motherhood, hidden from him also was the Lord's death; these were three mysteries to be shouted aloud, but accomplished in the stillness of God. And how was He made manifest to the ages? A star shone in the heavens, brighter than any other, of an ineffable light, and there was astonishment at its strangeness. And all the other stars, with the sun and moon, formed a chorus around this star—but it outshone all of them, and there was wonderment as to where it came from, so strange, so unlike the rest. And thus was destroyed all the fascination, all the chains of evil, ignorance was wiped away, and the ancient regime was crushed when God appeared in human form to bring us the new eternal life—and thus began what God had prepared. For thus were all things confused because He was plotting the destruction of Death. . . .

21   Pray for the community in Syria, from which I am being taken as a prisoner to Rome, though I am the least of all the faithful there, though I have been deemed worthy to do honor to God. My farewell to you in God the Father and in Jesus Christ, who is our common hope.

* For the text, see Kirsopp Lake, *The Apostolic Fathers* (Cambridge: Harvard University Press, 1959), I, 172 ff. Cf. also T. Camelot (Sources Chrétiennes 10, Paris: Editions du Cerf, 1951).

*Ignatius to the Trallians**

Hold deaf ears to anyone who speaks to you apart 9
from Christ Jesus, who was of the line of David, truly
born of Mary, who ate and drank, was truly tried by
Pontius Pilate, was really crucified, and died in the sight of
those who looked on from Heaven, earth, and from the
underworld; who was truly raised from the dead, when
his Father wakened Him, just as his Father will raise up
all of us who believe in him in Christ Jesus, without
whom there is no true life in us.

But there are men who do not believe in God, that is, 10
they have no faith. If, as they declare, His suffering was
only an illusion (it is they themselves who are mere illusion), why then am I a prisoner, and why do I pray to
fight with the beasts? I would then be dying in vain. I 11
would be lying to you about the Lord. So run away from
these wicked offshoots that bear poisonous fruit; whoever
eats of it dies at once. For these were not planted by the
Father. For if they were, they would appear as branches
of the cross, and their fruit would be immortal; for it is
through the cross that Christ in his passion calls all of
you to be his members. Hence the head cannot be born
without limbs, for God promises us union, that is, himself.

*Ignatius to the Romans**

Ignatius, also known as Theophorus, to her who has
won mercy in the majesty of the Father most high and of
Jesus Christ his only Son, to the Church beloved and enlightened by the will of Him who wills everything that
exists according to the love of Christ Jesus our God,
which holds the chief place in the land of the Romans,
most honorable, blessed, venerable, worthy of success, all
pure, and preeminent in love, named by Christ and the
Father, which I too greet in the name of Jesus Christ. . . .

My message to all the churches and my injunction to 4
all is that I am glad to go to my death for God's sake, if
only you would do nothing to stop me. Please do not be

* For the text see Kirsopp Lake, *op. cit.* In the following passage St.
Ignatius presents the first Christian version of the Christological
creed, in this case a profession of faith against the heresy of the
Docetes, who taught that Christ's body was merely an illusion, a
kind of phantom that was believed to walk the earth and suffer.

* Kirsopp Lake, *op. cit.*

an unseasonable kindness to me: let me be the food of the beasts, through whom I can attain the presence of God. God's wheat am I and I shall be ground by the teeth of the beasts, that I may become the pure bread of Christ. Rather coax the beasts to become my supulcher and have no trace left of my body, so that when I fall asleep I shall cause inconvenience to no one. Truly then shall I become a disciple of Jesus Christ when the world will not even see my body. . . .

5   From Syria to Rome by land and sea, night and day, I am fighting the beasts, bound to ten leopards—that is, to a squad of soldiers—and they get worse the better you treat them. Because of their cruelty I am becoming a disciple more and more, but not by this am I justified. I pray I may enjoy the animals that are ready for me and that I may find them quickly. Indeed, I am going to coax them to consume me as soon as possible—and I won't be like those whom they were afraid to touch; even if they do not want to I will force them to— Pardon me, I know what's good for me; I am just beginning to become a disciple. May nothing visible or invisible begrudge my attaining to Christ Jesus. Burning, crucifixion, wrestling with wild animals, the crushing of my bones, the mangling of my limbs, the crushing of my whole body, the Fiend's foul tortures—come what may, if only I can attain to Christ Jesus! . . .

7   The Prince of this world would like to take me captive and destroy my will to God, but let none of you there present help him. Take my part instead, I mean God's. . . . I take no pleasure in the food of corruption or in the pleasures of this life. I desire the bread of God, that is, the flesh of Jesus Christ of the seed of David, and for my drink I want his blood, which is immortal love. . . .

Ignatius to the Smyrnaeans *

6   Let no man be deceived. Even the heavenly beings, the glory of the angels, the rulers both visible and invisible, will face judgment if they do not believe in the blood of Christ. He that can take it, let him take it. No one should be puffed up because of his position; faith and love are all, and there is nothing higher. Learn how contrary to the mind of God are those who hold strange views about

* Kirsopp Lake, *op. cit.*

the grace of Christ Jesus who has come to us. They care
not for love, nor for the widow, the orphan, the oppressed, those who are in prison or have been released,
nor for those who are in hunger and thirst. They ab- 7
stain from the Eucharist and from prayer; they do not
admit that the Eucharist is the flesh of Christ Jesus our
Savior who suffered for our sins, the flesh that the Father in his goodness has raised from the dead. Quarreling
with the gift of God, they perish in their disputes, whereas it will profit them to love, that they too might rise
again.

You had better keep away from such men; do not
speak with them either in public nor in private. Rather
attend to the prophets, and above all to the Gospel, in
which the Lord's passion has been revealed to us and the
Resurrection has been accomplished. Avoid divisions; they
are the beginning of evil. All of you should obey the 8
bishop—as Jesus Christ obeyed the Father—and the body
of elders as you would the apostles. And revere the
deacons as God's will. No one should do any of the things
pertaining to the church without the bishop. That is to
be considered an authentic Eucharistic liturgy which is
celebrated by the bishop or his legitimate substitute. The
congregation should be present wherever the bishop appears, just as the Catholic Church is wherever Jesus Christ
is. It is not allowed to baptize or to conduct an agape
without the bishop. But whatever he approves is also
pleasing to God. In this way everything you do will be
true and valid.

*Ignatius to Bishop Polycarp of Smyrna**

If you love those who are good subjects, this is no 2
credit to you. Rather, by your own gentleness, rule those
who are more difficult. You cannot cure every wound with
the same bandage. Convulsions are stopped by moist ap-
plications. . . . The season bids you to reach unto God,
just as pilots look for the winds and the storm-tossed
sailor seeks the harbor. Live soberly; you are God's athlete. The prize is immortality and eternal life—of this
you are certain. In all things am I an offering for you, I
and my chains, whom you have loved.

Do not be shocked by those who teach new doctrines 3
but seem to be worthy of credence. Stand solidly like an

* Kirsopp Lake, *op. cit.*

anvil under blows. A good athlete suffers blows but wins. So too we must suffer all things for the sake of God, and then He will put up with us. Be more zealous than you are. Understand the times; and wait for Him who is above all time, the eternal, invisible one, who became visible for our sake, the untouchable, impassible one, who took on pain for our sake and in every way suffered for us. . . .

6   All should give heed to the bishop, that God may give heed to you. I am an offering for all who are subject to their bishop, their elders, and deacons, and I hope I shall have my share with them in God. Work together, struggle together, run the race together, suffer together, take your rest together, and rise up again as God's stewards, his assistants, and servants. Please the one in whose ranks you serve, and from whom you receive your pay, and let no one be found a deserter. Let your baptism be your armor, your faith the helmet, your love the spear, your fortitude your full panoply. And let your good deeds be your deposit paid in, that you may receive the savings that are your due. . . .

Polycarp to the Philippians*

Polycarp and the elders who are with him, to the Church of God at Philippi: mercy and peace from almighty God and from Christ Jesus our Savior be fulfilled in you.

1   I am very happy with you in Jesus Christ our Lord that you received the examples of true love and according to your opportunity helped those who were weighed down with holy chains. . . .

* See Kirsopp Lake, *op. cit.*, for the text. This early letter from Bishop Polycarp is an important addition to the corpus of Ignatius. After Ignatius had left Philippi for Rome, the community at Philippi wrote to Polycarp for copies of such letters as he had, and this request he complied with in the present letter, enclosing some of Ignatius' letters, we know not how many. Unfortunately, Polycarp's epistle is not completely extant in any one Greek manuscript, and the gaps must be completed by quotations from Eusebius, (*Eccles. Hist.* 3.36.13–15) and an early Latin version. There have been efforts to divide Polycarp's letter into two separate letters, one to introduce Ignatius' epistles (Chaps. 13–14), and the other (1–12) written much later to the Church at Philippi in order to settle a local crisis. The theory, however unproven, does account for the inconsistencies in the letter, but these are perhaps due rather to hasty revision and the hazards of manuscript transmission. Polycarp's writing reveals a deep knowledge of Christian doctrine and a fine sensitivity for the problems of the early Christian communities. It is unfortunate that so little of his work remains.

I write this, brothers, concerning righteousness, not on 3
my own initiative, but because you have requested it. . . .

Aware then that God is not mocked, we must walk 5
worthy of his commandments and his glory. Deacons, too,
should be innocent in his sight, as the servants of God
and of Christ, not of men; and they ought not to be
liars or deceivers, not money-lovers, but self-controlled in
all things, sympathetic, considerate, walking according to
the Lord's truth, for He was the servant of all. For if we
please Him in this world we shall receive from Him the
world that is to come, in accord with his promise that He
would raise us from the dead; and if we are honest
citizens of this city, we shall also share his throne, if we
but have faith.

The younger men, too, should be innocent in all respects, being careful above all of chastity and curbing
themselves from all sin. Indeed, it is right to abstain from
the passions of this world, for every passion is at war
with the Spirit, and the adulterers and effeminate and
the homosexuals and all who perform wicked deeds will
not inherit the kingdom of God [I Cor. 6.9]. Hence you
must abstain from all this, and be subject to the elders
and the deacons as to God and to Christ.

Virgins should walk with a pure and innocent con- 6
science. And the elders should be sympathetic, kind to
all, recovering those that have gone astray, visiting the
sick, taking care of widows, orphans, and the poor, always attempting to do what is good in the eyes of God
and man, abstaining from all anger, from partiality and
unjust decisions, keeping away from all avarice, not
quick to believe evil of others, not irresponsible in judgment, aware that we all owe a debt of sin. . . .

Ignatius wrote me, as well as yourselves, that if a mes- 13
senger was going to Syria, he could deliver the letters
from you. I shall do this if opportunity allows, either
myself, or through the person whom I am sending as a
legate for myself and for you. Acting on your request,
we are sending (attached to this letter) the epistles of
Ignatius that he sent us, as well as other ones that we had.
You shall be able to take great profit from them, for they
are filled with faith, fortitude, and all things which make
for edification in our Lord. . . .

The Martyrdom of Bishop Polycarp

Polycarp, the venerable bishop of Smyrna, had been a close friend and admirer of the great Ignatius of Antioch and was the custodian of Ignatius' letters after the Antiochene bishop had proceeded to Rome on his way to martyrdom. Polycarp himself was arrested by Roman authorities shortly after he returned from Rome, where he had been having discussions with Pope Anicetus about the date of Easter. And so, at the age of eighty-six, after forty years in the episcopate, this harmless patriarch was put to death on February 23, A.D. 156, under the reign of Antoninus Pius.[2] The Christian community at Smyrna composed an account of his martyrdom and sent it as a letter to the Church at Philomelion. Irenaeus (*Against Heresies* 3.3) said that he had "been trained by the apostles themselves and had spoken with many who had seen Christ." In Rome Polycarp was supposed to have met the brilliant Gnostic heretic Marcion and called him "the firstborn of Satan." Eusebius' *Ecclesiastical History* (4.15) contains a copy of much of the text of the *Martyrdom*; there are six Greek manuscripts, along with Latin, Syriac, and Coptic versions. The authenticity of the account is not doubted, except for miraculous details, like the dove issuing from the fire in Section 16.

The Martyrdom *

The Church of God at Smyrna to the Church of God at Philomelion and to all the communities of the holy Catholic Church everywhere: may the mercy, peace, and love of God our Father and the Lord Jesus Christ descend on you abundantly.

1   Brethren, we are writing to you in connection with the martyrs and blessed Polycarp; it was he who brought the persecution to an end, setting upon it the seal, as it were, of his own death. For one might say that practically all

---

[2] This traditional date has been questioned by some scholars who suggest the year 177 (e.g., H. Grégoire and P. Orgels), or sometime from 161 to 169 (H. Marrou). For the literature, see J. Quasten, *Initiation aux Pères de l'Eglise* (tr. by J. Laporte, Paris: Newman Press, 1955), I, pp. 92–93.

* For the text, see T. Camelot (Sources Chrétiennes 10 Paris: Editions du Cerf, 1951), pp. 242–74.

of the preceding events took place so that the Lord might once more demonstrate to us a martyrdom in accordance with the Gospel. For he, too, waited to be betrayed, like the Lord, so that we might imitate him not only for our own advantage but also for our brethren. This is the mark of true and constant love—that we wish not only our own salvation but the salvation of all our brethren.

Blessed indeed and noble are all the martyrs' deaths   2
that took place by God's will. For we must take care to attribute to God the power over all things. For who could fail to be moved by their magnificent fortitude and love of their Master? Torn by the whips till their flesh lay open, revealing their inner veins and arteries, they persevered, and even the bystanders pitied them and wept. Still others were so heroic that they uttered neither a sigh nor a groan, suggesting to us all that even in the midst of tortures these noble martyrs of Christ were absent from their bodies, or, rather, that the Lord himself was present to them and spoke with them. Attentive to the grace of Jesus, they despised the world's torments, purchasing eternal happiness with a single hour of suffering. Indeed, the fire applied by their cruel torturers felt cold to them as they focused their minds on the eternal inextinguishable fire they would escape; and in their mind's eye they saw the blessings stored up for those who persevere, *which eye has not seen nor ear heard, nor has it entered into the heart of man.* But of all this the Lord gave them a vision, since they were no longer men but angels. So too, those who were condemned to the amphitheater endured excruciating tortures, being stretched over sharp shards or subjected to other forms of varied torments, the idea being that the tyrant might thus reduce them to denying their faith through continuous punishment.

Thus the Devil used many tricks against them, but   3
(thank God) he failed in every case. The most noble Germanicus strengthened them in their faintheartedness by the fortitude he showed, fighting gloriously against the wild beasts. Indeed, when the proconsul tried to move him, telling him to have pity on his youth, he forced the animal to rush upon himself, that he might sooner escape this unjust and lawless life. At this point the entire crowd were amazed at the courage of the pious and devoted race of Christians and shouted, "Away with the atheists! We want Polycarp!"

There was a man named Quintus, a Phrygian who had   4
just come from Phrygia, and he was terrified when he

saw the beasts. It was he who had deliberately come forward, forcing others to come with him of their own accord. The proconsul, after a good deal of persuasion, convinced the man to offer sacrifice and swear he was not a Christian. Brethren, this is the reason why we do not approve of those who give themselves up; this is not the message of the Gospel.

5 But the venerable Polycarp, as soon as he heard all this, showed no alarm; in fact he wanted to remain in the city, but the majority prevailed on him to go away quietly. This he did, going to a small farm on the outskirts of the city. Here he stayed with several others, devoting his nights and days to praying for all mankind and for the Christian communities all over the world, as was his custom. Once, while at prayer, three days before his arrest, he had a vision. He saw his pillow ablaze. With that, he turned to those who were with him and said, "I am to be burned alive."

6 The search party that was looking for him kept on his trail, and so he moved to another farmhouse. The search party barely missed him, and when they failed to find him, they took hold of two slaves, one of whom confessed under torture. Thus it was impossible for him to hide when those who belonged to the same household would betray him. And the chief of police, who happened to have the precise name of Herod, was very anxious to bring Polycarp to the amphitheater, that he might fulfill his destiny and have a share with Christ. And as for those who betrayed him, may they suffer the same penalty as Judas.

7 It was a Friday, about suppertime, when the police set out with their cavalry under full armor, taking the slave along with them, as though they were after a robber. Late the same night they caught up with him, finding him in a cottage in bed in a room upstairs. Actually, he could have escaped to another hideout, but he did not want to, saying, "God's will be done." When Polycarp heard that they had arrived, he went downstairs and spoke with them. All present marveled at his age and his courage; and they wondered why it was so urgent to arrest a man of his age. Because of the hour, then, he immediately ordered the men to be served food and drink as much as they wanted; as for himself, he asked for permission to have an hour's uninterrupted prayer. When they agreed to this, he stood there and made his prayer, and he was so full of God's grace that he was unable to stop for two

hours, to the amazement of the bystanders. And many of them expressed regret that they had come out to arrest such a God-fearing old man.

He finally brought his prayer to an end, after calling 8 to mind all the people he had ever met, great or small, famous or lowly, together with the whole Catholic Church all over the world. When it was time to leave, they put him upon an ass and led him into the city. And it was a great Sabbath day. The chief of police, Herod, with his father Niketas, met Polycarp, took him into their carriage, and, sitting on either side of him, tried to persuade him.

"What is wrong," they said, "with saying that Caesar is the lord, burning incense, and all the rest of it—and so saving your life?"

At first Polycarp made no answer. And when they kept on, he told them, "I am not going to do what you tell me."

When they got nowhere trying to change his mind, they began to threaten him; and then they put him out of the carriage so suddenly that as he got out he hurt his shin. Polycarp did not turn around and kept going so vigorously that he did not notice it. Then he was taken to the amphitheater, where the noise was so loud that no one could be heard.

As Polycarp entered the arena, he heard a voice from 9 Heaven saying, "Have courage, Polycarp, and act like a man."

No one saw whoever it was who spoke, but those of our brethren who were there heard the voice. Finally he was brought forward, and there was a tremendous roar when it was learned that Polycarp had been captured. As he was brought forward, the proconsul asked him if he was Polycarp. And when he said he was, the proconsul tried to urge him to deny the faith.

"Think of your age," he told him, and the other things they usually say. "Swear by the emperor's genius. Change your mind. Say, 'Away with the atheists!' "

With a grave countenance Polycarp looked at the crowds of lawless pagans in the amphitheater; then, gesturing at them with his hand, he looked up to Heaven, sighing. "Away with the atheists!" he said.

The proconsul kept insisting, "Take the oath and I will let you go. Curse Christ."

"For eighty-six years," Polycarp replied, "I have been his servant, and he has never done me harm. How can I blaspheme my King and Savior?"

"Swear by the emperor's genius," the proconsul persisted.

"If you have any mistaken notion," said Polycarp, "that I am going to swear by the emperor's genius, as you say, pretending that you don't know who I am, then let me tell you plainly: I'm a Christian. If, however, you would like to learn about the doctrines of Christianity, set a day for this and hear me."

The proconsul said, "Convince the people."

But Polycarp replied, "According to our teaching, we are supposed to pay due respect to official authority as it is established by God, provided this does us no harm. I should have thought it worthwhile to discuss this with you. But as for the rest, I do not think it worth my while to defend myself before them."

11   Said the proconsul, "I have wild animals. And I shall throw you to them unless you change your mind."

"Bring them on," said Polycarp, "for it is forbidden to us to change from better to worse. But it will be good to change from violence to righteousness."

"Since you despise the beasts," said the proconsul again, "I shall have you burned by fire if you don't change your mind."

But Polycarp answered, "The fire you threaten me with burns for an hour and after a while goes out. You obviously do not know of the fire of eternal punishment and of the Judgment to come that is stored up for the wicked. Well, why are you waiting? Bring on whatever you like!"

12   Saying this and many other things, Polycarp was filled with courage and joy and his countenance was suffused with graciousness. He did not collapse in terror at what was told him; rather it was the proconsul who was amazed, and he sent his herald out into the middle of the arena to announce three times: "Polycarp has admitted that he is a Christian."

And when the herald had said this, the entire crowd, made up of the pagans and Jews of Smyrna, roared back in an uncontrollable burst of anger: "Here is your teacher of all Asia, the father of the Christians, the man who has destroyed our gods, teaching men not to sacrifice or to venerate them!"

This was what they shouted to Philip, the high priest of all Asia, and urged him to release a lion upon Polycarp. Philip said that this was not lawful for him to do, for it was he who had put a stop to wild-animal games. Then they began shouting to him all together to have Polycarp burned alive. And indeed what he had seen happening to his pillow in a vision was to be fulfilled, when he saw it all on fire during his prayer and turned and said prophetically to the brethren around him, "I am to be burned alive."

Quicker than the time it took to say the words, it 13 happened. The crowd straightway collected sticks and firewood from the baths and shops . . . and when the scaffold was ready, he took off all his clothes, loosening his girdle and attempting to remove his sandals, although he had not done this before, for there was always one of the faithful who would want to be the first to touch his flesh. Because of his exemplary life he had always before his martyrdom been treated with the utmost respect.

At any rate, Polycarp was immediately attached to the instruments on the scaffold, but when they were about to nail him, he told them, "Let me be. For He who gives me the strength to endure the flames will also help me to stay on the scaffold without moving. You do not need to secure me with nails."

So they tied him instead of nailing him. And he drew 14 his hands behind his back and was tied, like a noble ram from a great flock prepared as an oblation, a holocaust acceptable to God. And, looking up to Heaven, he said, "O Lord God almighty, Father of thy beloved and blessed child Jesus Christ, through whom we have come to know you, God of the angels, the powers, and of all creation and of all the race of the just who live in your presence: I offer thanks to you for thinking me worthy of this day and hour, to share with the multitude of martyrs in the chalice of your Christ, unto the resurrection of both soul and body to life everlasting in the incorruptibility of the Holy Spirit. I pray that I may be accepted in their number today in your presence as a rich and acceptable sacrifice, just as you, the God of truth who cannot deceive, have prepared all this beforehand, and have shown it forth, and fulfilled it. Therefore I praise you in all things, I thank you, and glorify you, through the eternal high priest of heaven, Jesus Christ, your beloved child, through whom be glory to you together with Him and the Holy Spirit now and forever. Amen."

He had just finished the prayer with the "amen," when 15 the executioners lighted the fire. As the great flame blazed up, we who were present were privileged to see a miracle, and we have been preserved in order to tell others what happened. For the flames were transformed into the shape of a vault, like the sail of a ship bellying in the wind. Thus it formed a wall all around the martyr's body, which was in the center, not as burning flesh but as bread baking, or like gold and silver being purified in a furnace. And we perceived a fragrant odor as of incense or some other precious spice.

16 Finally these evil men realized that his body could not be consumed by fire, and so they ordered an executioner to go up and stab him with a dagger. And as the man did this, there came out of the body a dove, with such a quantity of blood that the fire was extinguished. And all the crowd were amazed that there was such a difference between the unbelievers and God's chosen ones, of whom indeed the glorious martyr Polycarp was one—an apostolic teacher and prophet of our generation, bishop of the Catholic Church at Smyrna. And every word that he spoke has been fulfilled and will be fulfilled.

17 Now many of us desired to remove his body and to touch his sacred remains. But the vicious, jealous Evil One, the adversary of the family of the righteous, saw the magnificence of his martyrdom and how his blameless life from the beginning was now crowned with the wreath of immortality, winning an incontestable prize. And so he planned that we should not be able to take away his remains. And so he inspired Niketas, Herod's father and Alce's brother, to request the governor not to give up the body. "There's a danger," he said, "that they may abandon the Crucified and begin worshipping this man." . . .

18 And when the centurion realized this, he put the body right into the fire, as the custom was, and burned it. We then picked up the bones, more valuable than jewels and better than gold, and buried them in a suitable spot. There we gather as often as possible with joy and gladness, and the Lord allows us to celebrate the day of his martyrdom as his birthday, both in memory of those who have already fought in the contest, and as a training and preparation for those who will one day do so.

19 This then is the story of blessed Polycarp. Counting those who came from Philadelphia, he was our twelfth martyr in Smyrna, but he is the only one whom everyone especially remembers and talks about everywhere, even among the pagans. He was not only an extraordinary teacher, he was also an exemplary martyr, whose death

everyone wishes to imitate, following as it did the Gospel of Christ. He worsted the cruel proconsul by his fortitude and thus won the crown of immortality; and now he rejoices with the Apostles and all the just, glorifying God the Father almighty and blessing Jesus Christ our Lord, the Savior of our souls, the pilot of our bodies, and the shepherd of the Catholic Church throughout the world.

You had requested a complete account of all that 20 happened. Up to the present we had only given brief details through our brother Marcion. And so when you receive this, circulate the letter to the brethren who are more distant, so that they too may glorify the Lord, who chooses his elect from the number of his own servants.

And to Him who is able to bring us by his grace and goodness into his everlasting Kingdom, through his only child Jesus Christ, be glory, honor, power, and majesty forever. Our greetings to all God's people. Greetings from all who are with us, and also from Evaristus (who writes this letter) and his entire household.

Now the blessed Polycarp was martyred early in the 21 month of Xanthicus, on the second day; and it was the seventh day before the first of March [February 23], a great Sabbath, at the eighth hour. He was arrested by Herod; Philip of Tralles was high priest and Statius Quadratus was proconsul. But Jesus Christ was reigning forever, to whom be glory, honor, majesty, and domination forever from generation to generation. Amen.

6

THE SHEPHERD OF HERMAS

The authorship of this mysterious apocalypse has not been ascertained. The name Hermas may simply have been adopted to make the work seem to have come from the entourage of St. Paul. The material itself suggests different stages of composition, going back perhaps to the end of the first century; but the final redactor, who flourished perhaps under the emperor Trajan, appears to have been a Greco-Italian lay preacher from the region around Naples and Cumae. The suggestion contained in the famous Latin fragment known as the *Muratorian Canon* (that is, a list of books considered to be the canonical Scriptures), that Hermas was a kinsman of Pius I, Bishop of Rome in the middle of the second century, may not be far from the truth. Despite the confused text, there is a basic thematic unity throughout the work. Hermas preaches the rigorist doctrine of repentance, allowing but one act of penance once a man has committed serious sin after baptism. Hence the primary theme is a call to penitence. But there are a number of secondary themes: for example, a more rigorous view of sin, insofar as every act performed out of pleasure is sinful ("Similitudes" 6.5.5); the virtues to be practiced by the just; and the manner in which the Church grows in the Word. The title of the work comes from the figure of a mysterious Shepherd, who speaks to Hermas and seems now to be the Angel of Repentance and now the good Shepherd of the Gospel. But the work could just as easily have been entitled *The Ancient Lady,* for at first the focus of Hermas' visions is the Roman lady Rhoda, whose slave Hermas was supposed to have been. In subsequent apparitions, however, we see and hear an ancient matron, who appears, first holding a codex containing the mandate she is to give him. During the following visions, she becomes gradually more youthful and beautiful.

Now she represents the wisdom of the Church, and now her eternal beauty. The aged sibyl of the *Shepherd* foreshadows Methodius' archetypal woman (in the *Banquet*) and is obviously the symbol of mother church, the virgin spouse of Christ, and an antecedent of the dignified lady who appears to Boethius in the *Consolation of Philosophy*. The type recurs in the later poetry of the Church, and it plays a deeply moving role in Dante's Beatrice, especially in the *Commedia*. In fact, *Hermas* portrays all the virtues and vices as women dressed and adorned in different ways. *Hermas* owes little to the Gospels, but more to the epistles of St. Paul, and especially the epistle to the Hebrews. The work in general records Hermas' and his community's experience of guilt over their failure to live up to the fervent expectations of the Christian faith. Guilt is the ultimate impulse in the construction of the series of disturbed and confusing dreamvisions. Hermas lays the groundwork for the second repentance (which he feels the Church needs) in his vision of the healthy Vine and the Willow Tree, and for the collaborative work of all true Christians in the erection of the great Tower. Despite the rigorous spirit of the work, the ending seems optimistic. Hermas proposes to live chastely with the Twelve Good Maidens, who represent the virtues of the Christian; this is how the Woman who reminds him of his guilt shows him to live with the Church in its pristine beauty. The work manifests serious confusion about the persons of the Trinity, and there is no reference in it to the sacramental liturgy. Yet the simple colloquial style has a curious charm, which accounts for the wide distribution of the text in many different versions throughout Europe, Egypt, and Asia. As it spread, it acquired new variants and modifications. An almost complete Greek manuscript of the *Shepherd* is in the monastery of St. Gregory on Mt. Athos; a large fragment is contained in the Codex Sinaiticus in the British Museum; and, in addition to many small papyrus fragments, there are two distinct Latin versions, an important Ethiopic and several Coptic versions. All of these have been utilized in the most recent edition of the Greek text by M. Whittaker.[1]

[1] In *Griechische christliche Schriftsteller* 48 (Berlin: Akademie-Verlag, 1956). For recent bibliography and discussion, see F. L. Cross, *The Early Christian Fathers* (London: Gerald Duckworth & Co., Ltd., 1960), pp. 23–27; H. Musurillo, *Symbolism and the Christian Imagination* (Baltimore, Md.: Helicon Press, Inc., 1962), pp. 32–40; S. Giet, *Hermas et les Pasteurs: Les trois auteurs du Pasteur d'Hermas* (Paris: Presses Universitaires de France, 1963), with the bibliography cited.

The Shepherd*

1   The man who brought me up sold me in Rome to a lady named Rhoda. Many years later we met again, and I came to love her as a sister. After a certain time I saw her bathing in the river Tiber and I gave her my hand to help her out of the river. When I saw her loveliness I thought to myself, "Wouldn't I be happy if I had a wife of such beauty and character?" I merely reflected on this and nothing more.

Sometime later I was traveling to Cumae, glorifying God's creatures for their greatness, and beauty, and power, and as I was going along I fell into a trance. And a spirit took me and bore me through a pathless tract impassable to man, for the place was precipitous and broken into clefts by the water. It was a river, and when I had crossed it, I came to flat country. I knelt down and began to pray to the Lord, reciting the confession of sins. And while I was praying, the heavens opened and I saw the very woman whom I had desired, and greeting me from heaven, she said, "Hello, Hermas."

Looking at her, I said, "My lady, what are you doing here?"

"I was taken up," she replied, "that I might accuse you of your sins before the Lord."

Said I, "So now you are my accuser?"

"No," she said, "but listen to what I am going to tell you. God, who dwells in the heavens and has created all things out of nothing and increased and multiplied them for the sake of his holy Church, is angry with you because you have sinned against me."

I answered, "Sinned against you? In what way? Did I ever say a coarse word to you? Did I not always look on you as a goddess? Did I not always respect you as my own sister? How can you falsely charge me, my lady, with such wickedness and impurity?"

She laughed. "The desire for evil," she said, "did enter your heart. Or don't you think that it is wicked for an upright man when an impure desire enters his mind? No," said she, "it is a sin, and a great one. For the righteous man has righteous thoughts. So long as his thoughts are upright, his reputation stands steadfast in the heavens and he finds that the Lord will be favorable to him in all

* M. Whittaker, *op. cit.*

that he does. But those who think evil thoughts in their minds bring death and enslavement upon themselves, especially those who try to gain in this present life, who glory in riches and do not cling to the good things to come. Their souls will regret it; they have no hope, having despaired of themselves and their life. But as for you, pray to God, and He will heal your own sins and those of your entire household, and of all the faithful."

After she had said this, the heavens closed and I remained terrified and in grief. Then I said to myself, "If such a sin is to be recorded against me, how am I to be saved? For how am I to propitiate God for sins of mine which are fully deliberate? With what words will I be able to beg the Lord to forgive me?" 2

While I was pondering and debating this in my mind, I saw before me a great white throne of snow-white wool. And an elderly Lady clothed in shining white raiment came up with a book in her hands. She sat down by herself and greeted me, "Hello, Hermas."

I was grieving and in tears. "Hello, my lady," I said.

"Why so gloomy, Hermas?" she said. "You are always so patient and good-natured, and always laughing. Why so downcast and hardly cheerful?"

"Because of a very fine woman," I said, "who claims that I have sinned against her."

And she said, "Far be this from you, a servant of God! . . . But this is not why God is angry with you, but to bring you to convert your household, for they have sinned against the Lord and against you their parents. But you have been so fond of your children that you have not corrected them; you have allowed them to become worse. Hence the Lord is angry with you. . . ." 3

And when she stopped speaking in this way, she said to me, "Would you like to listen to my reading?"

I said, "Yes, my lady."

"Well, then," she said, "listen, and hear the glories of the Lord."

And I heard with attention and wonder things which I had no power to remember. For her words were all awe-inspiring and such as mere man cannot bear. Her last words, however, I recalled, for they were more gentle and suitable for us.

"Behold the Lord of hosts, who in his invisible power and might and great wisdom has fashioned the universe and has clothed his creation in loveliness following a glorious design. He has fixed the heavens with his word of power, established the earth upon the waters, and fashioned his holy Church by his wisdom and foresight, and blessed it. Behold now He is shifting heavens, mountains, hills, and seas, and everything will be leveled for the sake of his chosen ones, that He may fulfill the promise He made to them with great glory and joy, provided only they preserve the commandments of the Lord which they received in great faith."

4   When she finished reading, then, she got up from the throne, and four young men came and took the throne and departed for the East. Then she called me over, touched me on the breast, and said, "Did you like my reading?"

"My lady," said I, "I liked those last words of yours, but the first ones were hard and painful."

She said, "What I said last was for the good. The first words were for pagans and apostates."

While she was speaking with me two men appeared and grasped her by the arms and went off to the East, where they had taken the throne. And she was cheerful as she went, and as she was going she told me, "Hermas, act like a man!"

[The elderly Lady appears to Hermas several times and tells him he must "write out two small books and send one to Clement and another to Grapte. Then Clement must send it to distant cities, for that is his duty, and Grapte will preach to the widows and orphans. But you will recite it aloud to this city along with the elders who have the care of the Church." The city is Cumae. Later on she will explain the sufferings of martyrdom and the parable of the great tower. She tells him, "The Tower you see being built is myself, the Church." The rejected stones are the sinful or those who deny their Lord when persecution comes (*Shepherd* 5–17).]

18   When she stopped speaking to me, the six young men who had been working on the building came and carried her away to the Tower, and four others picked up the couch and carried it away also. But they were turned away from me and I did not see their faces. As she was going, I begged her to explain to me the three forms in which she had appeared to me. But her answer was, "You will have to ask someone else to explain this to you."

Now, brethren, the first time she appeared to me last year she seemed very elderly and was sitting on a throne.

In the second vision her face was more youthful, but her skin and her hair were old. She spoke to me standing up and she seemed more cheerful than before. In the third vision she was altogether younger looking and strikingly beautiful. Only her hair was that of an older woman. She was perfectly cheerful and sat upon a couch. I was very disturbed by all of this, since I wanted to understand the meaning of this revelation. One night I had a vision in which I saw the elderly Lady speaking to me.

"Every question you ask demands humility. Fast, then, and you will receive what you desire from the Lord."

And so I fasted for a day. That very night a young man appeared to me and said, "Why do you always want to have revelations ready to hand for your needs? Be careful; you will injure your body with so many requests. The revelations you have seen should suffice. Do you think you are able to endure greater revelations than the ones you have seen?"

My answer to him was, "All I ask, sir, is a complete explanation of the three forms of the elderly Lady." . . .

"Here is the explanation of the forms," he said, "that 19 you desire. Why did she appear to you in the first vision as an elderly lady seated on a throne? Because the spirits of you and your brethren are old and already shriveled up, impotent because of your weakness and your hesitations. Elderly people, who have given up all hope of growing young again, look forward to nothing but sleep. And so it is with yourselves, softened by worldly things you have surrendered to apathy and have not cast your cares upon the Lord. . . .

"And in the third vision you saw her as lovelier and 21 younger looking, cheerful and beautiful in form. . . . So too you have undergone a renewal of spirit because of the good things that you have seen. She was seated on a couch, for this suggests a secure position. A couch stands solidly on four legs, as the world is controlled by four elements. So those who have fully repented of their ways will become young again and firmly founded—those, that is, who have repented with all their heart.

"There you have the entire revelation. Do not ask about it again. If necessary, a revelation will be made to you."

Twenty days after the preceding vision, brethren, I had 22 a fourth vision, which was a foreshadowing of imminent persecution. I was traveling out to the country by the Campanian Way. The spot is about ten stades off the main road and is easily reached. As I walked along by myself, I asked the Lord to complete the visions and revelations that He had shown me through his holy Church, to make me strong and to grant a spirit of penance to his servants who had fallen, that his great and wonderful name might be glorified, because He had deemed me worthy of being shown these marvels. And I was glorifying Him and giving thanks, when the sound as it were of a voice replied, "Hermas, do not doubt."

And I began to reason with myself, saying, "Why should I doubt when I have been given such support by the Lord and have seen such glorious things?"

And I went a little farther on, and behold, brethren, I saw what seemed to be a cloud of dust reaching up to heaven and I started to say to myself, "It is probably cattle that are coming and stirring up this dust cloud."

It was about a stade away from me. But as the cloud grew bigger and bigger I suspected that it was from God. The sun shone for a bit, and behold I saw a monstrous beast like a whale, with fiery locusts pouring out of its mouth. The beast measured about a hundred feet long, and its head was shaped like a vase. Then I began to cry and ask the Lord to deliver me from it.

Then I recalled the words I had heard: "Hermas, do not doubt." And so, brethren, I put on the faith of the Lord and recalled the great things He had taught me; I took courage and faced the animal. And it kept coming on with a rush great enough to destroy a city. I went right up to it, and the huge monster stretched itself on the ground and all it did was to stick out its tongue without moving at all until I had passed by. On its head the beast had four colors: first black, then the color of blood and flames, then gold, then white.

23　　After I had passed by the beast and had walked about thirty feet, behold I was met by a young girl dressed as though she were coming from a bridal chamber, all in white with white sandals, veiled up to her forehead, with her head covered with a turban. And her hair was white. From my earlier visions I realized that this was the Church and I became very happy.

She greeted me, saying, "Hello, my man."

"Hello, my lady," I greeted her in return.

In reply she said, "Didn't you meet anything?"

"Yes, I did, my lady," was what I said; "a beast of such size that it could destroy men, but by the power and mercy of the Lord I managed to escape it."

"And well you did," she said, "because you cast your

care upon the Lord and you opened your heart to Him, believing that you can be saved by nothing but his great and wondrous name. For this reason the Lord sent his angel named Thegri, who is in charge of beasts; and it was he who stopped its mouth, so that it could not harm you. You have thus escaped great affliction because you believed, and did not doubt when you saw this huge beast. Go, then, and explain the great deeds of the Lord to his chosen ones and tell them that the beast is a symbol of a great persecution to come. . . ."

[Most of the other visions and revelations made to Hermas come from a mysterious Shepherd, who appears in Hermas' house, "clad in a white goatskin, with a wallet on his shoulders, and a staff in his hands." He has been sent, he says, "by the most venerable Angel to stay with you for the rest of your life" (*Shepherd* 25.1). He gives Hermas twelve great commandments (*Shepherd* 26–49): 1. Believe in God and fear Him. 2. Be sincere and single-minded. 3. Love truth. 4. Keep pure. 5. Be patient and understanding. 6. Practice self-control. 7. Fear the Lord and not the Devil. 8. Restrain oneself from adultery and all kinds of evil activity. 9. Petition the Lord without hesitation. 10. Avoid sadness. 11. Avoid false prophets. 12. Cast off all evil desires. In the third section of the work, called "Parables" or "Similitudes," the Shepherd illustrates the ideal Christian life by a series of visual symbols, i.e., the Vine, the Willow Tree, the great Tower, the twelve Mountains, and others. Various Christian practices are discussed in the course of the revelation, as for example fasting.]

I was fasting and while I was sitting on a certain mountain, thanking the Lord for all He had done for me, I saw the Shepherd sitting beside me. "You have come here rather early," he said. 54

"You see, my lord," I told him, "I am keeping a station."

"A station?" he said. "What is that?"

"I am fasting, my lord," I said.

"And why are you keeping this fast?" he asked.

I said, "It is what I have been accustomed to do, my lord."

He said, "You do not know how to fast to God. This fast you are keeping for Him is a useless one."

"How is that, my lord?" I asked.

He said, "Because this fast you think you are keeping is

not a fast. I will show you what a perfect and acceptable fast to the Lord is like."

"Indeed, my lord," said I, "you will make me very happy if I learn what fast is acceptable to God."

"Listen," he said. "God does not want such an empty fast. If you fast in this way you will achieve nothing in righteousness. This is the fast you should keep for God: Commit no evil in life, but serve the Lord with a pure heart. Keep his commandments, and live according to his precepts, and let no evil desire come into your heart. Put your trust in God that if you do this, if you fear Him and avoid every wicked deed, you will live for God. And if you do this you will be observing a great fast and one that is acceptable to God. . . ."

.   .   .   .

67   He showed me a great Willow Tree that overshadowed the plains and mountains, and underneath its shade came all who were called by the name of the Lord. And there stood by the Willow an angel of the Lord, glorious and very tall, with a great sickle in his hand. He was cutting branches from the Willow Tree and giving them to the people who stood underneath its shade. Little sticks he gave them, about a cubit long. When everyone had got a stick, the angel laid aside his sickle, and the tree was as sound as when I had first seen it. I was surprised, and I said to myself, "How can the tree be sound after so many branches were cut from it?"

The Shepherd said to me, "Don't be surprised that the Tree has remained sound even though so many branches have been cut from it. Wait till you have seen everything, and then it will be clear to you what this means."

The angel who had distributed the sticks to the people called them all back again. All of them were called in the order in which they had received them, and each one of them handed back the sticks. And the angel of the Lord took them and examined them. Some of the sticks he got back were dried up and, as it were, moth-eaten. The ones who gave back these sticks were ordered by the angel to stand aside. Others gave in dry sticks, but they were not moth-eaten; and these he ordered to stand apart. Others handed in sticks that were half dried out, and they stood apart. Others handed in sticks that were half dried out and cracked, and they stood apart. Others brought up sticks that were green and cracked, and they stood apart. Others gave in sticks that were half green and half dried out, and they stood apart. . . . Still others came and brought back their sticks green as they had received them from the angel; and these were the greater part of the multitude and they stood apart; and the angel was very happy over these. Others brought back their sticks green and budding, and they stood apart, and the angel was also very happy over these. Others gave in their sticks not only green and with buds, but the buds seemed to have some fruit; and those whose sticks were this way were very happy and the angel rejoiced and the Shepherd was overjoyed because of them.

.   .   .   .

I wrote down the commands and the parables of the 78 Shepherd, the Angel of Repentance; and then he came and said to me, "I want to show you what you were shown by the Holy Spirit, who spoke with you in the form of the Church. For that Spirit is the Son of God. This was not shown to you by an angel because you were too weak of body. Then when you had been made strong through the spirit and were full of your own strength, so that you even look upon an angel, the building of the Tower was revealed to you by the Church; this you received well and with due reverence, revealed as it were by a maiden. Now you are seeing it through an angel, and yet through the same Spirit. For you must learn it all more accurately from me. . . ."

And so he led me off to Arcadia, to a rounded mountain, and at the top he made me sit down. He pointed out to me a vast plain, and around the plain were twelve Mountains, each of a different shape. The first Mountain was as black as soot, the second one was bare of any vegetation, and the third was covered with thorns and briers. And the fourth Mountain had vegetation that was half dried up, being green at the top but dry at the roots, and some of the plants were becoming parched because of the heat of the sun. The fifth Mountain was very rough and had green vegetation. The sixth Mountain was entirely riddled with cracks, some large and some small; there was vegetation in the cracks, but it was not very flourishing and seemed rather withered up. The seventh Mountain was covered with gay foliage, and the whole Mountain was in a flourishing state, with all kinds of cattle and birds feeding on it; and the more the cattle and the birds ate, the more the vegetation on this Mountain grew. The eighth Mountain was full of springs, and every sort of creature of the Lord drank from the springs of the Mountain. The ninth had no water at all and was entirely a desert, but it contained wild beasts and poisonous reptiles that were dangerous to men. The tenth had large trees on it and plenty of shade; under the shelter of the trees lay sheep resting and chewing. The eleventh was full of trees and the trees had fruit; and each of these were heavy with different sorts of fruit, such that anyone who saw them would be eager to eat them. The twelfth Mountain was all white, of very gay appearance, and the Mountain itself was exceedingly lovely.

[The latter part of the so-called ninth parable to the end of *The Shepherd* is preserved only in the two distinct Latin versions, in an Ethiopic translation, and a few fragments. The following passage, from the final section of the tenth parable, is taken from the Old Latin version as printed in the text of M. Whittaker (*G. C. S.* 1956, pp. 104–13). The young Maidens whom the Shepherd sends to live with Hermas at the close are, of course, the spirits who stand at the corners of the great Tower: Faith, Self-control, Strength, Fortitude, Innocence, Purity, Joy, Truth, and so on. They are equivalent to the Pauline fruits of the Holy Spirit and bring joy to those who live by the Gospel and defeat the adversary. The rigorous tract on second repentance comes to a close as the young irresponsible hero learns to live in harmony and self-control with the chaste Maidens, who embody the principles of the Church; thus the ending is optimistic and forward-looking despite the rumbling of persecutions that the Christians would face under the Roman emperors. Though Hermas seems to presuppose the precepts of the four Gospels, there is little solid evidence to show that he was actually familiar with the text. And so this curious apocalypse ends, shrouded in the same mysterious atmosphere with which it began.]

111   When I had finished writing this book, the angel who had handed me over to the Shepherd came to the house in which I was staying and he sat down upon the couch, with the Shepherd standing at his right hand. He called out to me then and said, "I have handed you and your household over to this Shepherd, that he might protect you."

"Very good, my lord," said I.

"So then," said he, "if you want to be protected from all annoyance and cruel treatment, to succeed in every honest work and word, to have every virtue of righteousness, then live in accordance with those commands of his which he gave you, and thus you will be able to overcome all evil.

"For if you abide by his commandments, all the desire and sensuality of this world will be subject to you, and success will follow you in every good deed. Take unto yourself his modesty and maturity, and tell all men that he stands in great honor and dignity with the Lord, that he is powerful in the exercise of his function, and a patron of vast influence. Throughout the entire world he alone has been given authority over penitence. Do you think that he is powerful? And yet you think little of his wisdom and the humble attitude that he displays toward you."

"My lord," I said, "ask him whether I have done any-112 thing out of the ordinary to offend him since the time he has been in my home."

"As far as I am concerned," said he, "I am not aware that you have done, or will do, anything out of the ordinary. Hence I will tell you this, that you may persevere. For he has expressed to me his high opinion of you. But you are to tell the others these things, that those who have done penance, or intend to, may think as you do, and that thus he may have a good impression of them with me and that I may do so before the Lord."

"My lord," said I, "I shall tell every man the great deeds of the Lord. I only hope that all those who hear this, if they have committed sin before, will be happy to do penance and be restored to life."

"Continue then," said he, "in this ministry and bring it to completion. All who fulfill his commands will have life, and such a man will have great honor before the Lord. But those who do not keep his commandments shall not have life and are his enemies. Whoever does so, however, will have honor before the Lord. But whoever is against him, not observing his commandments, deliver themselves to death, and each one will be guilty of his own blood. But I say unto you, keep his commandments and you shall have a remedy for your sins.

"Now I sent these Maidens to live with you, for I saw113 that they were agreeable to you. And so you will have them as your assistants, the better to observe his commandments. For without these Maidens you cannot keep these commandments. Further, I realize that they enjoy being with you. I will, however, tell them not to depart from your home at all. Only you must cleanse your entire house, for they like to live in a clean home. For they are pure and chaste and hard-working, and all are in favor with the Lord. So if they find your home pure, they will stay with you; but if there should occur the slightest defilement, they will depart from your home at once. For these Maidens have absolutely no love for defilement."

"Sir," said I, "I trust I shall please them, so that they may dwell in my home forever and they may have nothing to complain of, just as the one who handed me over to you had not."

He said to the Shepherd, "I see that the servant of God wishes life and is eager to keep these commandments and to establish these Maidens in a chaste home."

After he had said this he handed me over to the Shepherd again and, calling the Maidens, he said to them, "Since I realize that you are happy to live in his house, I commend him and his household to you, so that you may never again leave it." And they were happy at what he said.

114   Then he turned to me, "Live courageously in this ministry. Show forth to every creature the great deeds of the Lord and you will enjoy his favor in this ministry. Whoever shall walk in these commandments will live and shall be prosperous in his life; whoever contemns them will not live and will be unhappy in his life. Tell everyone who can do good never to cease doing good, for this is useful for them. Indeed, I say that all men should be rescued from distress. For the man who is in want and suffers distress in his daily life is in great pain and difficulty. And so whoever rescues such a one from difficulty will gain great happiness for himself. For the man who is troubled with such distress endures as much torment as though he were in chains. For many, because of such suffering, commit suicide when they cannot endure such affliction. Hence the man who is aware of another's suffering and does not rescue him commits a great sin and becomes guilty of his blood.

"And so all of you who have been taught from the Lord, perform good works, for if you put off doing them, the tower may be completed. It is because of you that the work of building has been postponed. Hence unless you hurry to do good deeds, the tower will be completed and you will be shut out of it."

After he had spoken to me, he arose from his couch and, taking the Shepherd and the Maidens, he went away. But he said that he would send the Shepherd and the Maidens back to my house.

7

THE PAGAN REACTION

The Palatine Graffito

On the south brow of the Palatine Hill in Rome is an imperial building known as the Paedagogium, which was perhaps a training school for young officers of the administration or pages. The walls of the various chambers are covered with crudely scratched inscriptions, or graffiti, one of the most famous of which is the supposed caricature of Christ's crucifixion.[1] The drawing represents a man apparently offering worship to another man who is crucified, but the head of the crucified is that of an ass. Below, in Greek, we read: ALEXAMENOS WORSHIPS HIS GOD. Removed from its site in 1857 to the Kircher Museum of Antiquities in Rome, the caricature has been finally transferred to the National Museum (Museo delle Terme), where it now reposes. Though some scholars maintain that the inscription is a blasphemous jibe, others suggest that there might be a connection with the Gnostic sect of the Sethians, who identified Christ with Seth, Seth being also the name of an Egyptian deity depicted with an ass's head.

If the graffito is really blasphemous, the idea of the representation may have come from the manner of crucifying or executing Christians, for example in the time of Nero, by dressing them up in the skins of wild animals, or else from some satirical mime deriding Christianity. Tacitus (*Annals* 15.44) described Nero's use of the Christians as scapegoats for the burning of Rome in A.D. 64, for which he had himself been held responsible:

> But neither human resources, imperial gifts, nor offerings to the gods could remove the suspicion that the

[1] See the note and the picture in the article, "Graffito," *Enciclopedia italiana dell' arte antica, classica e orientale* III (Rome: Treccani, 1960), 997.

fire had been a command performance. And so, in order to suppress the story, Nero trumped up charges and punished with all sorts of ingenious tortures the sect popularly known as the Christians, a group that had become hated for their crimes. The name originated with a man named Christ who had been executed by the governor Pontius Pilate under the reign of the emperor Tiberius . . . But despite the temporary repression of the destructive superstition, it once more broke out, not only throughout Judea, where the evil practice started, but also in Rome. All kinds of frightful and shameful things flock to Rome from everywhere and flourish there.

At any rate, those who gave themselves up were first arrested, and then by their information, huge numbers of others were charged, but not so much for arson as for a general hatred of mankind. He turned their executions into a circus: they were ripped to pieces by dogs, crucified or set aflame, dressed in the skins of animals, and as daylight failed, their bodies were burned in place of torches after dark. Nero provided his own gardens for the show and put on performances in the Circus, standing in his chariot or mixing with the crowd in a charioteer's garb. Though the victims were guilty and deserving of extreme punishment, at the same time they roused pity, since they were being sacrificed to the sadism of one man and not for the common good.

Tacitus is indeed ambiguous, for though he cannot bring himself to condone Nero's brutality and is following a source which definitely charged him with the burning of Rome, at the same time he is obviously offended by Christianity and cannot understand its mission within the framework of the old Roman religion. The chapter in the *Annals* is written with a touch of acid, but it gives an authentic picture of the sadistic nature of the early Roman persecutions.

The Christians of Bithynia and Pliny

One of the earliest pagan accounts of Christianity comes from one of the greatest letter writers of antiquity, Pliny the Younger. After a boyhood of wealth and comfort, Pliny enjoyed a brilliant public career at Rome and was a trusted civil servant under Domitian and Nerva. Finally, in A.D. 111, when he was about 50, he was sent out by emperor Trajan as proconsul of the lucrative province of Bithynia and held court in the city of Amisus (mod. Samsun, Turkey) on the Black Sea. What is so interesting about the letters is the scrupulous fairness with which Pliny attempted to deal with the Christians who had been transferred to his court. Nonetheless he betrayed a confusion about the exact nature of the crime that the Christians were supposed to be committing. Clearly, there was at this time no explicit law against Christianity; yet, many suspicions were apparently associated with the "name," as, for example, that of illicit clubs, inciting riots, contempt and disobedience towards Roman officials, or contempt and refusal to be associated with Roman religious worship. Indeed, contemptuous refusal to venerate the images of the emperor might be interpreted as *laesa maiestas* or treason, with the possibility of capital punishment.

Pliny's account of the primitive Christian liturgy is fascinating and has aroused much discussion. He distinguished two meetings or synaxes. The first, which took place before dawn (and was therefore a kind of vigil service), had a *carmen* (hymn or prayer) recited or sung antiphonally to Christ; this was followed by a *sacramentum* or solemn oath in which all those present were pledged not to commit serious sin. The nature of Pliny's evidence is difficult to reconstruct. However, the earlier service seems to resemble an instructional or catechumen service combined with a vigil. The second meeting or synaxis corresponds to the communion service or the agape, and the harmless and ordinary food for which the Christians assembled the Eucharist. It is interesting to note the date, and the fact that as much as twenty years before (from about A.D. 90) Christianity was already firmly established in the area of Amisus along the Black Sea. The reference to *ministrae*, or "deaconesses," is uniquely this period's. Trajan's famous principle, *conquirendi non sunt* (they are not to be sought out) would remain in vogue until the time of the persecution of Decius in 250/51, just as Pliny's practice, perhaps the first of its kind, of demanding, as a test, the veneration of the statues, would occasion the great crises of the third century, when certificates (*libelli*) would be issued to all who sacrificed to the gods, as proof that they were not Christian.

Pliny's Letter to Emperor Trajan* (10.96)

My Lord:

It has been my custom to refer all my doubts to you, for surely no one else could control my hesitation or instruct my ignorance. Since I have never been present at the trials of Christians, I am not familiar with the nature and extent of the trial or its penalties. Indeed, I felt considerable hesitation on the question of whether there should be any distinction with regard to the age of the accused, or whether there should be no difference between those who are stronger and those who are more delicate; or again whether pardon should be granted in cases of remorse, or no allowance be made for anyone who has ceased to be a Christian; or, finally, whether being a Christian is punishable in itself even though there are no other crimes, or only those crimes that are associated with the name should be punished.

While awaiting your reply I adopted the following procedure in the cases of those who were brought before me. First I asked them whether they were Christian. Then, when they admitted this, I would ask them a second and third time, warning them of the penalty; and those who persisted I ordered to be led off to punishment. For I felt convinced that whatever it was they were admitting, surely their stubbornness and persistent obstinacy should be punished. Others infected with the same folly were Roman citizens, and so I arranged for their being dispatched to Rome.

Soon, in the course of events, as usually happens, the accusation became more widespread, and a larger number of cases came to my attention. An anonymous accusation was submitted, containing the names of many people. One class I decided to release. These denied they had ever been Christians; and then at my dictation they invoked the gods and with incense and wine venerated your statue, which I had ordered to be brought in with those of the gods precisely for this purpose; in addition, they reviled the Christ, a thing that real Christians, it is said, can never be forced to do. Others who had been listed in the report first admitted they were Christians

---

* For the Latin text, see R. B. A. Mynors, *Plinii Secundi Epistulae* (Oxford: Clarendon Press, 1964).

but then denied it, saying that though they had been Christians, they gave up the practice, some only three years before, others a longer time, and a few as many as twenty years ago.[2] All of these venerated your image and the statues of the gods and cursed the Christ. But they declared that all that their fault or error amounted to was the custom of meeting on certain days before daybreak and singing a chant[3] to the Christ as to a god, taking turns, and then binding themselves by solemn oath[4] not to commit any crime but rather to avoid robbery, theft, adultery, and not to break faith or repudiate a deposit when summoned to do so. When this was over, they used to disperse and meet later for a meal, of an ordinary and harmless kind, and as a matter of fact they had stopped doing this after my edict, in which, following your instructions, I have outlawed the existence of secret societies.

At any rate I felt it all the more imperative to discover the truth by torture from two servants whom they call deaconesses.[5] But I discovered nothing but an absurd and exaggerated superstition. Hence I adjourned the trial and determined to consult you. Indeed, I felt the case merited consultation especially because of the great numbers of the people involved; for those who are being indicted, or soon will be, are numerous and of both sexes, from every class of the people and every age group. For the infection of this superstition has spread not only to the towns and villages but also to the countryside. But I think it can be stopped and corrected. At any rate it is a well-known fact that temples that had been all but abandoned have begun to be filled again, and the people have resumed the celebration of sacred rites that had long been neglected; also, there has been a market for the food of sacrificial animals, whereas before there was hardly anyone to purchase them. This suggests that the bulk of

[2] Some manuscripts read "twenty-five."

[3] The Latin *dicere carmen* may mean "recite a set form of words," and not necessarily "sing." "Taking turns" must refer to antiphonal singing or recitation.

[4] That is, *sacramento*, but not necessarily with a Christian sense here.

[5] Latin *ministrae*, used of assistants to priests in religious worship.

mankind can be corrected if they are given a chance for repentance.

Trajan's Reply* (10.98)

My dear Pliny,

You have followed the right procedure, my Secundus, in your investigation of the cases of those who have been denounced to you as Christian. Actually, no general law can be laid down which would be applicable in all cases.[6] They are not to be sought out; but if they are delated and convicted, they are to be punished. However, anyone who denies he is a Christian and proves this in fact by venerating our gods, even though he may have been suspected in the past, should be pardoned because of his retraction. Anonymous reports, however, are not to be admitted in any case; they set a bad precedent and do not conform to the spirit of our age.[7]

Lucian of Samosata

The life of the pagan satirist Lucian covers the period from about A.D. 120 to shortly after 180, and his career as a wandering lecturer and Cynic philosopher took him around much of the Greek-speaking Roman empire from Syria to Gaul. He died after having served as a civil servant in Egypt under the reign of Septimius. His dialogues show him striking out at every human foible, the pretensions of the

* R.B.A. Mynors, *op. cit.*

[6] This and the following are the two sentences that suggest that there was no specific law against Christians as such in the time of Trajan and that Christians were punished only for specific crimes, such as belonging to clandestine societies, rioting, *lèse-majesté* towards the emperor or his family, and similar offenses.

[7] In his *Life of Agricola* (3) Tacitus justly praised the spirit of liberty and freedom which accompanied Trajan's reign: "Trajan daily augments the prosperity of our age, and the commonweal not only has a hope and expectation but a strong guarantee of fulfillment." What Gibbon said of the entire period was preeminently true of Trajan, speaking of those emperors "who delighted in the image of liberty, and were pleased with considering themselves as the accountable ministers of the laws," *The Decline and Fall of the Roman Empire* (2 vols.; New York: Modern Library, Inc., 1932), I, 70.

different schools of contemporary philosophy, charlatanism, and religious mania, and, like many of the clever Cynic philosophers of his own and an earlier period, attacking other positions without having anything constructive of his own to offer.[8] In his treatise *On the Syrian Goddess* he explained the peculiar cult of pillar climbing in Heliopolis (mod. Ba'albek, Lebanon), which may have influenced the holy Syrian stylite monks, who lived for years on lofty pillars. But his most interesting reference to contemporary Christianity occurs in his biography of the Cynic eccentric Peregrinus Proteus of Parium, Mysia (about A.D. 100–165). Lucian is the only source for all the details of his life, and therefore they may not all be reliable.[9]

Peregrinus ran away from his native city because he was accused of murdering his own father; in Palestine, he was converted to Christianity and (if we are to believe Lucian), cheated and bilked the Christians for as much as they were worth. The attendance of the various legates at his prison doors reminds one oddly of the special treatment accorded St. Ignatius of Antioch when he came to Smyrna on his way to death in Rome, and it may be that Lucian had somehow heard or read Ignatius' story.

At any rate, Peregrinus brilliantly exegeted the Christian "writings" (or Scriptures) and even, Lucian says, wrote a few of them himself. But the sumptuous prison banquets and "sacred discourses" by this new-found Socrates came to an abrupt end when he was discovered eating forbidden foods. His days of sponging were over, and, returning to Parium, Peregrinus demanded back his patrimony, which he had given the city in a moment of ascetic generosity. On the loose again, he came to Alexandria in Egypt about the year 150 in order to become the disciple of a Cynic named Agathobulus. There, with his head shaved on one side and his face smeared with mud, he would entertain passersby with his Cynic sermons, encouraging them to beat him with a stick. From Alexandria he went to Rome, but was expelled after criticizing the emperor Antoninus Pius. Finally, he turned up at the Olympic games in Greece, where he ended his wild career by preaching a last sermon against Rome and burning himself to death in Oriental fashion in the year 165. His career furnishes an interesting if neurotic side-

---

8 See M. W. Edwards, "Lucian," *Oxford Classical Dictionary* (Oxford: Oxford University Press, 1949), p. 515, with the bibliography.

9 D. Völter, *Polykarp und Ignatius* (Leiden: E. J. Brill, 1910), claimed that all the Ignatian epistles save *Romans* were composed by the Cynic Peregrinus, but this fantastic theory has been adopted by no one else.

light on the period in which the early Christians lived and suffered punishment and death.[10]

The Story of Peregrinus*

At this time Peregrinus became familiar with the won- 11 derful doctrine of the Christians, after meeting with their priests and scribes in Palestine. Well, in a short time, he showed what children they were, becoming a prophet, a leader of the community and the synagogue, and in fact everything, all by himself. He exegeted and explained some of the Scriptures, and many of them he wrote himself. They looked on him as a god, used him as a legislator, and inscribed him as their patron.

As a matter of fact, they still worship that great man who was crucified in Palestine for introducing a new religion into the world. At any rate, Proteus was shortly arrested and thrown into prison for this, bringing him in his later life a tremendous heightening of the charlatanism and notoriety that he doted on. Well, the Christians were greatly disturbed when he was put in jail and did all they could to have him released. And when their efforts came to naught, they performed every service they could, and not casually but with enthusiasm.

From dawn on could be seen old women (called widows) and orphaned children waiting at the prison doors; and those who had power among the Christians bribed the jailors and succeeded in sleeping inside with him. They had sumptuous dinners brought in, they held sacred discourses, and the good Peregrinus (for this was still his name) they called the new Socrates. Furthermore, some Christian deputies came from the cities of Asia, sent by the communities to help the prisoner, advise, and console him. They display an amazing speed whenever anything happens touching their congregation, and they become straightway lavish with all they hold. So too they sent a lot of money to Peregrinus because of his imprisonment, and he made quite a good thing of it. For these unfortunate people are persuaded they will live forever and become completely immortal. Hence it is that

[10] See the discussion of Peregrinus' philosophy in H. Musurillo, *The Acts of the Pagan Martyrs* (Oxford: Clarendon Press, 1954), pp. 269 ff., with the bibliography cited.

* For the text, see A. M. Harmon (ed.), *Lucian* (Cambridge: Harvard University Press, 1961), V, 2 ff.

they despise death, and many of them even give themselves up voluntarily.

Indeed, their first lawgiver convinced them that they would all be brothers of one another as soon as they had gone over and denied the gods of Greece and worshipped that crucified philosopher of theirs and lived in accordance with his precepts. They accept all this without any accurate proof and despise all things alike and hold their property in common. And so, if a clever trickster versed in worldly matters should slip in among them, he can make a lot of money in a short time, laughing at these simpletons. . . .

16   Peregrinus set forth on his wanderings a second time, having sufficient security in his Christian friends for expenses. Protected by them, he lived in absolute luxury and for a time he grew fat in this way. One day he committed some offense against them—I believe he was caught eating some forbidden food—and when they abandoned him he was in difficulties, and so, determined to take back the property that he had given to the city.[11]

---

[11] The forbidden food was probably the meat used in pagan sacrifice; it created a problem for many of the early Christians. The Council of Jerusalem in A.D. 50 had determined that converts should not eat food used in these sacrifices (see Acts 15.29). St. Paul was somewhat more lenient, but said that eating such food would bring scandal (I Cor. 8.8–13); see also I Cor. 10.14–33 on Christian participation at banquets).

8

INSCRIPTIONS FROM THE ROMAN CATACOMBS

Scholars have estimated that the forty odd catacombs under the city of Rome (there is one pagan and six Jewish cemeteries) measure more than sixty miles.[1] In the past, a cemetery would be erected on a definite piece of land, and when the available burial space was used up—which invariably came about, since the Christians and Jews buried the complete body—the practice arose of digging another floor underneath the existing level. Thus, in time, many of the cemeteries went down three and four levels at great depth. The largest of the catacombs, the cemetery of Domitilla, south of the city walls, consists of about eight miles of grave corridors. Though originally most of the Christian cemeteries began as private burial places, by the third century they had passed into the common ownership of the Church. The name "catacomb" came from the designation of the sunken valley now occupied by the catacomb of St. Sebastian as the cemetery *ad catacumbas,* from a Greek expression meaning "by the hollow." Thereafter all Christian cemeteries were called by the same name. The different types of grave, within niches or in more expensive sarcophagi, were often decorated with paintings, inscriptions, or other Christian symbols. The second to the third century, for example, left figures of the Good Shepherd, orantes, or praying figures, seasonal pictures, Daniel, Noah, Jonah and the whale, and others. After the Peace of the Church in the fourth century, scenes from the Old and New Testaments, pictures of Our Lord and the apostles, and allegorical scenes of great beauty replaced them. Interpretation

[1] See L. Hertling and E. Kirschbaum, *The Roman Catacombs and their Martyrs,* (tr. by Joseph Costelloe, Milwaukee: Bruce Publishing Company, 1956), especially pp. 15 ff.

of many of these pictures is hotly disputed by scholars.

The art of the catacombs figures importantly in any study of the popular beliefs of the primitive Church; consequently, there has been a vast literature on the representations of the Christian banquet, the agape, and on its frequent occurrence at this early period. Two of the earliest pictures come from the cemetery of Callistus and the cemetery of Priscilla, but they are difficult to date and may be late third or early fourth century. Representations of loaves and fishes (as for example in Callistus) perhaps go back further. There is a fine portrait of the Madonna and Child with the prophet Balaam in an arched vault in the cemetery of Priscilla; some scholars have dated it as early as the second century.[2] And in the same cemetery an appealing representation of the Wise Men worshipping the Child held in the lap of Mary seems to come from the same date. The praying figure called an orante—a male or female figure with hands uplifted to heaven in the Semitic prayer gesture—is everywhere to be seen, and there are different theories on its symbolism. At times the orante figure resembles an individual person; at others, however, it seems to represent merely the soul of the departed in an attitude of prayer in the Hereafter. Others have suggested that the figure stands for the prayers of the faithful for the departed soul. In all likelihood the symbolism varied and was not restricted to any one level.

The study of the primitive Christian inscriptions from the catacombs is fascinating. Apart from simple human interest value, these epitaphs, which Christian men and women chose for the adornment of their tombs, provide a glimpse of the growth of Christian doctrine and belief. Of course, we cannot look for profound dogma bearing on the great controversies of the first four centuries in the popular art of the catacombs and the simple memorials of the faithful departed. The rude pictures of the Christian love feast, and much less the chaste, unpremeditated inscriptions on the graves, cannot be expected to give us deep insight into the liturgy or the theology of the early Church. Yet they have an authentic, straightforward quality of their own and are essential for any complete portrait of the life of the early Church before the peace of Constantine and shortly after. After the death of Diocletian, there were more and more requests of the faithful to be buried "next to the martyrs"

---

[2] *Ibid.,* pp. 161 ff., on the art of the catacombs. As the authors shrewdly point out, no definite criteria have ever been established for the dating of catacomb art to the satisfaction of all scholars; hence the dates for any one picture will be widely divergent.

of the catacombs, situated outside Rome and Naples and scattered throughout Sicily. By the fifth century, the cemeteries had become places of pilgrimage, and by the eighth they were beginning to sink into that abandonment which lasted until the revival of antiquarian interest in the fifteenth century. The completely scientific approach to the excavation of the catacombs was begun by Father Giuseppe Marchi and John Baptist De Rossi in the middle of the nineteenth century under the aegis of Pope Pius IX, and many of the early archaeological finds were deposited in the Lateran Museum in Rome.

From the cemetery of St. Agnes:

SWEET FAUSTINA, MAY YOU LIVE IN GOD.[3]

HAPPY FLORENTIUS, LITTLE LAMB OF GOD.[4]

Graffiti on the walls of the Catacomb of St. Sebastian, in the crypt of the apostles Peter and Paul:

PETER AND PAUL, PRAY FOR VICTOR! [5]

PAUL AND PETER, REMEMBER SOZOMEN AND WHOEVER READS THIS! [6]

PAUL AND PETER, PRAY FOR NATIVUS FOREVER! [7]

From the cemetery of St. Callistus:

FABIAN, BISHOP AND MARTYR.[8]

PONTIANUS, BISHOP AND MARTYR.[9]

---

[3] This inscription can be found in the collection by Ernest Diehl, *Inscriptiones Latinae Christianae Veteres*, (3 vols., 2nd ed.; Berlin: Weidmann, 1961), 2196 A. It is now in the Lateran Museum; see O. Marucchi, *Christian Epigraphy* (Cambridge: Cambridge University Press, 1912), p. 89.

[4] See Diehl, *op. cit.*, 2481.

[5] *Ibid.*, 2333. This and the following invocations were crudely scratched in the stucco. Between the years 258 and 313, Christian pilgrims gathered for a memorial service here in honor of Sts. Peter and Paul, but the exact reason is not quite clear. Many scholars hold that this spot (in what is now San Sebastiano) was a temporary resting-place for the relics of Peter and Paul during one of the Roman persecutions. For a reproduction of the graffiti, see F. van der Meer and C. Mohrmann, *Atlas of the Early Christian World* (London: Thomas Nelson & Sons, 1958), plate 75b.

[6] Diehl, *op. cit.*, 2323.

[7] *Ibid.*, 2333 adn.

[8] From the so-called Chapel of the Popes, *ibid.*, 955; picture in van der Meer and C. Mohrmann, *op. cit.*, plate 97.

[9] Chapel of the Popes, Diehl, *op. cit.*, 253. Pontianus reigned from 231 to 235, Fabian, from 236 to 250. See Hertling and Kirschbaum, *op. cit.*, pp. 39 ff.

DEAR CYRIACUS, SWEETEST SON, MAY YOU LIVE IN THE HOLY SPIRIT! [10]

From the cemetery of St. Priscilla:
MODESTINA A O [—Alpha Omega, the beginning and the end].[11]

From the town of Grotta Ferrata:
[Pictures of Noah's ark, a dove with an olive branch, birds, and a dog:] AS I TOLD YOU. . . . PEACE! TO TIMINIA SITIRIS (?) OUR DEAREST DAUGHTER, EVERY KIND OF KISS, FROM POSIDONIUS AND V [. . . . ., her parents].[12]

The Magic Square

The following magic square, which goes back to Roman times, came from seven different locations: two from Pompeii (hence before August, A.D. 79, the date of Pompeii's destruction), one from Corinium (mod. Cirencester) in England, and four from the excavations at Dura-Europos (mod. Salahiyeh). Note that it reads the same up and down, backwards, and forwards:

```
S A T O R
A R E P O
T E N E T
O P E R A
R O T A S
```

It has been translated as "The sower Arepo (?) holds the wheels with care." In 1926 the German scholar F. Grosser pointed out that the letters could be arranged as follows:

---

10 From the catacomb of St. Callistus, Diehl, op. cit., 2230.

11 Painted in red on tile; ibid., 3982 C adn. The Alpha and Omega symbols from the Apocalypse represent Jesus. See O. Marucchi, op. cit., pp. 75–76.

12 Diehl, op. cit., 2273; first published in 1875.

That is, with the words "Our Father" spelled twice and the letters A and O (or alpha and omega, referring to Christ) repeated twice.[13] Now if, as Grosser contended, this could scarcely be mere coincidence, then apparently the magic formula was Christian and it goes back to a date before the fall of Pompeii (A.D. 79). Another interpretation, suggested by Père G. de Jerphanion, S.J., in 1935, is that the so-called Greek cross occupies a central place in the inscription, with the letters A and O repeated four times on either side. Thus:

These solutions are indeed ingenious, but most scholars tend

<hr />

[13] See his article, "Ein neuer Vorschlag zur Deutung der Satorformel," *Archiv für Religionswissenschaft* 24 (1926), 165–69.

to regard them as mere coincidence,[14] while others proffer the unlikely hypothesis that the two inscriptions at Pompeii were scratched on the walls much later than the date of the city's collapse. Nonetheless the inscription is interesting and unique among our documents.

[14] See F. L. Cross, *The Early Christian Fathers* (London: Gerald Duckworth & Co., Ltd., 1960), pp. 199–201, with the bibliography there cited. For the text of the inscription see *Ephemerides Epigraphicae* IX. 1001. See also the comments of G. de Jerphanion in *Recherches de Science Religieuse* 25 (1925), pp. 180–225, and in *Les voix des monuments* (Paris: Van Oeste, 1938), pp. 38 ff.; and J. Carcopino, *Museum Helveticum* 5 (1948), pp. 16–59, with the literature there cited.

9

THE AGE OF THE APOLOGISTS
AND GNOSTICISM

When for the first time Christianity found itself forced to answer the accusations of pagan and Jewish thinkers and, if possible, turn the argument against their opponents by pointing to the absurdities or inconsistencies in the non-Christian point of view, it had to adopt the categories of Hellenistic thinking in order to do so. Thus the form of the Christian apologia was taken from the legal brief delivered orally or in writing to the emperor in defense of a criminal accusation.

Some of the foremost pagan adversaries of the Christians in the second century were Marcus Cornelius Fronto of Cirta (mod. Constantine) in Africa, a close friend of the emperor Marcus Aurelius, who seems to have inaugurated the famous charges of atheism, incest, and cannibalism; Celsus, the author of the first complete treatise against the Christians entitled *The True Account* (about A.D. 180); and the vicious satirist from Samosata, Lucian, who died after 180. A Jewish group, whom Justin identified with the disciples of Trypho (or Tarpho), were less vocal. Finally, there were the defectors within the Christian camp, who had adopted some form of Gnosticism, and they were perhaps the most formidable of all adversaries—highly literate, energetic, and with a penchant for wide proselytizing.

Not much is known about the lives of the Christian Apologists. There was Quadratus the Asiatic, who addressed his work to Hadrian; an Athenian philosopher named Aristides; Aristo of Pella; Justin the Martyr (d. about 165), an itinerant preacher from Shechem (mod. Nablus) in Jordan; Tatian, a Syrian, who eventually defected to found his own Gnostic sect about 172; Miltiades, a rhetorician; Athenagoras, an Athenian philosopher, whose work marked the beginning of deeper sympathy for pagan Greek culture and thought; Theophilus of Antioch on the Orontes, who would later become bishop; Melito, Bishop of Sardis in Lydia; and many more. Although the struggle between the Christians and pagans continued into the late third century, when the controversy with the Neoplatonists took place, the word "Apologists" is usually reserved for the writers of the second century. Two other apologetic works which do not belong to this period but are of great interest are the *Satire* of Hermias, an attack on the pagan philosophers, and the better known *Epistle to Diognetus,* a work variously attributed to different authors (Quadratus, Pantaenus), and of problematic composition and tone.

The modern reader probably will find the literature that resulted from the confrontation with Gnosticism the most fascinating. "Gnosticism" does not designate a definite sect but rather a series of parallel heretical movements that sprang up throughout different parts of the world in the second century. According to writers like Irenaeus, to whom we owe much of our knowledge, the earliest Christian Gnostics came from the general area of Jordan and Syria; their founder was Simon the Magician, from Gitton in Samaria. Basilides, who later went to Alexandria in Egypt; Bardaisan, the first Syrian writer of sacred hymns; Saturninus of Antioch, one of the first to write against marriage; and a sect called the Ophites, because they worshipped the serpent of Genesis—these were some of the earliest teachers in the Syrian area. The most literate and productive group seems to have been the school at Alexandria. Basilides went there from Syria, and the great Valentinus (to whom Irenaeus devotes the most space), after an influential period at Alexandria, founded a school at Rome about the year 140. Valentinus had as disciples the two Italians, Ptolemy and Heracleon, among others. The great Marcion of Sinope (mod. Sinop) in Pontus also came to Rome. Yet Egypt and the Middle East remained the most fertile field for Gnostic activity.

Simon the Magician and Cerinthus, the earliest known Gnostics, both described a series of emanations from God; in Simon's system, for example, one of these emanations is a female deity called Thought, and the other is the Son. Most such systems have three tiers of supramundane beings descending from the Godhead; others postulate two ungenerated beings: a first principle or Father and a feminine principle called Silence, Grace, Thought, Virginal Spirit, and the like.[1] The genealogies of these Aeons, as they are called, can be most weird and confusing. Valentinus, for example, maintained that the world came into being through the fall of Sophia, one of the Aeons who was the Demiurge who created the world. But it was the Aeon Christ, united to the man Jesus at His Baptism, who redeemed men. Valentinus divided men into three classes: the "carnal," who cannot be redeemed; the "psychic," who can attain salvation by faith and good works; and the "pneumatic," (like the Valentinians, who return to God through their gnosis or higher doctrine. Although Valentinus' doctrines contain the seeds of many future heresies they form a phantasmagoria of confused mythologies.

Opinions differ as to the origins of Gnosticism. Some scholars have claimed it grew out of Hellenistic (especially Platonic) philosophy, others out of Oriental religious syncretism, and still others out of an Asiatic mystical Judaism, of the sort represented by the Essenism of the Dead Sea Scrolls. All of these influences, in varying degrees, were undoubtedly at work in different parts of the world, starting with the second century B.C. at least, and often (as, for example, in the cases of Valentinus, Basilides, and Egyptian Gnosticism) Christianity only supplied a further source for Gnostic speculation and served to sharpen (if this is the proper word) the then-current pre-Christian idea of purification and redemption.

One of the greatest potential sources for our knowledge of Gnosticism are thirteen Coptic manuscripts, which contain many previously unknown Gnostic works and were discovered near the town of Nag Hammadi along the Nile, not far from Chénoboskion (famous for an ancient Pachomian monastic foundation). They were acquired by the Coptic Museum in Cairo, but one of the manuscripts (Codex 13) was purchased by the Carl Jung Foundation of Switzerland, and from it was edited the *Gospel of Truth,* attributed with good probability to Valentinus.[2] Indeed, a preliminary breakdown of the manuscripts suggests that the collection is heavily Valentinian. But we must await the complete publication of the

[1] For a discussion of the systems, see H. A. Wolfson, *The Philosophy of the Church Fathers,* (Cambridge, Mass.: Oxford Univ. Press, 1956), I, pp. 504 ff. See also W. Schneemelcher (ed.) in E. Hennecke, *New Testament Apocrypha* (tr. by R. McL. Wilson, Philadelphia: Westminster Press, 1963), I, pp. 345 ff.; R. M. Grant (ed.) *Gnosticism: A Source Book of Heretical Writings from the Early Christian Period* (New York: Harper & Row, Publishers, 1961).

[2] For a preliminary survey of the discoveries, see Jean Doresse, *The Secret Books of the Egyptian Gnostics* (tr. by P. Mairet, New York: The Viking Press, Inc., 1960).

Cairo manuscripts—under the direction of P. Labib Ikladios, the present head of the Coptic Museum—in order to delve more deeply into the recesses of Gnostic thought.

Not only did Gnosticism draw on a vast range of Hellenistic, Jewish, and Christian thought, but it contained other interesting variations. Marcus, for example, was a Valentinian who apparently preached in Gaul. He was addicted to wealthy women, who, according to Irenaeus, offered him their persons as well as their wealth (*Against Heresies* 1.13 and 21). Other Gnostics, like Ptolemy (in his *Letter* to his sister Flora), urged strict asceticism; and Saturninus, Marcion, and the so-called Encratites, along with Justin's Syrian disciple, Tatian, prescribed abstinence from animal food and celibacy for all. Sects like the Ebionites were circumcised and followed a Jewish way of life, while, on the other hand, Marcion and his followers rejected the Old Testament law and worship, distinguishing between the evil God of the old law and the merciful God revealed by Jesus. The most extensive discussion of Marcion's theories can be found in Tertullian's treatise *Against Marcion,* composed in five books over a period of ten years and before the author himself adopted Montanism, a late form of Valentinian Gnosticism. The Gnostics of Syria seemed to have been the first Christians to compose their own hymns instead of restricting themselves to the psalms and canticles of the Old Testament. They in turn stimulated others, especially the Eastern Greek writers, to write devotional hymns to Jesus and to the Trinity.

Some modern scholars detect Gnostic influences in orthodox writers like Ignatius of Antioch and in other Fathers of the Church. Although this is surely an extreme position, the influence of Gnostic mysticism and asceticism was nevertheless felt in the Church for a long time. The Gnostics' doctrinal obscurity and genealogical fantasies forced clearer minds to sharpen the Church's Christology and Trinitarian theology, and this process lasted to the end of the Patristic period.

The Gospel of Thomas

The great Oxyrhynchus collection of papyri, which began with the discoveries made by Bernard P. Grenfell and Arthur S. Hunt as early as 1897 in the Egyptian Faiyûm, yielded three Greek fragments known as the *Sayings of Jesus,* or sometimes as the *Logia;* these were papyri 1, 645, and 655. By now, parallels to practically all of these texts have been discovered in the Coptic *Gospel of Thomas,* found among the Gnostic manuscripts from Nag Hammadi in 1945. The *Sayings* themselves seem unobjectionable and probably go back to a very early source, but their presence among the Gnostic documents indicates that their final adaptation was the work of a Greek-speaking Gnostic writer of the second century. We shall quote from the Greek papyri and give the corresponding numbers of the *Logia* from the Coptic version.[3]

Logion 5 (P Oxy., 654.27–31):
   Jesus says: [Know that which (?)] lies before your eye and [that which is hidden] from you will be revealed [to you, for nothing] is hidden that will not be manifest, and buried that will not be [raised up (?)].

Logion 6 (P Oxy., 654.32–39):
   [His disciples] ask Him, saying: How should we fast and how are we to pray and how [give alms (?)] and what ought we to observe [of the tradition (?)] Jesus says. . . .

Logion 27 (P Oxy., 1.4–11):
   Jesus says: If you do not fast to the world, you will not find God's kingdom, and if you do not celebrate the Sabbath, you will not see the Father.

Logion 28 (P Oxy., 1.11–22):
   Jesus says: I stood up in the midst of the world, and I revealed myself to them in the flesh, and I found them all drunk; and I found no one among them who was thirsty; and my soul is in pain over the sons of men, because they are blind in their hearts and see not [they are poor and do not realize their poverty].

Logion 77 (?–P Oxy., 1.24–31):
   [The Coptic text of Logion 77 does not perfectly correspond with the Greek text in the papyrus, but they both present the peculiar doctrine of the cosmic presence of Jesus.]
   [Jesus says:] Wherever there may be [two or three

---

[3] See W. Lock and W. Sanday, *Two Lectures on the Sayings of Jesus* (Oxford: Clarendon Press, 1897) and W. Schneemelcher, *op. cit.,* pp. 97 ff. with the bibliography there cited. For a discussion of the Coptic and Greek texts, see also R. M. Grant and D. N. Freedman, *The Secret Sayings of Jesus* with an English translation of *The Gospel of Thomas* (New York: Doubleday and Company, Inc., 1960).

(?), they are not] without God; and where there is one
alone, I declare I am with him. Lift up a stone and you
will find me there; split the wood and there shall I be.

Logion 31 (P Oxy., 1.31–36):
    Jesus says: No prophet is acceptable in his own coun-
try, nor does a physician perform cures for those who
know him.

A Hymn of the Naassenes

From Hippolytus Refutation of All Heresies*

5.10.2 The universe's all-productive Law
    Was first-born Mind, and next came outpoured Chaos,
    And third, the Soul, received its share of Law.
    Surrounded therefore with a watery shape,
    She grieves and must succumb to death. A queen
    At times, she sees the light; at other times
    She weeps. Now mourning, now rejoicing; now
    Again she weeps and then is judged; sometimes
    She stands condemned and sometimes dies.
    At times she finds no exit, when her path
    Has led her to a luckless maze of woe.

    Then Jesus said: "My Father, look! She wanders
    Far from your breath on earth, she tries to fly
    From the bitter Chaos and knows not how to do it.
    And so, dear Father, send me; bearing seals
    I shall go down, passing through the Aeons.
    I shall reveal the mysteries and show forth
    The forms of gods, and then I shall impart
    The Gnosis or the secret of sanctity."

* See P. Wendland (ed.) (Leipzig: Teubner, 1916).

The Secret Book of John

One of the most important Gnostic books is the *Apocryphon of John*. Contained in a Coptic papyrus which was found near Achmîm in Egypt and was purchased by the Berlin Museum in 1896, it lay largely neglected until scholars learned that the same book was copied several times in the Gnostic cache found at Nag Hammadi. Walter C. Till published an excellent edition of the Coptic text with translation and commentary, *Die gnostischen Schriften des koptischen Papyrus berolinensis 8502* (Berlin: Akademie-Verlag, 1955), and the following selection is based on his edition.[4]

The fount of the spirit flowed out of the living water of the light, and it gave forth all the Aeons and all the worlds absolutely. It recognized its own image, seeing it in the clear, surrounding water of light. And its Thought began to work and was made manifest. From the brilliance of the light, Thought stood before It, as the Power which is before the All, the Power made manifest, the perfect Forethought of the universe, light, copy of the light, image of the invisible. She is Power all-perfect, Barbelo, the perfect Aeon of glory. To It she gives praise, for she was made manifest through It, and she knows It. She is the first Thought, Its Image, she became a first man, the virginal spirit, three-men-in-one, with three powers, three names and three acts of generation: the Aeon that is ageless, the male and female one, which proceeded from It's Forethought. . . .

Barbelo turned towards It and brought forth a blessed light-spark, which was not, however, equal to her in greatness. He is the Only-begotten who appeared to the Father, the divine self-born one, the first-born son of the All out of the spirit of pure light. And the invisible spirit was happy because of the light that came into existence and had just become manifest through the first Power, Barbelo, that is, It's Forethought.

(marginal notes) 26 Till p. 92 28 30

[After the activity of Barbelo, the author, supposedly the apostle John, enumerates the successive emergences of various

4 Another English version also appears in the anthology of R. M. Grant, *op. cit.*, pp. 69 ff., tr. by E. R. Hardy.

supramundane beings, Aeons, and angels. Suddenly, in the last section, there is a dialogue between Christ and the writer. They discuss the serpent who deceived Eve, and Christ explains the first generations of mortals. The first Archon Ialdabaoth comes to paradise and, seeing the virgin Eve beside Adam, seduces her and thus begets two sons, Iahweh and Elohim. Thus was sexual generation taught to mankind. Then the mystic author questions Christ about the destiny of human souls.]

64   And I said, "Christ, will the souls all live longer than
Till the purity of light?"
p.   To me he said, "You have arrived at the perception of
168 great things, so hard are they to reveal to others except
for those who are of the race that falters not. Those upon whom the spirit of life descends, once they are united with strength, will be saved and become perfect, and they will become worthy of rising up to those great lights. For they will become worthy of purifying themselves with these from all wickedness and from the temptations of malice; thus they will be able to direct their eyes to that immortal assembly alone, and hence will be occupied with it apart from anger, jealousy, fear, concupiscence, and excess. By none of these will they be gripped nor by anything else with the exception of the flesh: of this they may make use while they wait to be delivered and taken up by the Receiver into the reward of the everlasting, immortal life and their calling. And so they endure and suffer all, that they may face the combat and inherit eternal life."

[As the dialogue continues, Christ explains to the apostle that the struggle in the human soul is between a divine Spirit and an imitation Spirit or *pneuma*, which draws souls to works of evil and delivers them to the powers which are subordinate to the Archon. Ultimately all of these go to a special place and are preserved for the final day, when they will be delivered to eternal torment. When asked the source of this imitation Spirit, Christ explains that it was created by the angels whom the wicked Ialdabaoth sent down for the purpose of seducing the daughters of men. After an ambiguous conclusion, Christ gives final orders to the apostle, and both depart.]

76   "I shall tell you what is to be. Indeed, I have given
Till you this so as to write it down, and it should be securely
p. laid away."
192   Then he said to me, "Cursed be the man who ex-

changes this for a gift or for food or drink or clothing or anything of the sort."

He delivered this mystery unto him and straightway disappeared. And he went to his disciples and began to tell them what the Savior had said to him.

[So ends] the Secret Book of John.

The Odes of Solomon

James Rendel Harris first discovered the so-called *Odes of Solomon* in a Syriac manuscript in 1905 and edited them four years later; [5] F. C. Burkitt noticed another manuscript in the British Museum that contained a few more Syriac odes of the same quality. Most scholars would concur that their original was actually Greek, but not all are in agreement as to the degree of Gnostic influence, even though five of the odes are found in the Gnostic Coptic work called *Pistis Sophia*. Some have associated Bardaisan with the poems, but there seems little real evidence that he was the author. The most plausible theory is that these were Jewish (even Essenian psalms, like the *Hadayoth* of the Dead Sea Scrolls), which were later recast by a Christian poet; however, since this theory has not found universal acceptance, the origin of these beautiful, mystical pieces, assigned to the late second century, is still controverted.[6]

Ode 3 is a love poem reminiscent of the Song of Songs as interpreted by Alexandrian allegory; Ode 12 is a lovely hymn to the Logos; Ode 17 tells of Christ's mystic descent into Sheol; and Ode 42 is a glorious hymn to the risen Jesus. They breathe the devout atmosphere of Asiatic or Syriac Christianity and were probably composed (or revised) for chanting during the vigils or the Liturgy.

[5] See his *Odes and Psalms of Solomon* (Cambridge: The University Press, 1909), reedited (2 vols.; Manchester: The University Press, 1916–20).

[6] For the bibliography, see J. Quasten, *Initiation aux Pères de l'Eglise* (tr. by J. Laporte, Paris: Newman Press, 1955), I, 182–89.

Ode 3: My Beloved is Mine and I am His*

. . . .

I cling to Him and He embraces me.
I should not be able to love the Lord,
Unless He had loved me first. For who can comprehend
What love is, save the lover? I embrace my Beloved
And my soul loves Him. Wherever He rests,
There also am I. No stranger am I,
For with the Lord there is no ill will.
To Him am I bound, for I shall find love
For my Beloved.

I shall become a son, because I love the Son.
Whoever clings to Him, who is immortal,
Shall never die. He who is accepted in the living One
Shall live. Such is the Lord's spirit
And He cannot lie. He teaches the sons of men
To know his ways. Be prudent, vigilant, and understand!
Alleluia!

Ode 17: The Descent into Sheol

I was crowned by my God: mine is a living crown!
I have been justified by my Lord, and He is my salvation
Forever. I am delivered from all folly, and I am not con-
      demned.
His hands cut off my stifling bonds
And now I have the face, the look of a new man.
I have entered in and I have been saved.
The thought of his truth had directed me.
I followed it and erred not.

* For my version I have used Harris, *op. cit.*, as well as the
admirable French version of J. Labourt and P. Batiffol, *Les Odes de
Solomon* (Paris: Gabalda, 1911). The sensuous tenderness of this
hymn recalls the Hebrew Song of Songs (or Song of Solomon), but it
is quite unique in Christian poetry of the second century and foreshadows the exegeses of Hippolytus and Origen. The Song's application
of the love story between God and the soul was first used by
Hippolytus and then in the *Commentaries* and *Homilies* of Origen,
from whence it passed to Ambrose and Gregory of Nyssa, to Bernard
of Clairvaux, and much later mystical and monastic literature. Such
a hymn as this surely does not seem primarily Gnostic, but
rather reflects the speculations of the Alexandrian and Asiatic
schools of Christian thought.

All who saw me were astonished;
And to them I seemed a stranger.
But the all-high God knew me, and brought me up
In all his perfection. By his kindness
He has honored me. And He has raised my mind
To the height of his truth. And from thenceforth
He showed me the way of his commandments.

I unlocked the closed gates, and shattered the iron bolts,
And my iron melted and dissolved before me.
Nothing seemed to me a mystery,
Because I was the Gate for all things.
I went out to all my prisoners,
That I might deliver them,
And abandon none who bind or who are bound.
Of my knowledge I gave freely, and my prayer
Was in all my love. In their hearts I sowed my fruit,
And transformed them into myself.
They received my blessing and lived;
Gathered unto me, they have been saved.
They were as my own members, and I am their head.

To you our Head, glory, O Lord Messiah! Alleluia!

Ode 19: The Virgin Birth and the Godhead

A cup of milk was offered me,
And I drank it in the delightful sweetness of the Lord.
The milk has come from the Father,
Drawn by the Holy Spirit.
His breasts are swelled with milk
Which He wished to pour forth in abundance. . . .

The Spirit opened the womb of the Virgin,
And she conceived and brought forth.
The Virgin became mother with abundant mercy.
She became great with Child and bore a Son
Without pain. And to avoid what she needed not (?),
She asked no midwife to assist her.
She brought him forth with a will, as though she were a
        man.
She bore Him openly, and she possessed Him
With great dignity. And she loved Him
In his swaddling bands, and tenderly protected Him,
And manifested Him in majesty. Alleluia!

Ode 30: Taste and See that the Lord Is Sweet!

Draw from the waters of the Lord's living spring,
For it has been opened to us.
Come all you thirsty and take this drink
And rest by the spring of the Lord,
For it is lovely and pure and gives peace to the soul.
Its waters are sweeter than honey:
Even the bees' honeycomb cannot compare.
For they pour forth from the Lord's lips,
And from the Savior's breast they take their name.
Invisibly, for all time, do they pour forth,
And none has seen them before they were put in the midst.

Happy are they who have drunk:
Happy those who have found their rest! Alleluia!

Ode 42: He Is Risen!

I have stretched out my hands, and I have approached
My Lord. His sign is the extension of my hands
And my stretching out is the outspread tree
Set up at the side of the Just One's way.

> No profit am I to those who grasp me not;
> But I shall be to those who bear me love.
> Dead are my pursuers, and they sought
> After me, those who thought me still alive.

I am risen, I am with them, and by their mouths
I speak. They have spurned their persecutors,
For I have laid on them the yoke of love.
Like the groom's arm upon the bride
So is my love on those who believe in me.
Like the marriage couch spread in the house
Of the bride and groom, so is my love
Over all who believe in me.

> I was not rejected, even when I seemed to be.
> They condemned me, but I perished not.
> Sheol saw me, and it was crushed.
> Death cast me forth, and many with me.
> I had gall and bitterness and I went down
> With him so far as there was any depth to go.
> And head and feet were let go
> Because they could not stand my countenance.

I held an assembly of the living amongst the dead.
And with living lips I spoke to them
And my work shall not be in vain.
They rushed towards me, those that had been dead.
They cried out and said: "Have mercy on us, Son of God,
And work in us according to your grace.
Free us from the bonds of darkness;
Open to us the gate by which we may come to you.
For we see our death has not touched you.
Let us also be saved with you; for you are our Savior."

I heard their cry, and over their heads
Was heard my name. For they are free men,
And they are mine. Alleluia!

The Gospel of Truth*

This Valentinian gospel, written about A.D. 180 was one of the most important works recovered from the manuscripts of Nag Hammadi. The present work was purchased in 1946 by the Jung Foundation and was published in a splendid edition by M. Malinine, H.-C. Puech, and G. Quispel. The codex is in the subachmimic dialect of Coptic and was transcribed about the end of the third century. The work is typical of the Gnostic apocalypses in that it transposes the message of the Gospel to that of redemption by illumination from the power of the wicked Aeons.

The Gospel of Truth is a joy for those who have f. VIIIv received from the Father the favor of knowing Him –IX through the power of the Word, which came from the Pleroma and is within the thought and Nous of the Father. He it is we call Savior, for that is the name of the work He is to accomplish for the salvation of those who did not know the Father. . . .

* See M. Malinine, H.-C. Puech, and G. Quispel, *Evangelium Veritatis* (Zürich: Rascher, 1956), with French, German, and English translations (the last by Helen Wall). There is also an excellent version, with notes, by W. W. Isenberg, in R. M. Grant, *op. cit.*, pp. 146–61, and this includes the four pages missing from the Jung codex and discovered with the rest of the cache in the Coptic Museum at Cairo. My own version is from the Coptic with assistance from the notes of the original editors.

The Gospel is the apocalypse of hope to those who seek Him. For the All sought for Him, from whom it emanated. And the All was within Him, who is incomprehensible, inconceivable, and beyond all thought. Ignorance of the Father created anxiety and fear. And anxiety became as thick as fog, so that no one could see. Thus error became strong. . . .

Redemption Is Essentially Illumination

f. XIII^v   For every man loves the truth, for truth is the Father's mouth. His tongue is the Holy Spirit, who unites man to truth, attaching him to the Father's mouth by his tongue, when he receives the Holy Spirit. This is the manifestation of the Father and his revelation to his Aeons: He revealed of himself what was hidden, and He explained it. For who is He who is, save the Father alone? All the spaces are emanations from Him. They have known that they have come forth from Him as children from a perfect man. . . .

We Are Redeemed As Though from a Dark Nightmare

f. XV   What then does He wish man to think? That "I am as the shadows and phantasms of the night." When the day breaks, this man understands that the fear with which he was gripped was nothing. So too were they who did not know about the Father, Him whom they did not see. Because of this they were in fear and confusion, unsettled, divided and split in mind, and there were many illusions . . . as though they were in a deep sleep and were obsessed by disturbing dreams: They are running away somewhere, or they are forced to chase someone, though they are weak; or, again, they get into a quarrel and strike blows, or, on the contrary, are themselves beaten, or they fall from a great height, or else fly into the air without wings. At other times, it seems as though someone is trying to kill them, even though there is no one there to chase them, or else it is as though they were killing their neighbor and are red with his blood.

---

[7] The doctrine of redemption from "dreams" resembles the Epicurean discussion of dreams of an earlier period, save that here dreams are associated with the darkness and anxiety from which the Gnostic doctrine delivers us. For a discussion of dream symbolism, see my *Symbol and Myth in Ancient Poetry* (New York: Fordham University Press, 1961), pp. 159 ff.

Up to the time that those who experience this (passing through this in confusion), wake up, they see nothing; for such imaginings are nothing.[7]

The Life of the Initiate: Conclusion

This is the place of the blessed. May the others, then, f.XXI^v each in their own place, know that it is not fitting for me to speak further, now that I have been to the place of rest. And indeed, I shall be in it to devote myself forever to the Father of all and to my true brothers, over whom the love of the Father shines, and nothing of Him is wanting in their midst.

These are they who are manifest in truth, since they dwell in that true and eternal life, and they speak of the perfect light which is filled with the Father's seed, which is in his heart and his Pleroma, while his Pneuma rejoices in Him and glorifies Him, in whom it exists. For He is good.

His children, too, are perfect and worthy of his name. For they are the sort of children that He, the Father, loves.

"Light Serene"

The lovely, ancient Greek hymn, *Phôs hilaron*, "Light Serene," most probably originated in the second century in Egypt or Palestine as a counterbalance to the heretical Gnostic songs of the same period.[8] It still is part of the Byzantine liturgy today.

[8] See J. Quasten, *op. cit.*, p. 181. An Oxyrhynchus papyrus (1786, published by Grenfell and Hunt in 1922) from the latter half of the third century contains the text and musical notation for a fragment of a Trinitarian hymn, clearly from the orthodox theological school. For the music and a discussion, see Egon Wellesz, *Classical Quarterly* 39 (1945), 34–45. After mentioning the "brilliant stars" and the "murmuring streams," it concludes:

> As we too hymn the Father and the Son
> And Holy Spirit, let all the powers sing
> In harmony, Amen, Amen! Power, Glory
> To Him the Giver of all good things. Amen, Amen.

Written in the hypophrygian mode, this fragment is probably representative of the liturgical worship of the second century in Egypt and is therefore not too far in spirit from the "Light Serene."

O light serene of the eternal Father's glory,
Christ Jesus! Now that we have come to the hour of sunset,
Seeing the evening star appear, we sing
To the Father, Son, and Holy Spirit of God.
It is truly meet to praise your name forever
In holy hymns, O Son of God, You who gave
Your life. For this the world sends up its glory.

St. Justin the Martyr

Justin, who was born early in the second century at Shechem in Samaria (now Nablus in modern Jordan), was one of the most important apologists of the primitive Church. At an early age, he was converted from paganism, probably in Ephesus, and spent the rest of his life as an itinerant preacher in Asia and in Rome, where he founded a school. His *Dialogue with Trypho* was written during the dramatic revolt of the Jewish messiah Bar Kokhba (132–35); the setting was Ephesus and his opponent was a Jewish savant and Palestinian religious leader—probably the same Rabbi Tarphon mentioned in the Mischna. More important, however, are Justin's two *Apologies*. The *First Apology*, comprising some sixty-eight chapters, was written about A.D. 150 and addressed to the emperor Antoninus Pius (cf. Eusebius *Eccl. Hist.* 4.18). In addition to its defense of Christianity, it contains the earliest lengthy treatment of the Liturgy (in Sections 65 and 67), and concludes with an authentic rescript that the emperor Hadrian issued about the year 125 to the governor of Asia, prohibiting the persecution of Christians. The shorter *Second Apology*, addressed to the Roman senate, is probably merely an appendix of the first. It offers a short disquisition on the Christian attitude towards death and persecution, answers the attacks of a Cynic philosopher named Crescens, and concludes with a balanced request to the emperor to prohibit all illegal prosecution of Christians without evidence that crime has been committed.

A number of early Greek apologetic works have been wrongly attached to Justin's name, as for example, the *Exhortation to the Pagans*, the brief *Speech to the Pagans*, *On God's Monarchy*, and several others which are extant only in fragments.

The First Apology*

And after baptizing him who has been joined to our 65
number in faith, we bring him to those who are
called our brethren, to the place where they are
gathered together to offer communal prayers both
for ourselves and for him who has been enlightened,
as well as for everyone everywhere, with the sincere
intention that we who have learned the truth may be
deemed worthy to be faithful citizens by our good
works and obedient to the commandments, that we
may attain eternal salvation.

After the prayers are finished we greet each other with
a kiss. Then they bring to the one who presides some
bread, a cup of mixed water and wine, and he takes
this. He offers praise and glory to the Father of all
through the name of his Son and of the Holy Spirit.
And he says a long thanksgiving prayer, that He has
given us all these things. After he has finished the
prayers and the thanksgiving, everyone present ex-
presses his approval by saying "amen" (meaning, in
Hebrew, "may it be so"). And after the president has
given thanks and all the people shout their assent, men
whom we call deacons distribute bread, over which
the prayer has been said, and wine with water to be
consumed; and they carry some to those who are
absent.

And this food we call the Eucharist, and no one is 66
allowed to partake of it unless he believes our doctrine is true and has been washed in the laver for re-
generation and the forgiveness of sins, and so lives as
Christ has taught. For we do not partake of this as
ordinary food and drink; but just as the Word of God
incarnate, Jesus Christ our Savior, took on flesh and
blood for our salvation, so too the food over which
the thanksgiving prayer has been pronounced through
the word which came from Him, and by which our
flesh and blood are changed and nourished—this food
we have been taught is the very flesh and blood of
Jesus. For the apostles in the memorials which they
wrote, called the Gospels, declared that Jesus ordered
them to act in this way. Jesus, taking bread, gave thanks
and said, "Do this in commemoration of me: this is my

* For the text see J. Quasten, *Monumenta Eucharistica et Liturgica
Vetustissima* (Bonn: Florilegium Patristicum, 1935) I, 13 ff., with notes.

body." And, likewise, taking up the cup, He gave thanks and said, "This is my blood," and shared it with them alone. . . .

67   And so on the day called Sunday there is an assembly in one place of all who live in the cities or in the country; the memorials of the apostles or the writings of the prophets are read as long as time allows. After the reader has finished, the presiding officer verbally instructs and exhorts us to imitate these shining examples. Then we all rise and pray together. Next, as I said before, when we finish the prayer, bread, wine, and water are brought up. The presiding officer once again offers up prayers of thanksgiving according to his strength, and then the people cry out "amen." Then there is a distribution and partaking of what has been blessed with the Eucharistic prayer, and the deacons bring a share to those who are not present.

Those who are wealthy and others who wish each offer a donation according to their choice, and what is collected is brought to the presiding officer, and with this he assists orphans, widows, and those who are in need through illness or any other reason; also those who are in prison, strangers from other lands, and, in short, he takes care of all those who may be in want.

We all hold this common assembly on Sunday because it is the first day of the week, on which God made the world, changing darkness and matter, and on which Christ Jesus our Savior rose from the dead. On Friday He was nailed to a cross, and on the day after Saturday, the day of the Sun, He appeared to his apostles and taught them these things that we have proposed for your attention.

The Dialogue with Trypho*

1   One morning I was walking along the paths of the Colonnade, when a man in company with several others came up and spoke to me.

"Good morning, philosopher," said he.

He then turned around and walked along with me and his friends. I turned and addressed him.

"What can I do for you, sir?" I said.

[The mysterious stranger tells Justin that he studied under an Academic philosopher at Argos by the name of Corinthus and that he is Jewish, named Trypho, has escaped from Palestine during a recent uprising, and since then has been

* See J. Otto (Jena: F. Maucke, 1847) for the text.

living mainly at Corinth in Greece. Justin leads him at once into a discussion on the nature of the Godhead, as discussed by the philosophers and taught by the sacred books, and the nature of the soul's immortality. Justin is speaking.]

Is not your doctrine the same as Plato teaches in his 5 *Timaeus*? There he says that the world is corruptible because it has been created, but that it will not be subject to death or be destroyed because that is what God wants. Don't you think that we could say the same thing about the soul, and about all other things? For whatever exists or will in future exist apart from God, these must be destructible by nature, capable of being destroyed and ceasing to exist. God alone is uncreated and incorruptible: that is why He is God. But everything else is created and destructible. . . . So it is impossible that there should be many uncreated beings. If there were, they would have to be different; but then you could not by any amount of inquiry discover the reason for this. But if you would permit your mind to roam through infinity, it would finally, after all its effort, arrive at some one uncaused being—and this, you would agree, would be the cause of all things. Now Plato and Pythagoras were wise men; were they then ignorant of these truths, which are the very walls and bastions of our philosophy?

"I pay no attention," he replied, "to Plato, Pythagoras, 6 or to anyone else who holds these views. . . ."

[After this discussion of God as the uncaused cause, Justin takes his friend through various details of the Old Testament, as for example, Isaiah's prediction of Christ's passion as a new form of sacrifice of purification from sin (13); he discusses the Jews' rejection of the Messiah, the final coming, Christ as King, Priest, and God (34), and other important points of Christian doctrine. Justin insists on the divinity of Christ and the Jews' need to recognize Him as their promised one (64). The prophecy of Malachi (1.10–12) applies only to the Christian prayers and eucharistic offerings (117), in which "there is made a commemoration of the passion of the Son of God for their sake." In the end Trypho and his Jewish companions thank Justin for his explanations and pray that his voyage may be free from all calamity. Justin replies that he can wish them no greater blessing than that they could believe that Christ is God (141). And so this fascinating debate between Christian and Jew ends on a note of mutual tolerance and love.]

10

IRENAEUS OF LYONS

Irenaeus, one of the most profound of the Fathers of the second century, was born most probably in Smyrna, where, according to his account, he sat at the feet of St. Polycarp. By the year 177/78 he was active as a priest at Lyons in Gaul and was sent as an envoy to visit Pope Eleutherius in Rome in connection with the Montanist controversy. He then succeeded Photinus as bishop of Lyons and later interceded with Pope Victor I to effect a compromise with the Christians of Asia Minor in their celebration of Good Friday and Easter. Gregory of Tours, who was naturally interested in the early bishops of Gaul, claimed that Irenaeus converted the whole country and that his life ended in martyrdom; indeed, it is not unlikely that he was martyred, though the evidence is inconclusive.[1]

Irenaeus wrote in Greek, but of all his works only two survive: the *Proof of the Apostolic Preaching,* a summary of Christian doctrine and an apologia for the Church, extant only in an Armenian version,[2] and the more important treatise *Against Heresies,* extant completely in a literal Latin version of perhaps the fourth century, together with some fragments in the original Greek, some in Syriac, and two entire books in Armenian. All the versions are important for a restoration of the original text of Irenaeus.

The five books of the *Against Heresies* form a sprawling

[1] See J. Quasten, *Initiation aux Pères de l'Eglise* (tr. by J. Laporte, Paris: Newman Press, 1955) I, 329 ff.; F. L. Cross, *The Early Christian Fathers* (London: Gerald Duckworth & Co., Ltd., 1960), pp. 110–15.

[2] Published in R. Graffin and F. Nau (eds.), *Patrologia Orientalis* (Paris: Firmin-Didot, 1919), Vol. 12 and translated into English by J. P. Smith, *St. Irenaeus: Proof of the Apostolic Preaching,* (Ancient Christian Writers 16, Westminster, Md.: Newman Press, 1952), with excellent introduction and commentary.

(*Above*). Jerusalem, Hashemite kingdom of Jordan. View from the tower of the Lutheran Church of the Saviour, looking over the facade of the Church of the Holy Sepulcher. The traditional site of Jesus' tomb is under the large cupola; the facade of the church is still defaced by metal supports. Moslems, Copts, Armenians, Greeks, and Roman Catholics all have rights to various parts of this ancient shrine built upon Constantinian foundations.

(*Below*). A fourth-century cubiculum (burial chamber) from the catacomb of St. Domitilla, Rome. Note the decorated arcosolium for the placement of a sarcophagus; the lovely peacocks symbolize the life of the blessed in heaven.

(Left). A fourth-century painting of Christ from the catacomb of St. Domitilla, Rome. It is the typical portrayal of Christ as a preaching philosopher in Roman costume.

(Below). The sacred fountain of Pirene in Corinth, notable landmark of the city in the time of St. Paul. Not far from here is the spot where tradition has it the apostle spoke before the Roman governor Gallio (Acts 18.12).

(Above). A Roman theater in the city of Caesarea, Israel. Paul was imprisoned at Caesarea under Festus (Acts 25.4), and the city later became important for its theological school, made famous by Eusebius and Origen.

(Below). Scene from an ancient street in Caesarea; the statues are from the late imperial period. The city is still being excavated by a team of archaeologists of the Israel Department of Antiquities. Much of the earlier work had been done by members of the local kibbutz, Sooth Yam.

(Above). Remains of the apse of the early Christian basilica at Caesarea, Israel, still in course of excavation.

(Below). Ephesus, Turkey: the great avenue of marble, the most beautifully preserved thoroughfare of the ancient city, near the modern Turkish town of Selçuk. The avenue is not far from the site of the ancient church where the Ecumenical Council of Ephesus was held.

(Above). The author and a friend before the chapel of Meryem Ana on the hill Panaya Kupulu, near Ephesus. The chapel was built by the de Foucauld Fathers on the foundations of a house of the first century, believed to have belonged to the Virgin Mary.

(Left). Famous statue of Artemis found in the ruins of Ephesus, now in the archaeological museum in Selçuk. Worship of Artemis was one of St. Paul's chief targets in his missionary work at Ephesus (Acts 19.35).

(Above). Ruins of the Basilica of St. John the Apostle, Ephesus. Built under Emperor Justinian in the sixth century on the traditional site of the apostle's tomb, it has been restored by American archeologists.

(Below). The Roman theater at Miletus, near modern Balat, Turkey, completed in the third century after Christ. This ancient Ionian city became a thriving Roman colony and in the time of St. Paul was an important Christian center. (See Acts 20.15 ff. for the meeting of the presbyters at Miletus.)

(Above). A magnificent view of the Acropolis and Areopagus, Athens, as seen from the hill of the Pnyx. It was at Athens that St. Paul spoke of the "unknown God" before the Epicurean and Stoic philosophers (Acts 17.15–33).

(Below). A view of the great mountain of Acrocorinth as seen from the marketplace of Corinth. It was famed for its temple of Aphrodite and servant priestesses. The Christian community at Corinth, comprising both Jews and Greeks, was founded by St. Paul (Acts 18.1–11).

(*Above*). Rome: the Roman forum and the Sacred Way as seen through the third-century triumphal arch of Septimius Severus. The low shed protects the so-called Black Stone and the oldest Latin inscription of Rome. Paul wrote his epistle to the Romans before he visited there (Rom. 15.29) and was finally imprisoned there on appeal to the emperor (Acts 28.16 ff.).

(*Below*). Ostia: the site of a chapel erected to the Ostian martyrs near the Roman theater. Ostia, the port of Rome, had a flourishing Christian community in the first centuries of the Church and was made famous by Minucius Felix and Augustine.

attack on Gnosticism, summarizing its doctrines (especially in Book 1) and contrasting them to the teachings of the Church and reason in Books 2–5. Of great interest is the fifth book, in which Irenaeus spoke of the Last Things and developed the doctrine of millenarianism—or the final reign on earth of Jesus for a thousand years—along the same lines as Methodius of Olympus and other early authors before the peace of the Church developed it. In other respects Irenaeus was quite orthodox. He was interested in the succession of bishops as a guarantee of the truth of Christian tradition. He stressed the role of Christ's dual nature and his death in the work of the Atonement, underlined the importance of baptism (even for infants) and the Eucharist, and pointed to the canon of the Scriptures as well as the apostolic teaching as a source of faith. As opposed to any Gnostic ideas of the redemption, Irenaeus developed the teaching implied in John and Paul, which has Christ's achievement and sacrificial death overthrowing the work of Satan and restoring man to the image of God, which Adam possessed by an incorporation into Christ. Christ is the recapitulation, at once the culmination of humanity and the restorer of the original state intended by God. Irenaeus was an intensely biblical theologian, whose speculations paved the way for later dogmatic thought both in the East and the West.[3]

Against Heresies*

Now the Church, spread throughout all the world even 1. to the ends of the earth, received from the apostles 10. and their disciples her belief in one God, the Father al- 1 mighty, who made the heavens, earth and sea, and all that is in them; in the one Jesus Christ, the Son of God, made flesh for our salvation; and in the Holy Spirit, who declared the ordinances of God through the prophets, and his visitations, and the birth from a virgin, his passion and resurrection from the dead, and the bodily assumption of Jesus Christ our beloved Lord into heaven, and his

---

[3] Among recent comprehensive studies should be mentioned J. Lawson, *The Biblical Theology of St. Irenaeus* (London: The Epworth Press, 1949), and A. Houssiau, *La Christologie de Saint Irénée* (Louvain: Presses Universitaires de Louvain, 1955), but for complete bibliographies, one must consult the works of Quasten, Altaner, and Cross (see Bibliography).

* For the text see R. Massuet (Paris, 1710); J. P. Migne *Patres Graeci* 7 (1857 ff.).

final coming from heaven in the Father's glory for the recapitulation of all things, and the elevation of the flesh of all mankind, that according to the will of the invisible Father every knee might bend of those in heaven, on earth, and in hell, that every tongue might confess to Him. . . .

1.
10. Receiving this kerygma and this faith, as we have
2. said, the Church has carefully preserved it, as though dwelling in a single house, even though she has been spread over the entire world. In these things does she believe as though she possessed the same single heart and soul, and she consistently proclaims them, teaching and handing them down, as though she had but one mouth. For the languages throughout the world are all diverse, but the message of her preaching is one and the same. Hence the churches that have been established among the Germans believe and teach the same; so too those among the Iberians, the Celts, in the Orient, in Egypt, in Libya, and those which have been founded in the very center of the world. God's creature, the sun, is one and the same throughout the whole world; so too, that light which is the proclamation of the truth shines everywhere and enlightens all men who have the will to come to the realization of the truth. . . .

3.3.
1–2. Anyone who wishes to see the truth can observe the apostles' tradition made manifest in every church throughout the whole world. We can enumerate the men who were appointed bishops in their churches by the apostles and their successors down to our own day. Never did they teach or know of the absurd doctrines which these heretics bring forward. For even had the apostles known of hidden mysteries or had taught them privately and secretly to the initiate, they would surely have transmitted them to those to whom they entrusted the charge of their churches. . . . But it would take too long in a work of this sort to offer detailed lists of succession in all the churches. Indeed, we shall confound those who hold unauthorized assemblies (whether out of unfounded self-esteem, or vanity, blindness, or perverse doctrine) by pointing to the tradition of the church that is the greatest, most ancient, and best known to all men, founded and established at Rome by the two most renowned apostles, Peter and Paul. It is from the apostles that this church has its tradition and the faith announced to all men, showing its succession of bishops right down to our own day. And therefore all the churches (that is, the faithful

everywhere) must agree[4] with Rome because of its special priority, for those who spread everywhere have maintained in her [5] the tradition received from the apostles.

After laying the foundations and building the Church, the blessed apostles handed over the role of administration to Linus—Paul mentioned this Linus in his letters to Timothy—and he was succeeded by Anancletus, and after him, in the third place after the apostles, Clement was appointed to the episcopacy. Clement, too, had seen the apostles and had conferred with them; he still held the vivid preaching and teaching of the apostles before his eyes, and he was not alone among the men who still survived in those days, who had actually been instructed by the apostles. It was under Clement, then, that a considerable conflict broke out among the community of Corinth, and thus the Church of Rome dispatched a very strong document to the Corinthians, urging them to peace and a renewal of their faith and the teaching which they had but recently received from the apostles. . . . *3.3. 3*

The only-begotten Word is always present to the human race; united and mingled with his own creation, as the Father willed, and becoming incarnate, He is Jesus Christ our Lord, who suffered and rose again for our sake; and He will come once more in the glory of his Father to raise up all men as a testimony to salvation, and He will mete out the rule of just judgment to all his creatures. *3. 16. 6*

Thus, as we have shown, there is but one God the Father, and one Jesus Christ our Lord, who came to complete God's plan for all men, recapitulating all things in himself. Mankind is absolutely God's creation. Hence Jesus fulfills man in himself. Being invisible, He became visible; incomprehensible, He became comprehensible; unable to suffer, He became passible; He was the Word and became man, fulfilling all things in himself. . . .

Eve indeed had Adam as her husband, though she was still a virgin (for they were both naked in paradise and *3. 22. 4*

---

[4] The Latin *convenire* is difficult; it may mean, "agree with," "join with," or "resort to" (in cases of judgment).

[5] Again the Latin, *in qua*, may not accurately represent the original Greek text, and hence the entire last sentence becomes vague. The *in qua* might be taken to mean, "*insofar* as they have maintained the tradition," etc., and not (as I have taken it) "*in her* they have maintained the tradition received from the apostles."

were not ashamed), for since they had only been created they did not yet understand the process of generation; they first had to grow more mature and then proceed to multiply. But, becoming disobedient, she became
the cause of death both to herself and to the entire race of
men. So too Mary, having a betrothed husband and still
a virgin, by her obedience became the cause of salvation
both to herself and to the entire race of men. This is why
the Law speaks of her, espoused as she was and still a
virgin, as the wife of him to whom she was betrothed,
thus suggesting the completion of the cycle from Mary
to Eve. . . . Thus the knot of Eve's disobedience was
untied by the obedience of Mary; and what the virgin
Eve had bound by her lack of faith, this was loosed by
Mary's act of belief. . . .

4.   God differs from man insofar as God creates, but man
11. is created. He who creates remains always the same,
2 whereas that which is made must receive its beginning, its
middle, its addition, and increase. God is the author of
good; man receives its benefit. God is perfect in all things,
in all respects the same and consistent, since He is all
Light, all Mind, all Substance, and the source of all
good. . . .

5.2.   We are his members and we are fed by his creation.
2–3 Hence He who makes his sun rise and his rain fall
as He wills offers us his creatures: this cup, his creature,
He has said is his very own blood which was shed and
nourishes our blood; this bread, his creature, He has
said was his very own body, which nourishes our bodies.
   And so, when the prepared cup and that which was made
bread receive God's Word and become the Eucharist, the
body of Christ, from which the substance of our flesh
grows and subsists, how can they deny that the flesh
can receive God's favor, life eternal, seeing that it is fed
by the body and blood of Christ and is his member? [6]
For the blessed Paul, saying in his Epistle to the Ephesians that we are members of his body, of his flesh, and
his bones, is not speaking of the spiritual and invisible
man, for the Spirit has neither bones nor flesh, but of a
real, human organism made up of flesh, sinews, and
bones. This is what is fed by the cup which is his blood
and by the bread which is his body.

[6] Irenaeus is here arguing specifically against the Docetes.

A shoot of a vine that is buried in the earth bears fruit in its proper season; a grain of wheat that falls to the ground and dissolves rises again, multiplied in form by the Spirit of God that embraces all things; then by the wisdom of God it becomes useful to men, and, receiving the Word of God, becomes the Eucharist, which is the body and blood of Christ. So too our bodies, fed by the Eucharist, although buried within the earth and crumbling within it, shall rise again in due season, since the Word of God will give them the grace of resurrection for the glory of God the Father, who clothes mortality with everlasting life, gives incorruptibility to corruption, for God's power is thus made perfect in weakness.

11

MELITO OF SARDIS

Eusebius cited a letter of one of the bishops of Ephesus to Pope Victor (189–98), which mentioned Melito, bishop of Sardis in Lydia, as one of the recently departed great churchmen of Asia Minor. Melito, who apparently flourished during the reign of the emperor Marcus Aurelius (161–80), is said to have made what was the earliest known pilgrimage to the Holy Land. Aside from a long list of works and some fragments preserved by Eusebius and others, little was known of Melito until the discovery of extensive Greek papyri of his sermon *On the Pasch,* or the symbolic meaning of the Christian Passover. One large fifth-century papyrus is divided partly between the Chester Beatty collection (edited by F. G. Kenyon in 1941) and the Michigan University collection (edited by Campbell Bonner in 1940); [1] another almost complete papyrus with the name of Melito and the title *On the Pasch* turned up in the famous Bodmer collection in Switzerland.[2] In addition, there are fragments of a Coptic version,[3] a Syriac version, and a Latin epitome appearing among the sermons of Leo the Great.[4]

[1] *The Homily on the Passion by Melito Bishop of Sardis with Some Fragments of the Apocryphal Ezekiel* (London: Christophers, 1940). For the details of the discovery and the division of the leaves between the Dublin collection of Chester Beatty and the Michigan papyrus, see pp. 3 ff.

[2] Michel Testuz, *Papyrus Bodmer XIII: Méliton de Sardes* (Cologny-Genève: Bibliotheque Bodmer, 1960), with the history of the problem on pp. 7 ff.

[3] One large fragment is the Crosby Codex in the University of Mississippi (Miss. Coptic Codex I), now being prepared, according to report, by Prof. W. H. Willis; see Testuz, *op. cit.,* pp. 11–12.

[4] In J. P. Migne, *Patrologia Latina* (54.493–94); see H. Chadwick, "A Latin Epitome of Melito's Homily on the Pascha," *Journal of Theological Studies* (1960), 76–82.

The homily is written in a curiously rich and rhythmic style unique in the Greek sermons of the early Church, and some scholars have suggested that it may ultimately be a translation of the Syriac (e.g. P. Kahle), while still others, such as P. Nautin, felt that the homily could not have been written so early and should be placed in the third or fourth century and attributed to another author. The majority view, however, is that the sermon is authentic. The actual genre of the sermon has also been hotly debated. Most plausible of all views is F. L. Cross's,[5] which states that the opening words of the tract refer to the reading of the passage from the book of Exodus in Hebrew, followed by a paraphrase in the vernacular. Melito's work then is an exegesis of the mystery of the Paschal Lamb in terms of Christ's passion and death and the continuing Christian mystery of the Liturgy. Hence Melito constantly refers to the "mystery of the Pasch," and even falsely links the Hebrew word *pasah* with the Greek *pascho* (to suffer). In any case, Melito's tract—it is not strictly a sermon or homily—is a unique example of a Christian Haggadah, an explanation of the mystery in much the same way that the president of the passover meal would explain the important elements of the meal to those who shared it with him.

Theologically, the work of Melito is not important, but as a document *On the Pasch* is one of the most moving exegeses of the Christian mystery; and the hypnotic, rhythmic quality of the Greek clauses conveys the extraordinary power of the preachers of the Asiatic Church. The central doctrine of the treatise is the transformation achieved by Christ in slaying the "man-slayer Death." Before Christ, men are pictured as prey to "insatiable pleasure, adultery, fornication, sexual pleasure, lust, avarice, murder, bloodshed, oppression" (50). Melito exaggerated the vices of the pagan world: "father lusting for his daughter, son for mother, brother for sister, man for man, and everyone for his neighbor's wife" (53) It was Jesus who came and, clothing Death with shame, bound the devil in anguish, smote iniquity, and made wickedness barren (68). The work, taken altogether, is a veritable hymn to the mystery of salvation and foreshadowed the baroque style of Methodius of Olympus and the Oriental imagery of Ephraem the Syrian. This style would be shortlived within the primitive Church.

[5] See *The Early Christian Fathers* (London: Gerald Duckworth & Co., Ltd., 1960), pp. 103–9, with the literature, and Testuz, *op. cit.*, pp. 19–20.

On the Pasch *

1   The Scriptural passage concerning the Exodus of the
Hebrews has been read, and the words of the mystery
have been translated (telling us) how the sheep is sacrificed and how the people are saved. And so, my dearly
beloved, understand how the mystery of the Pasch is both
old and new, eternal and passing, material and spiritual,
mortal and immortal. It is old according to the Law, but
new by the Word, passing according to its type, but
eternal by grace, material through the sacrifice of the
lamb, but spiritual through the life of the Savior, mortal
by his burial in the earth, but immortal through his
resurrection from the dead. . . .

48   Now man being disposed by nature to both good and
evil, like a piece of land capable of receiving seed of both
kinds, received the hateful and shameless counselor and,
touching the tree, disobeyed the commandment and
sinned against God. For this reason he was cast out into
the world as a condemned man is cast into prison.

And when he had become aged and prolific, because
he had eaten of the tree, and having spread over all the
earth, he left his children an inheritance. But the
heritage he left them was not chastity but fornication,
not immortality but corruption, not honor but scorn, not
freedom but slavery, not royalty but tyranny, not life
but death, not salvation but destruction. And the destruction of men on earth had become terrifying and
strange. For this is what befell them: they were seized
by tyrannous sin and dragged into the turmoil of their
passions, in which they were submerged by insatiable
desires: by adultery, fornication, immorality, avarice, murder, bloodshed, by a wicked and lawless oppression. For
the father drew his sword against his son and the son
raised his hand against his father, and the wicked struck

53   the breasts that gave him suck. . . . One could find even
further than this many things still more horrible, more
terrifying and licentious among men: a father lusting
after his daughter, a son for his mother, brother for sister, one man for another, and everyone sinning with his
neighbor's wife. At all this Sin rejoiced; for she, being
the collaborator of Death, went before him into the souls
of men and prepared for him his food, the bodies of the

* For the text, see Testuz, *op. cit.*

dead.[6] Sin left her mark on all souls, and every soul which she had marked had to die. And so all flesh fell into the power of Sin and every body into the hands of Death. . . .

For man had been divided by Death: a new calamity, 56 a new destruction encompassed him. He was dragged away as a captive by the shadow of Death, and the image of the Father lay deserted. This is the reason why the mystery of the Pasch was accomplished in the body of the Lord. . . .

"It is I," says Christ, "who destroyed Death, triumphed102 over the enemy, trod Hades underfoot. . . . And so come to me all you families of men, who are sullied by sin, and receive forgiveness of sins. For I am your forgiveness, I am the Pasch of salvation, the Lamb that was sacrificed for you, I am your redemption,[7] your life, your resurrection, your light, your salvation, your King. . . ."

This is He who made the heaven and earth and shaped104 man in the beginning. . . . He is the alpha and omega, the beginning and the end, the ineffable beginning and the incomprehensible end. Here is the Christ, the King, Jesus, Leader, Lord, He who rose from the dead, sat at the right hand of the Father; He bears the Father and the Father bears Him. To Him glory and power forever. Amen.

The Work of Melito On the Pasch

Peace to him who writes and to him who reads this and to those who love the Lord in simplicity of heart.

[6] The image of hungry Hades or Death is familiar from Greek tragedy (see Sophocles, *Oedipus Tyrennus* 29–30); but the image of Sin being the wife serving food for her husband Death is unique.

[7] Or, as others translate, "your lustral water." The Greek text is doubtful; the Latin version, however, has "redemption."

12

THE ADDRESS TO DIOGNETUS

The epistle or apologia addressed to Diognetus (perhaps the tutor of Marcus Aurelius) has remained one of the unsolved mysteries of early Christian literature. The text was first edited by Henri Estienne in 1592 from the unique manuscript in the city library of Strasbourg; but the manuscript was destroyed when the city was besieged during the Franco-Prussian war in 1870 and the fragment has never been found in any other source, citation, or manuscript.[1] To complicate the matter further, it seems all but certain that the *Address* comprises merely Sections 1 to 10, while Sections 11 to 12, displaying a somewhat different style, derive from an ancient homily of another author.[2] The *Address*, which is a rhetorical defense of Christianity, first shows that the Christian religion is superior either to Judaism or paganism; the absurdity of worshipping idols, the Sabbath, circumcision and food laws of the Jews all come under fire. Next, the author (5–6), in a famous passage, demonstrates that Christians externally are like the rest of men, but "they are to the world what the soul is to the body" (6.1). Finally (7–10), he develops the idea that Christianity is the love and service of the one true God, who has revealed himself and saved mankind through his Son.

For all its charm, there is something highly contrived about the *Address* and there is really nothing in it—save an apparent reference to the *Apology* of Aristides (about A.D. 140)—that would force us without hesitation to place

[1] See F. L. Cross, *The Early Christian Fathers* (London: Gerald Duckworth & Co., Ltd., 1960), pp. 27–28.

[2] The best argument for the unity of the piece has been advanced by H. Marrou in his edition, wherein he attributes the entire work to Pantaenus, the teacher of Clement of Alexandria. See also J. Quasten, *Initiation aux Pères de l'Eglise* (tr. by J. Laporte, Paris: Newman Press, 1955), I, 281–86.

the work in the second century after Christ, and perhaps a date in the third century would be closer to the truth.

The Address to Diognetus*

Excellent Diognetus!   1
I see that you are most eager to learn about the religion of the Christians, raising sharp and careful questions as to what God they believe in and how they worship Him, seeing that they despise the world, have contempt for death, neglect the gods whom the Greeks believe in, and do not observe the superstitions of the Jews. You inquire, too, about the love they bear one another, and what is the nature of this new people, this new way of life that has just now and not before come into existence. I welcome this enthusiasm of yours and I pray that God, who gives us the power both to speak and to listen, may enable me so to speak that you may become the better by listening, and that you may hearken to my words in such wise that you may not grieve the speaker. . . .

[The author attacks the idolatry of the pagans (2–3) and proceeds to the "errors and fussiness" of the Jewish religion (4).]

Now Christians are not different from the rest of men in   5
where they live, in their speech, or in their clothing. For they do not dwell in their own private cities, they use no special language, nor does their external life present anything remarkable.[3] They have no doctrine invented by the thought or reflection of inquisitive mortals, nor do they champion (as some do) any human teaching. They live as luck will have it either in Greek or non-Greek cities; they follow local usage in their dress, food, and way of life; and yet they manifest a marvelous and admittedly strange way of life in their society. They live in their own native cities, but as though they were strangers. They participate in everything as citizens, and yet carry out their obligations like aliens. Every foreign city is their native land, and every native city a foreign country. They marry and have babies like the rest of men, but they do not expose their infants. They share a common table, but not a common bed.

---

* I have followed the Greek text of H. Marrou (Sources Chrétiennes 33, Paris: Editions du Cerf, 1951), which occasionally differs from earlier editions.

[3] Surely a strange remark for a writer of the second century.

Though in the flesh, they do not live according to the flesh; though living on earth, their citizenship is in heaven. They obey the established laws, yet in their private lives they go beyond the laws. They love all men, yet all men persecute them. Though unknown they are condemned; though put to death, they live. Though poor, they make many others wealthy. . . . The Jews make war on them as though they were Philistines, the Greeks persecute them, and those who hate them cannot explain their hostility.

6   In short, Christians are to the world what the soul is to the body. The soul is dispersed throughout all parts of the body, just as the Christians are spread throughout the world. The soul lives in the flesh but it is not of the flesh; so Christians live in the world but are not of the world. The invisible soul is imprisoned in a visible body; so Christians are known to exist in the world, but their worship remains invisible. . . .

[The author recalls the Designer of the universe, who is known by the order that shines in the stars and the planets and the phenomena of the earth (7); it was He who conceived of the plan to sanctify the world through his Son (8–9).]

9.2   And when our sins reached their highest point and it became perfectly clear that the only recompense to be expected was chastisement and death, then came the time which God had set down for the future manifestation of his goodness and omnipotence—ah, the surpassing kindness and love of God for men! He did not hate us; He did not reject us or hold it against us; rather, He was magnanimous and endured us, and in his mercy He himself took on our sins. He himself delivered up his own Son in ransom for us, the holy one for the criminal, the innocent for the wicked, the incorruptible for the corrupt, the immortal for those doomed to die. What else could have concealed our sins but his righteousness? How else were we to be justified, sinful and ungodly as we were, save alone through the Son of God? What a lovely substitution, what a mysterious process, what an unforeseen bounty! That through one just man the crime of the many should be buried and that the uprightness of one should justify so many sinful men! . . .

[In return for this love of God, our Father, Teacher, Physician, and Life, man must live up to the image God has formed in him by becoming "an imitator of God" (10.4).

We must realize that our true life is in Heaven, and real death "is reserved for those who are to be condemned to everlasting fire" (10.7). The document breaks off, and then begins the Appendix, in which the preacher says that "having been a disciple of the apostles, I am now become a preacher to the pagans" (11). The final section (12) teaches that all who believe in the Lord will become "a paradise of delight," bearing all kinds of luscious fruit, and then concludes with the usual doxology.]

13

THE AFRICAN CHURCH

The Acts of the Scillitan Martyrs

Knowledge of the earliest acts of the martyrs come from transcripts of the court proceedings leading up to their conviction and condemnation. Only later were these accounts embroidered for the edification of the faithful. The precious document that describes the trial of twelve Christians of Scillium in Africa Proconsularis is preserved in several Latin recensions and a Greek version and is the oldest document that we possess from the primitive church of Numidia. The original Latin text gives the date of the trial at Carthage as July 17, A.D. 180, that is, in the reign of the emperor Commodus, whose attitude towards the new sect was hardly as tolerant as Trajan's. The Latin of this document, one of the finest in the early church, is beautifully austere and simple.

The Acts*

On July 17, when Calusian and Praesens were consuls, the latter for the second time, Speratus, Nartzalus, Cittinus, Donata, Secunda, and Vestia were arraigned at Carthage in the court.

* For the original Latin text and the other recensions, see J. Armitage Robinson, *The Passion of Perpetua with an Appendix on the Scillitan Martyrdom* ("Texts and Studies" 1, 2, Cambridge: The University Press, 1891), 104–21. On the problem of the literary form of the martyr acts, see H. Delehaye, *Les passions des Martyres et les Genres Littéraires* (Brussells: Bureaux de la Société des Bollandistes, 1921); cf. also H. Musurillo, *The Acts of the Pagan Martyrs* (Oxford: Clarendon Press, 1954).

Saturninus, the proconsul: If you come to your senses, you will gain the pardon of our Lord the emperor.

Speratus: We have never hurt anyone. We have never committed any crime. We have never libeled anyone. But when we were mistreated, we showed our thanks, because we reverence our own emperor.

Saturninus, the proconsul: We Romans are also a religious people. Our religion is very simple: we swear by the *genius* of our Lord the emperor and pray for his well-being. This is what you also ought to do.

Speratus: If you would only listen to me quietly, I would explain to you the mystery of simple belief.

Saturninus: If you are going to deride our sacred ceremonies, I shall not listen to you. Swear, instead, by the *genius* of our Lord the emperor.

Speratus: I do not recognize the kingdom of this world. Rather, I serve the God whom no one has seen nor can see. I have committed no theft. I pay the taxes on everything I buy. And this because I recognize my Lord, the king of kings and emperor of all mankind.

Saturninus, the proconsul, then said to the others: Cease to adhere to this belief.

Speratus: Any doctrine that teaches that we should commit murder or bear false witness—this would be evil.

Saturninus, the proconsul: Take no part in this business—it is madness.

Cittinus: The only one we fear is the Lord our God in Heaven.

Donata: Respect Caesar as Caesar, but fear God.

Vestia: I am a Christian.

Secunda: I want to be none other than what I am.

Saturninus, the proconsul, to Speratus: Will you persist in remaining a Christian?

Speratus: I am a Christian.

(And all the rest agreed with him.)

Saturninus, the proconsul: Would you like some time to think this over?

Speratus: Where our duty is so clear there is nothing to think over.

Saturninus, the proconsul: What do you have as the documents in your case?

Speratus: The sacred writings, and the epistles of a saint named Paul.

Saturninus, the proconsul: You may have a thirty-day reprieve to think this over.

Speratus again said: I am a Christian.

(And all the others were of the same mind.)

Saturninus, the proconsul, then read out the sentence from his tablets: Whereas Speratus, Nartzalus, Cittinus, Donata, Vestia, Secunda, and the others, have admitted that they live in accordance with the religious rites of the Christians, and whereas they have persevered in their stubbornness even when given the opportunity to return to the Roman religion, it is hereby decreed that they should die by the sword.

Speratus: Thank God!

Nartzalus: Today we shall be martyrs in heaven—thank God!

The proconsul Saturninus ordered the following proclamation to be read by his herald: I have ordered the execution of Speratus, Nartzalus, Cittinus, Veturius, Felix, Aquilinus, Laetantius, Januaria, Generosa, Vestia, Donata, and Secunda.

All said: Thank God!

And in this way all of them were crowned with martyrdom together, and reign with the Father, Son, and Holy Spirit forever. Amen.

Tertullian

Quintus Septimius Florens Tertullianus was born in Carthage, Africa, about the year 155, and his father was a centurion in the proconsular cohort. He probably practiced law in Rome before his conversion to Christianity, at the age of about forty, and then returned to Carthage. The rest of his life is obscure, and we do not know whether to believe St. Jerome's report (*On Famous Men* 53) that he was ordained a priest; in any case, Tertullian never referred to it himself. Shortly after Tertullian's birth, a Phrygian Christian named Montanus proclaimed that he was the new emissary of the Holy Spirit, and he attached himself to two women, Prisca and Maximilla, with whom he would fall into prophetic ecstasies. Their doctrines based on new visions and revelations were strongly related to a severe asceticism that frowned on marriage or any sensual pleasure. About the year 207 Tertullian moved in the direction of Montanism at Carthage and remained an adherent until his death, some time after 222. Some scholars claim that this African sect inspired the *Passion of Saints Perpetua and Felicitas* (A.D. 203); indeed, this fits Tertullian's style, and the stress on new visions and the operation of the Spirit suggests a moderate form of Montanism.

Tertullian's enormous and brilliant output (over thirty treatises, treating all aspects of Christian life) are normally divided into three periods. There is the Catholic period (197–206), which saw classics like the *Apologia for Christianity* (Apologeticus), *On the Games, The Adornment of Women.* Next came the beginning of the Montanist influence, often called Tertullian's semi-Montanist period (A.D. 207–13), with such works as the treatise *Against Marcion, The Exhortation to Chastity,* and *On Idolatry.* The last period, which reveals an intransigent attitude towards the orthodox Church and lasted until his death (213–22), was marked by the treatise *Against Praxeas, On Fasting,* and *On Monogamy.*

Tertullian's sharp, legal mind forged a new Christian terminology out of classical Latin, but his achievement transcended the linguistic level. His terminological solution of the problem of the two natures in Christ (as, for example, in the treatise *Against Praxeas* and elsewhere), remarkably anticipated the final solutions of the council of Chalcedon in 451, and his clear comprehension of the problem of the three distinct persons, who share the unity of the divine nature of the Godhead, became normative for many centuries to come in both East and West. His logical mind drew the correct inferences from the Gospels and the earlier Christian tradition; and when the conclusions of faith seemed to contradict the data of reason, his reply was, as given in *The Body of Christ* (5): "We must believe because it is absurd" (*Credendum quia absurdum est*). And if the logic of the Greeks seemed to clash with the humble doctrine of Jesus, he would say, "What has Athens to do with Jerusalem?" (*On the Exclusion of Heretics* 7). The evolution and perfection of Tertullian's teaching on the nature of Christ and the mystery of the Trinity form one of the greatest intellectual achievements of the primitive Church and merit a separate study.[1]

---

[1] One may consult the careful treatment of H.A. Wolfson, *The Philosophy of the Church Fathers* (Cambridge: Harvard University Press, 1956), I, 322–32, despite the somewhat unorthodox thesis of the book (see pp. 177 ff.). For a complete study of Tertullian's synthesis of the nature of the Godhead, see René Braun, *Deus Christianorum: Recherches sur le Vocabulaire Doctrinal de Tertullien* (Paris: Editions du Cerf, 1962), with the most recent bibliography, pp. 595–623. Emerging from the book is the conclusion that Tertullian was the most original thinker of the western Church before St. Augustine and that in many ways his daring pioneer work even surpassed the work of the latter.

Tertullian's precise connection with the African branch of Montanism has not been established.[2] The movement arose in the communities of Phrygia, led by an obscure, itinerant preacher named Montanus, who was assisted by a group of women who claimed to have clairvoyant powers. They maintained that the Spirit was revealing a new, definitive doctrine through them and, rejecting the hierarchic foundation of the Church, they asserted that the true Church was made up of *pneumatici*, or "men of the spirit," who lived according to an austere asceticism and avoided marriage; first marriages were tolerated but second marriages were equated with fornication and adultery. Of Montanus Tertullian said: "He has dispelled all the doubts of the past . . . through his clear and open explanation of the entire mystery, through the new revelation which comes down in abundant streams from the Spirit" (*On the Resurrection of the Body* 63). According to Jerome, an Asiatic bishop named Apollonius said that "Montanus and his crazy prophetesses died by hanging" (*On Famous Men* 40). Apollonius also accused them of gambling and usury, and (presumably the women) of dyeing their hair, using makeup, and wearing jewels and fine clothing. Unfortunately, Tertullian's reply to Apollonius' attack has been lost; it would have been a valuable comment on one of the earliest illuminationist movements of this primitive period.[3]

Tertullian was the first Latin patristic writer to use the Latin word *sacramentum* for what we now familiarly refer to as the sacraments; for the Greek Fathers the word had been *mysterion*, the "mystery" of the Eucharist, of Baptism, and so on. At least until his Montanistic period Tertullian had held a solidly comprehensive view of the orthodox Church, such as had come down from St. Ignatius of Antioch, and Irenaeus, i.e., the community of those who had been washed in the cleansing waters, who shared the sacred banquet and the mystical sacraments, directed in their unity by the hierarchy of bishops, priests, and deacons. The organizational, external body was part of the great mystery represented by the total body of Christ. Tradition does not

[2]For a selection of texts, with commentary, from this early period, see Paul F. Palmer, *Sacraments and Forgiveness: History and Doctrinal Development of Penance, Extreme Unction and Indulgences* (Westminster, Md.: Newman Press, 1959), pp. 23 ff.

[3]A vivid and fascinating portrait of Montanism and other early movements is painted by Ronald Knox, *Enthusiasm: A Chapter in the History of Religion, with Special Reference to the Seventeenth and Eighteenth Centuries* (New York: Oxford University Press, 1950).

tell us how this great man was converted; possibly he was influenced by the staunch behavior of the Christians whom he had observed under persecution in Rome and elsewhere. But it must also have been his own fascination with the Christians' new doctrine of chastity (of which he would write so often), and especially with the Trinitarian and Christological dogmas, which he was to do so much to advance even after he had broken with the visible Church and propounded the independence of the "spiritual man." Ultimately, Tertullian's transformation must remain a mystery; perhaps, like the later Luther, some psychological cataclysm was the chief cause of the amazing rupture from the Church of one who had done so much to advance her doctrines for future ages.[4]

On Flight in Time of Persecution*

[This treatise, written during Tertullian's semi-Montanist period, about the year 212, advances the idea that it is sinful to escape persecution by taking to flight. Some forty years later, however, when the bishop Cyprian did precisely this during the persecution of Decius, he defended it as being for the good of the African Church. Some of the dogmatic passages of the treatise are important, especially the following discussion of Jesus' Atonement. In some of his works, Tertullian held the so-called mystical theory of the Atonement, that is, that the process was primarily an elevation of the human race by the fact of Christ's participation in human flesh (see, for example Section 4 of *The Body of Christ*: "In loving man He loved his flesh and his process of being born"). But for the most part he taught the rescue or ransom theory, based on the concept of a series of contracts, such as he described in the following passage.]

He did all this that He might wean us from our sins. 12. The sun yielded the day of our purchase, we were ef-2-3 fectively released in the underworld, a contract was made

---

[4] I have used many of the recent editions of Tertullian, but the texts are in most cases based on the edition by F. Oehler (Leipzig: Weigel, 1853–54). For a brief introduction to some of the problems, see F. L. Cross, *The Early Christian Fathers* (London: Gerald Duckworth & Co., Ltd., 1960), pp. 135–45. See also the preface to the works of Tertullian in the *Corpus Christianorum* (Turnholt: Brepols, 1954), I, iv–xxv.

* See J. J. Thierry, *Corpus Christianorum* (Turnholt: Brepols, 1954) for the text.

for us in Heaven. The eternal gates were lifted up, that the King of glory might enter in. For it was He who purchased man from the earth, from the underworld, to place him in Heaven.

What kind of a man is it, then, that struggles against Christ, who lowers and dirties the property that He has bought at so great a price, the price, that is, of his own most precious blood? Surely it would be better to run away than to have one's price lowered—for this is precisely what a man does who puts on himself a lower price than Christ did. For the Lord ransomed man from the angelic powers who rule the world, the spirits of wickedness, the darkness of this world; he ransomed him from the eternal judgment and from everlasting death.

On the Flesh of Christ*

This is a vehement defense of the reality of Christ's body directed at the Gnostic heretics, and written in the semi-Montanist period or earlier, in a style of great purity and beauty. In this treatise, Tertullian expressed the view that Christ was physically an ugly man (see Isaiah 53.2). But more important was his sharp delineation of the doctrines of the Incarnation and Atonement, which set the standard for the western Church for many ages to come.

4.   Surely Christ loved man, the man that is hardened in
3–4a womb in the midst of uncleanness and comes forth through the parts of shame, the man who must grow up through all the indignity of being a baby. It was for man that Christ came down to earth, preached and humbled himself even unto death, the death of the cross. . . . In loving man He loved his flesh and his process of being born. . . .

He remakes our birth by a new, heavenly birth; He cures our flesh from all the ills that afflict it; He cures it when defiled with leprosy, he gives it new light in its blindness, new power when paralyzed; He exorcizes the demons that obsess it; He raises it to life from the dead. . . .

5.2   Reply, then, you who slay the truth. Was not God truly

* E. Kroymann, *op. cit.*

crucified? Did He not really die, being really crucified? And did He not truly rise, being really dead? . . . God's Son was truly born—there is no shame here because this was his shame. God's Son died—absurd, and hence wholly believable. He was buried and rose again—impossible, and hence absolutely certain. . . .

No angel ever came down to earth to be crucified, to [6.5] experience death, and to rise from the dead. There never was such a reason for angels to assume bodies; and that is why they never took on flesh through the process of birth. Since they did not come to die, they did not come to be born. But since Christ's mission was to die, He necessarily had to be born, so that He would be able to die. Only that which is born can die, according to the general principle. Birth and death are mutually connected. . . .

Since the devil had captured that which was the image [17.] and likeness of God, God undertook to restore it by a [4-6] contrasting process. For that word which was the builder of death had slipped into Eve while she was still a virgin. In similar fashion, God's Word was to be introduced into a virgin as the architect of life. In this way, that which had been destroyed through women should be restored to salvation through the same sex. Eve believed the serpent; Mary believed Gabriel. And if one sinned by believing, the other by belief destroyed that sin. . . . And while Eve bore a devil who murdered his brother, Mary brought forth a man who would one day bring salvation to Israel, his own fleshly brother and his own murderer.

Against Praxeas*

If you hold fast to the fact that I have always adhered [9.] to the principle by which I believe that Father, Son, and [1-2] Holy Spirit are one, you will understand how each point of doctrine can be asserted. For I declare that Father, Son, and Spirit are distinct; but any untutored or perverse person would misunderstand this if he thought that this distinction implied the complete separation of Father, Son, and Holy Spirit. And yet it must be said, seeing that those who adhere to a theory of monarchy against that of a proper division contend that Father, Son, and Spirit are one and the same person. Yet the Son is not other than

* E. Kroymann and E. Evans, *op. cit.*

the Father by separation from him, but by diversity of function, not by complete division but by distinction; for the Father and Son are not identical but distinct by way of degree. Now the Father is the entire substance; the Son a share and portion of the whole, as He himself confesses: The Father is greater than I [John 14.28]. And in the psalm it is sung that He has been subordinated by the Father a little less than the angels. So the Father is distinct from the Son as being greater than the Son insofar as the begetter is distinct from the begotten, the sender from him who is sent, and the creator from him who is the agent of what is made.

On the Prayer*

6.2   "Give us this day our daily bread" should be understood in a spiritual sense: Christ is our bread, because He is our life and bread is life. He said, "I am the bread of life," and a little earlier, "This is bread, the word of the living God which descended from Heaven." Further, we believe that his body is in the bread: "This is my body."

The Adornment of Women*

Divided in two books, each somewhat independent of the other, this was written during Tertullian's Catholic period and had a deep influence upon Cyprian. Tertullian's observation of the women of his day was quite acute and, though he goes to extremes at times, there is no hint of Montanism in the work.

6.   I am aware that women have been dyeing their hair
1–3 blonde by using saffron; so far as their hair is concerned, they renounce their native land, for they are ashamed of their country, ashamed that they had not been born in Germany or Gaul. It can scarcely be considered propitious that they prefer to have flame-colored hair; they take for beauty something that merely taints them. Actually these dyes are so powerful that they can harm the hair; indeed, the continual application of any natural wet material can harm the head itself, just as the heat of the sun can be harmful if excessive, even though it can dry the hair and give it vitality. . . . Indeed, you can even find persons

* G. F. Diercks, op. cit.
* E. Kroymann, op. cit.

who are ashamed that they are old, and try to turn their white hair to black. Are you not ashamed of such vanity? Here you try to hide the fact that you have finally attained the age for which you longed and prayed, and sigh instead for the youth that was a time of sin. . . .

[There is little that escapes Tertullian's attention: the makeup, the false hair and wigs, the excessive jewelry, immodesty of dress. His impatience with the follies of his time suggests that women have changed very little—and, indeed, how could they?—since his day; only their male critics, perhaps, have developed a better sense of humor.]

*Apologia for Christianity**

Tertullian followed the usual apologetic form for this early treatise, but the defense has the author's own special bite, and the attack against the pagans themselves is ironic and sharp. In addition, Tertullian went more deeply into the details of Christian dogma than most other apologists. A few examples follow.

Of those of you who stand around panting for the 9. blood of Christians (even you judges who have been most 6-8 righteous, most severe towards us), there are many whose consciences I could prick for the infants you killed at birth! Here too there is a difference in the manner of death, and it is surely more vicious to kill them by drowning than to expose them to cold, hunger, and the dogs. Even an older person would prefer to die by the sword.

Now for us Christians murder is forbidden on all counts, and we are forbidden to terminate the life of the womb once the blood has been drawn for the conception of a man. To prevent the child from being born is merely premature murder: it makes no difference whether one takes away the life of a man already born or stops it on its way to birth. What is to be born is already human; the full fruit is already present in the seed.

[Tertullian then defended the Christians against the charge of cannibalism and incest and pointed to their widespread reputation for chastity. He enumerated the various forms of death (12) to which Christians had been subjected: the cross, tearing with hooks, burning, and being cast to the

* E. Dekkers, *op. cit.*

beasts. He ridiculed the rumor that the Christian worshipped
an ass's head (16). He dwelt on the antiquity of the Scriptures,
and finally turned to the important topic: "We must now
say a few words about Christ as God" (21).]

21.7   This Christ, the Son of God, came, as it was foretold
–17 of him that He would come, from God, to enlighten and
reform the world. The Son of God had already been announced as the lord and master of this dispensation of
grace, the leader and enlightener of the race of men, but
He was not born in such a way that He might blush at
the name of Son or at his Father's seed. . . . The Son of
God had a mother by no act of lust; indeed, even she who
seemed to be his mother had not married.

But I must first explain his nature, that the quality of
his birth may be understood. We have already taught that
God constructed the entire universe by his word, his
reason, and his power. Even your philosophers believe
that the demiurge of the universe was the Logos, that is,
Word and Reason. . . . Now we also attribute to this
Word, Reason, and Power, by which God, as we said,
created everything, a proper spiritual substance, in whom
there is the Word when declaring, Reason when arranging,
and Power when accomplishing. And we have been taught
that this Spirit was uttered by God, was generated in the
utterance; hence He is called the Son of God by the unity
of substance. Thus this Spirit is also God. . . . So Spirit
comes from Spirit, God from God, as light is kindled from
light. . . . And the Spirit that is from the Spirit, God from
God, brings about a duality, by reason of the order, not
the status of each, for the second came forth from the
first but did not separate from it. Thus this ray of the
Godhead, as was constantly foretold in the past, descended
into a certain virgin, was molded into flesh in her womb,
and was born as man mingled with God. And this flesh,
informed with a soul, is nourished, grows, begins to speak,
teaches, works—and this is the Christ. . . . And so He
whom they thought to be merely a man, by reason of his
lowliness, they followed because they thought He was a
magician in his power, when with a word He cast demons
out of men, brought back sight to the blind, cleansed the
lepers, restored the paralyzed, and finally raised the dead
to life with a word, even ruled the elements, curbing
storms and walking on the waves—it was thus He proved
that He was the Word of God, the original, the firstborn,

filled with Reason and Power and supported by the Spirit, the same one who by a word made and can make all.

[Tertullian discussed Christ's arrest and death and resurrection, the mission of the apostles, and the emperors' persecutions even to his own day. He spoke of the innocence of the Christian agape, the orderliness, the modesty, and the prayers. After touching these and other points, he concluded with the boast that though Christians were dying, they were winning the battle: "our truth is manifested to all men" (46); the "blood of Christians is the seed" of the coming new harvest (50). His work forms one of the strongest appeals for Christianity in history.]

The Passion of Saints Perpetua and Felicitas

This beautiful account, composed shortly after the martyrdom and incorporating the testimony of eyewitnesses, exists in a Latin and in a Greek version; the Latin was undoubtedly the original. On March 7, 203, under the emperor Septimius Severus' reign, six young catachumens of Carthage were arrested and eventually executed. The group consisted of a young matron of good family, Vibia Perpetua, twenty-two years of age, her personal slave-girl Felicitas (who was pregnant at the time of her arrest and gave birth before her execution), two other young people named Saturninus and Secundulus, a slave named Revocatus, and another young catechumen, named Saturus, who gave himself up of his own accord.[5] After an introduction by the writer (1–2), there follows what purports to be the personal account of Vibia Perpetua herself (3–10); next, comes a linking section by the author (11), and then the story of Saturus (11–13), and finally the author's conclusion (14–21), containing a stirring eulogy of the martyrs.[6] Perpetua's visions in prison provide a vivid insight into the eschatological beliefs of the primitive African community—beliefs which, if some scholars are right, were sympathetic with the heresy of Montanism. The last charge is

[5] Their names are also found on inscriptions in Carthage: see Ernest Diehl, *Inscriptiones Latinae Christianae Veteres* (3 vols.; Berlin: Weidmann, 1961), 2040–41.

[6] For a discussion, see my *Symbolism and the Christian Imagination* (Baltimore, Md.: Helicon Press, 1962), pp. 47–50, and for the literature, J. Quasten, *Initiation aux Pères de l'Eglise* (tr. by J. Laporte, Paris: Newman Press, 1955), pp. 205–7.

difficult to prove, but since much of the style and some of the ideas in the *Martyrdom* find easy parallels in the work of Tertullian, possibly Tertullian was responsible for its final version. In any case, the tone of the document seems orthodox on the surface, and any overt plea for Montanism it may have certainly went unnoticed by Augustine and many of the early writers who admired the charm and spirituality of the piece.

The Passion of Saints Perpetua and Felicitas*

1   The ancient stories about the faith were a proof of God's favor and achieved the spiritual strengthening of man as well, and they were set forth in writing precisely in order that comfort might be given to men and honor to God by the recollection of the past through reading. Why then should not recent examples be set down that contribute equally to both ends? Indeed, these two will one day become old and needful for the ages to come, even though in our own time they may enjoy less prestige because of the prior claims of antiquity.

Let those then look to this, who would restrict the power of the one Spirit to times and seasons. For the more recent things should be considered the greater, being later than the last. And this is a consequence of the extraordinary graces promised at the last stage of the world. For, says the Lord, in the last days I will pour out my Spirit upon all flesh and their sons and daughters shall prophesy, and on my menservants and my maidservants I will pour my Spirit, and the young men shall see visions and the old men shall dream dreams [Acts 2.17–18; Joel 2.28–29]. So too we hold in honor and acknowledge not only new prophecies but new visions as well, according to the promise; and we consider all the other powers of the Holy Spirit as intended for the advantage of the Church, to which this same Spirit was sent to bring all gifts to all as the Lord allows to each person; ⁷ and hence we would set these forth and make them known for the glory of

---

* I have followed the Latin text of C.J.M.J. van Beek, *Passio Sanctarum Perpetuae et Felicitatis* (Bonn: Hanstein, 1938).

⁷ Precisely this stress upon the continuity of the outpouring of the Spirit after Pentecost suggests a Montanistic source for the document; the Montanists saw the government of the Church as proceeding by "new prophecies and new visions." If this is indeed the tone of the work, then it is reemphasized in the conclusion (21): "these new examples of virtue are proof that one and the same Spirit is still working. . . ." But the exact intent of these remarks remains unclear.

God. In this way no one of weak or despairing faith may think that supernatural grace was present only among those of ancient times, either in the grace of martyrdom or of revelations. For God always achieves what He promises, as a witness to the nonbeliever and a blessing to the faithful.

And so, my brethren and little children, that which we have heard and have touched with our hands we proclaim also to you [I John 1.2–3] so that those of you who were witnesses might recall the glory of the Lord, and those who now learn of it through hearing might have fellowship with the holy martyrs, and through them with the Lord Christ Jesus, to whom splendor and honor for all ages. Amen.

Some young catechumens were arrested, Revocatus and   2 his fellow slave Felicitas, Saturninus and Secundulus, and among them Vibia Perpetua, a recently married matron of respectable family and upbringing. Her mother and father were living, and of her two brothers one was a catechumen like herself; and she had an infant son at the breast and was about twenty-two years old. (From this point on the entire account of her ordeal is her own, according to her own ideas and the way she wrote them down.)

"I was, at the time," she said, "under arrest, and my   3 father out of love for me was trying to persuade me and move me from my resolution. 'Father,' I said, 'do you see this vase here, or waterpot, or whatever?'

" 'Yes,' he said.

"And I told him, 'Could it be called by any other name than what it is?'

"And he said, 'No.'

" 'Well, so too, I cannot be called anything other than what I am, a Christian.'

"At this my father was so angered by the word 'Christian' that he moved towards me as though he would pluck my eyes out. But he left it at that and departed, vanquished with his diabolic arguments.

"For a few days afterwards I gave thanks to the Lord that I was parted from my father, and I was comforted by his absence. During those few days we received baptism, and I was inspired by the Spirit not to ask for any other grace after the water but that of physical perseverance. A few days later we were lodged in the prison, and I was terrified, as I had never before been in such a dark hole. What a difficult time it was! The heat was stifling because of the crowd, and soldiers blackmailed us. To crown everything, I was tortured with worry for my baby.

"Then Tertius and Pomponius, those blessed deacons who were attempting to take care of us, bribed them to allow us to go to a better section of the prison to refresh ourselves for a few hours. Everyone then left that dungeon and shifted for themselves. I nursed my baby, who was faint with hunger. I spoke to my mother anxiously about the child, encouraged my brother, and gave my child to their charge. I suffered because I saw them suffering out of pity for me. These were the trials I endured for many days. And I got permission for my baby to stay with me in prison. I recovered my health at once, relieved as I was of the worry and anxiety over the child; and my prison had suddenly become a palace, so that I preferred to be there rather than anywhere else.

4   "Then my brother said to me, 'Dear sister, you are in great esteem; surely you might ask for a vision to discover whether you are to be condemned or released.'

"And I faithfully promised that I would, for I knew that I could speak with the Lord, whose great blessings I had come to experience. And I said, 'I will report to you tomorrow.' And so I made my request, and this was the vision I had.

"I saw a stairway made of bronze of tremendous height, reaching all the way to the heavens, but so narrow that only one person could climb at a time. And on the sides of the stairway were attached all sorts of iron weapons: there were swords, spears, hooks, daggers, and spikes, so that if anyone would climb up carelessly or without paying attention, he would be mangled and the flesh would cling to the weapons.

"And below the stairway lay a dragon of enormous size, and it would attack those who wanted to climb up and terrify them from doing so. And Saturus went up first, for he had later given himself up of his own accord; and he had been the cause of our strength, though he was not present when we were arrested. And he arrived at the top of the staircase and he turned and said to me, 'Perpetua, I am waiting for you. But be careful lest the dragon bite you.'

"And I said, 'He shall not harm me in the name of Jesus Christ.'

"And from underneath the stairway the dragon slowly stuck his head out as though he were afraid of me. And, using him as a first step, I trod on his head and went up.

"And I saw an immense garden, and in it a gray-haired man sitting in shepherd's garb, a tall man, milking the sheep. And standing about him were many thousands of people clad in white. He raised his head, looked at me, and said, 'I am glad you have come, my child.'

"He called me over and he gave me, as it were, a mouthful of the milk he was milking, and I took it into my joined hands and ate. And all those who stood by said 'Amen!' And at the sound of this word I came to, with the taste of something sweet still in my mouth. I at once told this to my brother, and we realized that we would have to suffer, and from now on we would no longer have any hope in this life.

"A few days later the story went about that we were 5 going to be given a hearing. My father also arrived from the city, worn with worry, and he came up to see me with the idea of persuading me.

" 'Daughter,' he said, 'have pity on my gray hairs; have pity on your father—if I deserve to be called your father, if I have favored you beyond all your brothers, if I have nurtured you to reach this prime of life. Don't abandon me to the disgrace of men. Consider your brothers, consider your mother and your aunt, consider your child, who will not be able to live once you are gone. Give up your pride. Do not be the ruin of us all—for none of us will ever feel free to speak again if anything should happen to you!'

"This was the way my father spoke in his love for me, kissing my hands and casting himself at my feet. It was with tears in his eyes that he no longer addressed me as his daughter but as a woman. I was sorry for my father's sake, because he alone of all my kin would not be happy in my suffering.

"And I tried to comfort him, saying, 'It will all happen on that platform as God wills; for, know that we are in his power and not in our own.'

"And he left me in great sorrow.

"On another day, when we were having our meal, we 6 were suddenly hurried off for a hearing. We came to the forum, and suddenly the rumor went through the area connected with the forum, and a huge crowd gathered. We mounted the platform, and the others, when questioned, all admitted their guilt. My turn came, and there my father appeared with my son, dragged me from the step, and said, 'Perform the sacrifice. Have pity on your baby.'

"And Hilarianus the governor, who had then received the power of life and death as the successor of the proconsul Minucius Timinianus, who had died, said to me, 'Have pity on your father's gray hairs. Have pity on your infant son. Offer sacrifice for the health of the emperors.'

" 'I will not,' I replied.

" 'Are you a Christian?' Hilarianus asked.

"And I said, 'I am.'

"And when my father persisted in trying to dissuade me, Hilarianus ordered him to be thrown to the ground and struck with a rod. And I was sorry for my father, almost as if I had been struck. I was so grieved for his pathetic old age.

"Then he passed sentence on all of us: we were condemned to the beasts, and we went back to the prison in great spirits. But my baby had been accustomed to be nursed at my breast and to stay in the prison with me; and so I immediately sent the deacon Pomponius to my father to ask for the baby. But father refused to give him over. And as God willed, the baby had no further desire for the breast, nor did I suffer any inflammation; and so I was relieved of any anxiety for the child and of any discomfort in my breasts.

7   "A few days later we were all at prayer and all of a sudden in the midst of the prayer I spoke out and uttered the name Dinocrates. I was surprised, for the name never had come into my mind until that moment. And I was pained when I recalled what had happened to him. And I at once realized that I was privileged to make a petition for him. I began to pray much for him and to lament before the Lord. Straightway, on that same night, I had the following vision. I saw Dinocrates coming out of a dark place, in which there were many others, very hot and thirsty, pale of countenance, and dirty. And on his face was the wound which he had when he died.

"This Dinocrates had been my brother according to the flesh, and he died miserably of cancer of the face when he was seven years old, and his death was a source of loathing to everyone. It was for him then that I made my prayer. There was a great gulf between us, so that neither could approach the other. And in the spot where Dinocrates was there was a pool full of water, and its edge was higher than the height of the child, so that Dinocrates had to stretch to drink. I felt sorry because the pool ought to have had water in it and at the same time Dinocrates could not drink because of the height of the rim. And I woke up realizing that my brother was in difficulty. But I was confident that I could help him in his trouble, and I prayed for him every day until we were transferred to the military prison. For we were supposed to fight with the beasts in the military games on the occasion of emperor Geta's birthday. And I prayed for him night and day with tears and sobs, that he might be granted to me.

"During the day, while we were kept in chains, I had 8 this vision shown to me. I saw the same place that I had seen before, and there was Dinocrates all clean, well dressed, and refreshed. I saw a scar where there had been the wound; and the pool which I had seen before now had its edge lowered to the child's waist, and he kept drinking water from it, and there above the rim was a golden bowl full of water. And Dinocrates came forward and began to drink from it, and the bowl remained full. And when he had drunk enough of the water, he began to play as children do. I awoke, and I then realized that he had been released from his punishment.

"A few days afterward, a military adjutant named 9 Pudens, who was in charge of the prison, began to show us great esteem, realizing that we possessed some great power within us. And he began to admit many visitors to see us for our mutual comfort. Now the day of the contests was approaching, and my father came to see me and he was overcome with sorrow. And he began to tear the hairs from his beard and to cast them on the ground; he threw himself upon the ground and began to curse his years and to say many things that were enough to move all creation. I was sorry for his unhappy old age.

"On the day before we were to fight I saw the follow- 10 ing in a vision. The deacon Pomponius came to the gate of the prison and knocked violently. I went out and opened the door for him; and he was dressed in a white tunic without a cincture and wore very fancy sandals.

"And he said to me, 'Come Perpetua, we are waiting for you.'

"And he took my hand and we began to walk through rough and winding country. At last we arrived with difficulty at the amphitheater, out of breath, and he led me into the center of the arena.

"And he told me, 'Don't be afraid. I am here with you, struggling with you.' And he left.

"And I looked at the enormous crowd, who watched in astonishment. And I was surprised that no beasts were let loose on me, because I knew that I was condemned to die by the beasts. And out came an Egyptian against me, foul of aspect with his minions, to fight me. There also came up to me handsome young men to be my seconds and assistants.

"My clothes were stripped off and I became a man; and my assistants began to rub me down with oil as they are accustomed to do before a contest. And I saw the Egyptian on the other side, rolling in the dust. And there came forth a man of marvelous height, so that he rose above the top of the amphitheater. And he was clad in a purple tunic without a belt, with two stripes, one on either side, running down the middle of his bosom, and wearing sandals that were wondrously made of gold and silver. And he carried a wand, like a trainer, and a green branch on which there were golden apples.

"And he asked for silence, and said, 'If this Egyptian defeats her, he will slay her with the sword; but if she defeats him, she will receive this branch.' And he withdrew.

"And we came close to one another and began using our fists. My opponent wanted to get hold of my feet, but I kept on striking him in the face with the heels of my feet. And I was lifted up into the air, and began to rain blows on him without, as it were, touching the ground. But when I saw that there was a lull, I put my two hands together and, linking the fingers of one hand with the fingers of the other, I got hold of his head. And he fell down upon his face, and I stepped upon his head. And the people began to shout and my seconds began to sing psalms. And I came forward to the trainer and received the branch.

"And he kissed me and said to me, 'Peace be with you, my daughter.'

"And I began to walk in triumph towards the gate of Life. And I awoke. And I realized that I would not fight with the wild animals but with the Devil; but I knew that I would win the victory. This is what I did until the time of the contest. About what happened at the contest itself, let him write who will."

11   The blessed Saturus has also made known his own vision, and he has written it out in his own hand. "We had gone through our suffering," he said, "and had put off the flesh, and we began to be carried towards the east by four angels, who did not touch us with their hands. . . ."

[Saturus has a vision of Paradise, as the martyrs come before the good Shepherd and receive the kiss of peace before his throne.]

Such were the famous visions of the blessed martyrs, 14 Saturus and Perpetua, which they themselves wrote down with their own hands. As for Secundulus, God called him from this world to depart earlier, while still in prison, not without grace, that he might not have to face the animals. Nevertheless, his flesh, if not his spirit, knew the sword.

As for Felicitas, she too enjoyed the favor of the Lord 15 in this wise. She had been pregnant when she was arrested and was now in her eighth month. As the day of the spectacle drew near, she was very grieved lest her martyrdom would be put off because of her pregnancy, since it was unlawful for pregnant women to be executed. Thus she might have to shed her holy, innocent blood afterwards, among others who were criminals. Her fellow martyrs were also saddened, for they were afraid that they would have to leave behind so good a companion and fellow traveler alone on the way to the same hope. And so, in one torrent of common grief, they poured forth a prayer to the Lord two days before the contests. And straightway after the prayer her birth pains came upon her. She suffered a good deal in her labor because of the natural difficulty of an eight months' delivery. And hence one of the prison guards said to her:

"You're suffering so much now—what will you do when you will be tossed to the beasts? You thought little of them then when you refused to sacrifice."

And she replied, "What I am suffering now I suffer by myself. But then another will be inside of me, who will suffer for me, because I also am to suffer for Him."

And so she gave birth to a girl, and one of the sisters brought her up as her own daughter.

And so, since the Holy Spirit has permitted the story of 16 the contest to be written down, and by so permitting has willed it, we shall carry out the command or rather the commission of the most holy Perpetua, however unworthy we might be to add anything to this glorious story, at the same time adding one example of her perseverance and nobility of soul.

The military tribune had treated them with unusual severity, because, on the information of very foolish people, he became afraid that they would be spirited out of the prison by some magic spells.

Perpetua spoke to him directly, "Why can't you even allow us to refresh ourselves properly, since we are the most distinguished of the condemned, seeing that we belong to the emperor and we are to fight on his very birthday? Won't it be to your credit if we are brought forth on that day in healthier condition?"

The officer was disturbed and grew red. And so it was that he gave the order that they were to be more humanely treated, allowing her brothers and other persons to visit, so that the prisoners might dine in their company. By this time the head of the prison was himself a believer.

[On the day before their martyrdom the prisoners share their last supper as a love feast, an agape. On the final day they are led into the amphitheater together, and Perpetua refuses to put on the robe of a devotee of Ceres. Saturus is not dispatched by the leopard, the bear, and the wild boar that are set upon him, and so he retires unhurt (17–19).]

20   For the young women the Devil had prepared a mad heifer, an unusual animal, but selected so that their sex might be matched with that of the beast. They were stripped and then placed in nets and so carried into the arena. The people were disturbed, seeing on the one hand a delicate young girl and on the other a woman fresh from childbirth, with the milk still dripping from her breasts. Hence they were brought back again and were dressed in tunics without cinctures.

The cow first tossed Perpetua and she fell on her back. Sitting down she pulled the torn tunic from her side to cover her thighs, thinking more of her modesty than of her suffering. Next she asked for a pin and fastened her unruly hair, for it was not right that a martyr should die with her hair in disorder, lest she might seem to be in mourning in her hour of glory.

Then she got up. And, seeing that Felicitas was bruised, she came up to her, gave her her hand and raised her up. And the two stood side by side. And the people's cruelty was by now appeased, and so they were called back through the gate of Life. There Perpetua was held up by a certain Rusticus, a catechumen at the time, who kept close to her. She awoke from a kind of sleep (she had been so absorbed in ecstasy in the Spirit), and began to look around her. And she said to those who were in amazement, "When are we going to be thrown to that cow?"

She was told what had already happened, but she refused to believe it until she noticed some of the marks of her rough experience on her person and on her dress.

Then she called for her brother and spoke to him and to the catechumens, saying, "All of you love one another and stand fast in the faith; and do not be weakened by our sufferings."

At another gate, Saturus was earnestly addressing the 21 soldier Pudens. "It is exactly," said he, "as I foretold it and predicted. Not one animal has so far touched me. And now you may believe me with all your heart: I am going thither and I shall be finished with one bite of the leopard." And immediately as the spectacle was coming to a close, the leopard was set upon him, and with one bite Saturus was so drenched with blood that as he came away the crowd roared in witness to his second baptism.

"Well washed! Well washed. . . ."

Then he told the soldier Pudens, "Good-bye. Remember me, and remember the faith. These things should not disturb you, but rather confirm you."

And with that he asked for a ring from Pudens' finger, dipped it into his wound, and handed it back again as a legacy, leaving it as a pledge and as a memorial of his bloodshed.

Shortly after, he was thrown lifeless with the others in the usual spot, to have his throat cut. But the crowd asked for their bodies to be brought out into the open, that their eyes might be guilty witnesses to the sword that pierced their bodies. Hence the martyrs got up of their own accord and went to the spot the people wanted them to; and, kissing one another, they consummated their martyrdom with the ritual kiss of peace. The others took the sword in silence and without moving—especially Saturus who, being the first to climb the stairway, was the first to die. Now once more he was waiting for Perpetua. Perpetua, however, had yet to taste some pain, and she screamed as she was struck on the bone. She took the wavering hand of the young gladiator and guided it to her throat. It was as though so great a woman, feared as she was by the unclean spirit, could not be killed unless she herself were willing.

Ah, most valiant and blessed martyrs! Truly called and chosen for the glory of Christ Jesus our Lord! And any man who exalts, honors, and adores his glory should read for the comfort of the Church these new examples, which are no less significant than the tales of old; for these new manifestations of virtue will bear witness to the one same Spirit, who still operates, and to God the Father almighty, to his Son Jesus Christ our Lord, to whom is splendor and immeasureable power for all the ages. Amen.

14

MINUCIUS FELIX: OCTAVIUS

Faustus Sabaeus unknowingly published this jewel-like dialogue, the *Octavius,* in Rome in 1543. Mistakenly believing it to be the eighth book of Arnobius' *Against the Pagans,* he printed it in that work's first edition and was thus probably responsible for its preservation. Marcus Minucius Felix, the author and main speaker of the dialogue, was a Roman lawyer (this is how St. Jerome identifies him in his work, *On Famous Men* 58), but, because of his style and his affinity with Tertullian and Cyprian, most scholars today would guess that his origins were African. With very little solid evidence to go on, Minucius is difficult to date, but his apparent borrowing from Tertullian and the absence of any clear reference to actual persecution suggest a date early in the third century, that is, before the persecution of Decius. Indeed, it is tempting, like H. Dessau, to identify the Caecilius Natalis of the dialogue with the Caecilius who erected a triumphal arch at Cirta (mod. Constantine) in honor of the emperor Caracalla, and this would further narrow the date down to the second decade of the third century. Nevertheless, the question of date remains an open one.

The dialogue is not only a skillful apologia for Christianity but also, as the opening hints, a pious memorial in honor of the recently deceased Octavius Ianuarius. Thus Sections 1 to 4 provide the setting, in which Octavius, Minucius, and Caecilius of Cirta debate about Christianity on their way from Rome to Ostia and the seacoast. It is a charming, almost pastoral scene, full of nostalgia for days gone by. Sections 5 to 13 present the case of the pagans against the Christians, as put into the mouth of Caecilius. Caecilius attacks the Christians for their nonconformity, as well as their dogmatism in areas that he would consider open to philo-

173

sophical discussion. In such dilemmas, Caecilius argues, it is best to adhere to the traditional beliefs. In Sections 14 to 15 Minucius acts as referee, warning against the use of rhetoric as a means of obscuring the truth; to this Caecilius objects and suggests that Minucius is not an impartial judge. Then in Sections 16 to 38 (a portion more than twice as long as Caecilius' speech) Octavius Ianuarius makes his rebuttal. Without appealing to Scripture or any explanation of Christ's mission, he begins by criticizing the pagan gods and their oracles; he shows how the philosophers had anticipated the best of Christian teaching and finally demonstrates not only that the stories about the Christians are grossly distorted but also that the Christian ideal of living is far superior to the pagan ideal. In Sections 39 to 40 Caecilius saves Minucius the trouble of making a decision by admitting his defeat, as well as his own decision to become a Christian, and Minucius concludes the dialogue with joy in his heart. Caecilius, we suspect, has given in much too easily; but the dialogue form (almost like the Roman *controversia* of the rhetorical schools) is only a mask for a subtle apologetic aimed at pagan Romans of the cultured and conservative class. Although Minucius is neither an ardent evangelist nor a profound thinker, he manages to cover many topics then under debate with charm and persuasiveness.

Like Arnobius' *Against the Pagans*, the dialogue survives only in the ninth-century Paris manuscript (Paris. lat. 1661), of which there is one known copy, the eleventh or twelfth century Brussels codex (Bibl. royale 10847), which some date to the sixteenth. The text has been edited many times and translated into many languages.[1]

Octavius [*]

1   Going back in thought and recollecting the memory of a dear and loyal companion of my youth, Octavius, his personal charm and my deep affection for the man has been so firmly rooted in my mind that I feel I am somehow still living in the past and not merely remembering things that are now past and beyond recovery. Indeed,

[1] For the bibliography, see J. Quasten, *Patrology* (Westminster, Md.: Newman Press, 1953), II, pp. 155–63, and the English version with commentary by R. Arbesmann in (*Fathers of the Church* 10, New York: Fathers of the Church, Inc., 1950), 313–402.

[*] I have followed the text of G. Quispel, *Marcus Minucii Felicis Octavius* (Leiden: E. J. Brill, 1949), with the introduction and commentary.

removed as he is from my sight, the more deeply is his picture stamped upon my heart and, as it were, upon my inner senses. Nor is it without reason that the passing of this extraordinary, holy man has left us with a feeling of infinite regret. For his love for me was so sincere that whether in amusement or things more serious, we always shared our likes and dislikes in perfect accord. . . .

He had traveled to Rome on business and also to visit 2 me. He had left at home his wife and children, children who were still in that charming age of innocence when they were just starting to speak and their speech was all the sweeter for the mistakes of a lisping tongue. When Octavius arrived I cannot express in words how incredibly happy I was, and my joy was all the more intense because my dearest friend was unexpected.

For a day or two, our constant companionship made up for the eagerness of our affection and we filled in the gaps in each other's knowledge because of our separation. Then we decided to visit the charming city of Ostia, where I felt the sea bathing would be just the sort of pleasant therapy I needed for the drying up of bodily humors. Besides, it was the time of the harvest holidays and there would be no worries about the law courts. Summer had just passed, and the weather was passing into a mild autumn.

One morning at dawn, we started walking along the river bank towards the sea; the gentle breeze, we felt, would invigorate our limbs, and the soft sand yielding to our footsteps was quite delightful. Caecilius happened to notice a statue of Serapis and, following the common superstition, put his hand to his mouth and kissed it.

At this, Octavius said, "Brother Marcus, here is a man 3 who is your constant companion in and out of the house; now it is hardly worthy of a good man to leave him in such blind and vulgar ignorance. How can you allow him on so fine a day as this to fall and worship stones, even though they are in human shape and are anointed and garlanded? Surely you know that you will be held as much responsible for this error as he will."

As he was speaking, we had already covered the stretch between the city and the sea and were now close to the open seashore. The waves were gently breaking over the edge of the sand, as though they were leveling out a place to walk. As usual, the water was rough even though there was no wind, and though the sea did not break on the shore in white, foaming waves, we enjoyed it as it churned and curled constantly around our legs as we dipped them into the water's edge. And the sea sent in waves to play about our legs as they were driven into shore or sucked them back again as the water retired and slipped away.

We made our way, walking slowly and leisurely along the gently curving shoreline, beguiling the time with stories. The stories were really Octavius'; he was telling us about his sea voyage. When we had gone a good way, talking all the while, we then retraced our steps and went back again. We came to a spot where a few small boats had been hauled up on land and placed on oakwood blocks to keep them from rotting on the ground. We saw some boys there having a contest, throwing shells into the water. The idea of the game consists in picking up from the beach a shell that has been worn smooth by the waves, holding it flat at the edges and bending over, making it skip as far as possible over the waves. The missile either skims the surface of the sea as it slips along, or else, cutting the tops of the waves, it darts up and springs into the air. The winner is the one whose shell goes the farthest and makes the most skips.

[Caecilius Natalis proposes a discussion with Octavius on the nature of Christianity. As they sit on the rocks on the Ostian seashore, Marcus Minucius Felix serves as their referee. Caecilius then begins with a devout pagan's view of Roman religion: philosophy has cast doubt upon the existence and benign providence of the gods. Hence, in the midst of uncertainty, "it is the wisest thing to accept the teaching of our ancestors as a criterion of truth, to respect the religious rites they have handed down to us, and to adore the gods whom your parents taught you to fear rather than know familiarly" (6.1). Caecilius' argument consists of a reference to the unanimous belief in the existence of the gods, which has grown up in association with the ritual, poetry, and art of the ancient world. He voices the feelings of the highest strata of pagan society when he is shocked that "an outlawed and criminal gang rebels against the pagan gods. They number the most boorish people from the lowest dregs of society, pious women who are an easy mark because of their feminine instability; thus they organize a vicious mob of conspirators who come together at nightly meetings, binding themselves by solemn fasts, filthy meals, and not by a sacred rite but by an atrocious crime. They are the sort who lurk in corners and shun the light of day, silent in public but quite talkative in secret. They ridicule our temples as though they were tombs, insult our gods, and make fun of our ceremonies" (8.4). Caecilius continues his attack, and in this clever way, Minucius can portray the contemporary criticism of Christianity.]

"Evil is always quick to spread. So now, as their vicious 9 morals spread from day to day, the foul secret meeting places of this ungodly society are increasing in number throughout the entire world. They form a conspiracy and they must be rooted out and cursed. The members recognize one another by secret symbols; they come to love each other after barely meeting. Among them everywhere there prevails a kind of religion of lust; and indeed, they call one another brother and sister indiscriminately, so that under the cloak of a holy name a not infrequent violation becomes incest. Thus does this mad and foolish superstition boast of its crimes.

"And so far as their crimes are concerned, there must be some basis for them; surely rumor, which is ever shrewd, would not otherwise have spread such scandalous stories about them that I apologize for mentioning them. I hear they worship the head of an ass, the lowest of animal creation, because of some foolish belief or other. And their religion is exactly in keeping with its origin from such customs. . . .

"The stories about the initiation of their neophytes are as disgusting as they are well known. Before the person to be initiated is placed a little baby deceptively covered with a crust of dough. The novice is urged to strike harmless blows upon the surface of the crust, and thus the baby is killed at the hands of the initiate by wounds inflicted unintentionally and invisibly. Then (horrible sight!) everyone thirstily drinks up the baby's blood, they have a contest in tearing it limb from limb, and it is by this victim that they are bound in fellowship and sworn by common guilt to mutual silence. Such are their sacred rites—and they are fouler than the worst sacrilege.

"Everyone knows about their banquets, the story is spread everywhere, as a fellow citizen of mine from Cirta bears witness in a speech of his.[2] On a given day they attend the banquet with their mothers, sisters, and chil-

---

[2] The reference is to Marcus Cornelius Fronto (*ca.* 100–*ca.* 166), a Numidian rhetorician who was one of the teachers of emperor Marcus Aurelius; a collection of his *Letters* is extant, but his *Oration against the Christians* is lost.

dren, and both sexes and all ages are commingled. Then
after a sumptuous banquet, when the company has grown
excited and drunkenness has added fuel to the fire of
incestuous lust, they tie a dog to one of the lamps, then
tempt him to dash and leap beyond the range of his
leash by a piece of food. Thus the lamp, which would be
a witness, is upset and put out, and in the ensuing darkness, which is a temptation to shamelessness, they unite
promiscuously in any shocking embrace. . . ."

[And so the pagan Caecilius goes on (10–13), making a
rhetorical case against Christianity. He concludes with an
attack on the Christian belief in the Judgment and last
conflagration, and finally pleads for the simple ignorance of
a Socrates. As Minucius notes (14), Caecilius seems relieved
after his vehement outburst and challenges his opponent
Octavius to see what he can do to answer him. Minucius
cautions him and in general warns against the evils of
rhetoric. "There are always two sides to every question," he
says (14.7), and one must be careful not to obscure the truth
by making an overwhelming case for one side. Caecilius
counterattacks by accusing Minucius of partiality; but he
still is eager to see what Octavius will reply (15). Octavius
then embarks on a proof of the existence of a provident
Creator from the order of the universe, a doctrine anticipated by the poets and philosophers of old (16–19). Next
Octavius attacks the ridiculous mythology and absurd ritual
practices of the pagans (20–27), after which he attempts to
refute the false charges against Christian practice and belief
(28–35). Finally (36–38), he dwells on the virtues of the
Christians themselves and the high morality which they
hold up as their ideal. The conclusion is a masterpiece of
quiet writing, crowned by an unexpected denouement:
Caecilius, for all his vicious attack, has been hiding the
secret that he too is to become a Christian.]

33 "Let us not deceive ourselves [Octavius continues]
on our numbers: we may seem to be numerous, but we
are but few in God's sight. Men distinguish between nations and tribes; to God this entire world is one family.
Rulers are made aware of what is going on in their
kingdoms through their ministers: God has no need of
such information, for we live not only in his sight, but
in his bosom. But what good was it, you object, for the
Jews to worship one God on their altars and in their
temples with such intense scrupulosity? Here you err

out of ignorance: you recall only their later history, either forgetful or ignorant of what took place before. For their God is our God, indeed the God of all mankind. And so long as they worshipped Him in purity, innocence, and devotion, and observed his salutary commandments, they grew numerous from their small numbers, they became wealthy out of their poverty, and rulers instead of slaves. Though small in number and unarmed they put to flight and crushed multitudes of armed fugitives, all by God's help and the assistance of the elements. Read their scriptures; or if you prefer Roman authors, let us pass over the ancient writers and try Flavius Josephus or Antonius Iulianus for what they say about the Jewish people.[3] Here you will find that it was their own sinfulness which brought on their downfall, and that nothing happened that had not been foretold would happen if they persisted in their obstinacy. They abandoned God, you understand, before He abandoned them. Their God was not taken into captivity with them; rather they were handed over by God for giving up his covenant. . . ."

[In Section 34 Octavius eloquently defends the Christian doctrine of a future life.]

"Do you think that simply because our weak sight does 34 not see something it is also lost to God? All bodies are thus removed: they dry up, dissolve in moisture, or crumble into dust, or pass off in vapor, but all their elements are still preserved in God's sight. Nor is it true, as you believe, that we are afraid of a harm that may come from the manner of burial; it is simply that we practice the older and better custom of complete burial.[4]

"Consider how all nature consoles us by the suggestion of a future resurrection. The sun sets and rises again, the stars rise and set, flowers die and live again, shrubs grow old and then blossom again, seeds can only sprout after

---

[3] Josephus, a priest of aristocratic Jewish ancestry, though pro-Roman in his sympathies, was a zealous apologist for Jewish religion and culture in his *History of the Jewish War* and *Antiquities of the Jews*. Iulianus also took part in the siege of Jerusalem in A.D. 70, but his writings are not extant.

[4] The choice between the two methods of burial in the Roman empire, cremation or inhumation (burial of the entire body in a tomb or below the earth), often depended upon economy or convenience. Both Jews and Christians objected to cremation, a factor that had much to do with the early appearance of the catacombs at Rome, Naples, and elsewhere.

they have died. Thus the body lying in the earth of this
world is like the trees in winter, they conceal their live
sap underneath a deceptive dryness. Why force it to return and revive while it is still in the dead of winter?
So too we must wait for the springtime of the flesh. I
realize, of course, that many men of evil conscience
hope against hope that there is nothing after death; they
would prefer to become annihilated rather than be restored for the sake of punishment. Thus their error is
compounded because God in his infinite patience allows
them complete freedom in this life; but his judgment
will come, and it will be no less just because it will
come late. . . .

37   "How charming a sight it is for the Lord when the
Christian grapples with pain, braves threats, torture and
execution, when he looks down with an ironic smile upon
the terrifying executioner and the noisy preparations of
death, when he upholds his freedom in the face of kings
and princes, yielding to God alone whose creature he is,
and when, bold and triumphant, he stands in defiance of
the very judge who passes sentence on him. . . . How
many of our number have allowed their right hands, indeed their entire bodies to be burned without the slightest
whimper of pain, even when they had it in their power
to be released? And it is not only our men who can be
compared with Mucius, Aquilius, or Regulus.[5] Even our
tender women and children, in their truly inspired en-
durance of pain, make a mockery of torture and crucifixion, the wild beasts, and all the other terrifying forms
of execution. Misguided men, little do you realize that
no man would undergo suffering without a motive, nor
could he sustain such torture without the help of God.
. . .

"We are all born equal; it is moral goodness alone that
distinguishes us. Hence, judging ourselves as we do by
our moral behavior, we rightly keep away from your processions, your shows, and other sources of evil pleasure.
We know their ritual origin and their evil seduction. Indeed, who would not be nauseated by the mad frenzy of
the crowds at the chariot races as they squabble among
themselves, or the systematic murder that takes place
in the gladiatorial games? You see the same insanity in

---

[5] Mucius Scaevola, Aquilius Nepos, and Marcus Atilius Regulus
were all historical examples of the fortitude of Roman heroes under
torture; Scaevola's right arm was burned, Aquilius had gold poured
down his throat, Regulus gave himself voluntarily into captivity.

the theater and an even wider range of vice. Sometimes an actor will either describe adultery or even act it out; sometimes a homosexual actor will inspire love even though he is only playing a part; he disgraces your gods by portraying their hatreds, their desires, and their sinful loves; and he tempts you to tears by acting out make-believe sorrows with stupid motions and gestures. So it is that you weep at a play, but demand murder in real life. . . .

"It is clear to everyone that we love the flowers of 38 springtime: we pluck the rose in season, the lily, and any other blossom of sweet odor or hue. We like them scattered about or untied, and we make soft wreaths of them to wind about our necks. You will pardon us, but we do not use them for chaplets on the hair, we like to drink in their sweet perfume with our nostrils and not inhale it with the hair of the head. And we do not place chaplets upon the dead. In fact, I am surprised that you do this: on the one hand you put a torch to the dead person as though he had no sense of feeling, and yet you give him a chaplet as though he did. If he is happy, he needs no flowers; if he is unhappy, he will not enjoy them. Our burials are distinguished by the same sense of peace as our lives. We plait no chaplet which will wither away; rather we await from God a fresh crown of eternal blossoms, filled with faith in his ever-present majesty, humble yet confident of our future glory through the kindness of our God. Thus we shall rise one day in blessedness, yet we live today in the vision of what will come. . . ."

Octavius ended his speech, and we looked at him in- 39 tently for a while in silence. As for me, I was overwhelmed with an intense admiration for his ability to take things which are more easily felt than expressed and to support them with arguments, examples, and quotations from authorities, to turn against the ill-disposed the very philosophical weapons which they had used against us, and thus show that the truth was not only easy to discover but also on our side.

As I was thinking all of this to myself, Caecilius interrupted: "Sincere congratulations to my friend Octavius—and to myself. No, I won't wait for the decision. For we have both won—since I may boldly claim a victory as well. He has defeated me—but so too I have defeated error. Hence, on the main point of our debate I yield the victory, both with regard to the exist-tence of God and his providence, and I completely agree on the authenticity of the new religion, which is now my own. There are, however, some difficulties that remain, not really obstacles to the truth but essential for complete understanding. But since the sun is near setting, we can discuss them in detail tomorrow with more dispatch now that we are in agreement on the whole."

"As for myself," I said, "I'm the happier now for all of us, now that Octavius has won me this victory, for I've been relieved of the odious task of passing judgment. My words are insufficient to do justice to his good qualities. For the testimony of a single human being is meager praise. The extraordinary gift he has is from God; it was his inspiration and assistance that helped him win his case."

After this, we left in high spirits: Caecilius was happy because he now believed, Octavius because he had won, and I for both of them—the victory of the one and the faith of the other.

15

HIPPOLYTUS OF ROME

Though Hippolytus, who died as a martyr in A.D. 235, was one of the most prolific writers of the early Church and was even elected rival Bishop of Rome in 217 by a group that opposed Pope Callistus, relatively little is known about his career, and very meager fragments of his vast output are extant today. He is the only Father of the Church whose contemporary statue has been found; brought from the Lateran Museum, it now reposes in the entrance hall of the Vatican Library, with a complete list of the saint's works inscribed upon the base. Hippolytus was very deeply influenced by the Alexandrian tradition in exegesis, and his commentaries on the Scriptures are highly allegorical; as a reaction against those who tended to deny a strict Trinity in God (the Monarchians or Patripassians as they were called), he adopted a subordinationism that was very similar to the positions of Origen, Justin, and Methodius. He believed that the Logos or Son of God is a divine spirit who is somehow subject to the Father, in whose divinity he shares. His attack on the pagan cults and Gnostic heresies owes much to the work of Irenaeus of Lyons; and his austere asceticism which recalls the spirit of *Hermas,* also brings to mind his contemporary, Origen. Indeed, he opposed the election of Pope Callistus because he was shocked at the prospect that those guilty of adultery and other serious sins could find relatively easy reconciliation with the Church.[1] His reign in Rome continued throughout the pontificate of Pontian (230–35), when suddenly they were both exiled to Sardinia, and there, after a presumed reconciliation,

[1] There is an interesting summary of the recent controversies on Hippolytus and his works in F. L. Cross, *The Early Christian Fathers* (London: Gerald Duckworth & Co., Ltd., 1960), pp. 155–67.

both died as a result of the treatment received in the Roman prisons. Thus Hippolytus' name found a venerable place in the earliest martyr lists of the Church.

A good number of his exegetical works have long been known in translation. For example, the important *Commentary on the Song of Songs,* completely extant only in Georgian, is a lovely allegorical work which deeply influenced St. Ambrose, and a *Commentary on Daniel,* in which Susanna and the two elders represent the Church, paganism, and the Synagogue, is extant in Palaeoslavic or Old Church Slavonic. The *Refutation of All Heresies,* originally in ten books, is preserved in Greek and remains an excellent source for our knowledge of the early Gnostic movements. But of all his works,[2] perhaps none has aroused so much interest as the *Apostolic Tradition.* The original text has been lost, but after a half century of research by various scholars, R. H. Connolly showed in 1916 that it was substantially preserved in a Latin version of what had originally been called an *Egyptian Church Order,* thought to be from the fifth century.[3] Once restored to Hippolytus, the *Apostolic Tradition* becomes a vivid source for our knowledge of liturgical practice in the early third century.

The Apostolic Tradition*

[After a brief prologue, the author treats of the election and consecration of a bishop. He quotes the prayer for the bishop's consecration and immediately follows it with the text of an early liturgy.]

4   And when he has been made bishop, everyone is to give him the kiss of peace, saluting, seeing that he has been made worthy. Let the deacons then bring forward the offering. And he with all the priests shall lay his hand on the offering and say, giving thanks, "The Lord be with you." And the people shall say, "And with your spirit. Lift up your hearts. We have them with the Lord. Let us

[2] See the listing, with bibliography, by J. Quasten, *Patrology* (Westminster, Md.: Newman Press, 1953), II, 165 ff.

[3] For a brief account of the controversy, see Cross, *op. cit.,* pp. 94–96, and 156–58, with the literature there cited. Recently P. Nautin has attempted to deny the authenticity of some of Hippolytus' works, especially the *Refutation of All Heresies,* but the tide of scholarly opinion has not run in his favor.

* For the text, see B. Botte, *Hippolyte de Rome: La Tradition Apostolique* (Sources Chrétiennes 11, [Paris: Editions du Cerf, 1946]).

give thanks to the Lord. It is just and worthy." And then he shall continue as follows.

"We give thanks to you, O God, through your beloved Child Jesus Christ, whom You did send to us in these last days as a savior and redeemer and a messenger of your counsel; who is your inseparable Word, through whom You made everything, and in whom You were well pleased; whom You sent from Heaven into a virgin's womb, and He, conceived within her, was made flesh, and showed himself to be your Son, born of the Holy Spirit and the virgin; who fulfilled your will and prepared for You a holy people, and stretched forth his hands unto suffering, that He might free from suffering all who have believed in You; who, when He was betrayed to his voluntary suffering to abolish death, crush hell, enlighten the just, establish his commandment, and manifest the resurrection, took bread and, giving thanks to You, said: 'Take, eat; this is my body which is broken for you.' Similarly the cup, saying: 'This is my blood which is shed for you. When you do this, make it a memorial of me.'

"Keeping, therefore, this memorial of his death and resurrection, we offer to You the bread and the cup, making thanksgiving to You because You have found us worthy to stand before You and minister as priests to You.

"And we beseech You to send your Holy Spirit upon the offering of your holy Church, grant to all your saints who partake of it to be united with You, that they may be filled with the Holy Spirit for the confirmation of their faith in truth, that we may give You praise and glory, through your beloved Child Jesus Christ, through whom may You have glory and honor with the Holy Spirit in your holy church now and forever. Amen." . . .

[In Sections 20 to 23 the author gives a description of the baptismal ceremony of the early third century, with its accompanying Liturgy. The ritual contains an excellent example of an early Roman Creed; the administration of baptism, by total immersion, is divided into three dippings, spaced between the questions. There seems to be no actual formula, "I baptize you in the name of the Father, etc." After the baptism there follows the rite of confirmation, administered by the bishop. Then at the Mass of the Faithful, which follows, three deacons bring up three chalices with water, honey and milk mixed, and the cup of wine and water.

Only the last is consecrated. After the faithful have partaken of the bread, they drink of the three chalices, concluding with a sip of the consecrated wine.]

20   5. Those who are to be baptized should be instructed to wash and purify themselves on the fifth day of the week. 6. And menstruous women should be kept apart and baptized on another day. 7. Those to be baptized should fast on Friday and Saturday. . . . 9. And they are to pass the entire night watching; the Scriptures are to be read to them and they are to be instructed. . . .

21   1. And at cockcrow they are first to pray over the water; 2. when they approach, the water is to be pure and flowing. 3. And they are to remove their clothes. 4. And the little children are to be baptized first; and if they can make the responses for themselves, they are to do so; if not, their parents or someone else from the family should answer for them. 5. Next they are to baptize the adult men; and lastly the women, who will have untied their hair and removed any gold ornaments. No one is to go down to the water with any foreign object on him. . . .

12. And when he goes down to the water, the one who is baptizing should lay his hand on him, saying: "Do you believe in God the Father almighty?" 13. And the one to be baptized shall say: "I do believe." 14. Let him then immediately baptize, with his hand laid upon his head. 15. And after this he should say: "Do you believe in Jesus Christ, the Son of God, who was born of the Holy Spirit and the Virgin Mary, was crucified in the time of Pontius Pilate, and died, and rose on the third day living from the dead, and ascended into Heaven, and sat at the right hand of the Father, and will come to judge the living and the dead?" 16. And when he says, "I do believe," he is to baptize him a second time.

17. Once again he should say: "Do you believe in the Holy Spirit in the holy Church, and the resurrection of the flesh?" 18. And the one being baptized should say: "I do believe." And so he should baptize him a third time. 19. And, coming up afterwards, he shall be anointed by the priests with the oil of thanksgiving, saying: "I anoint you with holy oil in the name of Jesus Christ. . . ."

[After the new Christians have dressed, the bishop lays his hand on them, anoints them with oil on the forehead, and kisses them. Then the sacred Liturgy begins.]

5. From then on they shall pray together with all the 22 faithful. But before they have gone through all these things they must not pray with the faithful. 6. And after the prayers, they are to give the kiss of peace.

1. And then the offering is immediately to be brought 33 to the bishop by the deacons. And he shall first eucharistize the bread unto the representation of the flesh of Christ, and the cup with a mixture of wine unto the antitype of the blood which was shed for all who believed in Him; 2. and milk and honey mingled together to fulfill the promises made to the forefathers, in which He said, "I will give you a land flowing with milk and honey." This Christ indeed gave in his flesh, with which believers are fed like little children, sweetening the bitterness of the heart by the sweetness of his word; 3. and water, too, as an offering signifying the washing, that the inner man, the spiritual man, may receive as well as the body. 4. And the bishop is to give an explanation of all this to those who receive. 5. And when he breaks the bread to distribute a piece to each one he shall say: "The bread of Heaven, in Christ Jesus." 6. And the one who receives should say, "Amen."

7. Then the priests (and also the deacons, if the former do not suffice) are to hold the cups and stand by in orderly fashion and reverently: first, one with the water, secondly one with the milk, thirdly one with the wine. 8. And those who communicate are to taste of each cup three times, as the one who offers it says: "In God, the almighty Father." And the one receiving shall say: "Amen." 9. "And in the Lord Jesus Christ, and 10., in the Holy Spirit in the holy Church." And he shall say, "Amen." 11. And this is the way it is to be done in each case. . . .

16

CLEMENT OF ALEXANDRIA

The beginnings of the school at Alexandria are shrouded in obscurity.[1] According to tradition, Titus Flavius Clement was born at Athens—the name suggests a family of Roman citizens—and after much traveling he finally settled in Alexandria, to sit at the feet of Pantaenus, whom he called the "Sicilian bee." He remained there about twenty years, being ordained a priest and lecturing to those who attended the Alexandrian Museum for the study of literature, science, and philosophy. Eusebius wrote that he left Alexandria during the persecution of the emperor Septimius Severus about A.D. 202, and, some years later, Alexander, bishop of Jerusalem, mentioned him as the bearer of letters from his prison in Cappadocia. Apart from the fact that he died between 211 and 215 (the dates of two of Alexander's letters that mention Clement), next to nothing is known about his final years. He never returned to Alexandria.

A person of vast erudition, Clement labored to achieve a consistent Christian theology, structured upon rational foundations instead of the attitude fostered by teachers like Tertullian, whose cry was "we must believe because it is absurd" (*credendum quia absurdum*). Hence, although Clement's attack on paganism was sharp and acute, he attempted to support Christian philosophy and belief by borrowing from Stoicism [2] and Platonism. Yet his method was definitely his own, and seems at times to have been a revolt against traditional approaches. Although he believed in the hier-

[1] For a discussion, see E. F. Osborn, *The Philosophy of Clement of Alexandria* (London: Cambridge: University Press, 1957), pp. 3 ff., with the sources cited.

[2] See M. Spanneut, *Le Stoïcisme des Pères de l'Eglise* (Paris: Editions du Seuil, 1957), pp. 166 ff., and *passim*.

archic, sacramental Church, Clement stressed piety of the heart based on a rational approach to faith; and for the initiate, or the "gnostics," as he preferred to call them, he revealed a special doctrine or intuitional knowledge of Christianty. Sincere in his asceticism, he anticipated the austerity of Origen's teaching; loyal to those who bore witness by martyrdom, he remained firm in his insistence on a single repentance after baptism (in the spirit of the *Shepherd* of Hermas). He inveighed against luxury even though he may have had a wealthy audience, and he was one of the few Greek Fathers who extolled the married state, as well as celibacy and virginity.

Some of Clement's works that have been preserved are the *Paedagogus*, dedicated to Christ the Teacher, and the *Protrepticus* or *Exhortation to the Pagans* in honor of the Logos who exhorts or converts souls to himself. The longest is the *Stromateis*, which means "tapestries," or "miscellanies," according to the best explanation.[3] It is unfinished and is a sprawling, massive treatment of philosophy, the Christian "gnostic," conversion and faith, asceticism, marriage, martyrdom, and the folly of paganism. Also left are his wonderful homily on verses 17 to 31 of the tenth chapter of Mark, *Who Is the Rich Man Who Is Saved?*, some excerpts from Gnostic writings entitled *Excerpts from Theodotus* and *Prophetic Selections*, in addition to a number of fragmentary pieces.

From the Paedagogus

Hymn to the Savior*

Rein of indomitable steeds, wing of birds   3.12.101
Secure, fast tiller of ships, O Shepherd

---

[3] For a discussion of the work and its meaning, see C. Mondésert, *Clément d'Alexandrie: Les Stromates: Stromate I* (Sources Chrétiennes 30 Paris: Editions du Cerf, 1951), 6 ff. For the texts I have followed O. Stählin, *Griechische christliche Schriftsteller*, Vols. 12, 15, 17 (Berlin: Akademie-Verlag, 1936, 1939, 1909). For the bibliography, see J. Quasten, *Patrology* (Westminster, Md.: Newman Press, 1953), II, 5 ff.

* Stählin, *op. cit.*, pp. 291–92. This intensely beautiful lyric, from the end of the *Paedagogus*, reflects the fervent acclamations of the early Church. It is loosely constructed, in anapaestic meter; for a bibliography, see J. Quasten, *Initiation aux Pères de l'Eglise* (tr. by J. Laporte, Paris: Newman Press, 1955), I, 180.

Of royal sheep! Wake up your pure children
To praise and hymn you in all holiness
With chaste lips, leader of your offspring, Christ!

King of the blest, all-conquering Word
Of the Father Most High, O Prince of Wisdom
Our support in labor, source of eternal joy!
Jesus, Savior of mankind and Shepherd,
Sower, our rein, tiller, celestial pinion
Of a hallowed flock, Fisher of mortals snatched
From a vicious sea, snaring holy fish
From the enemy wave by the bait of a life most sweet.
Lead the blessed flock of spiritual sheep,
Lead them, O King of these immaculate babes!

Christ's footprints are the path to heaven. Eternal
Word, everlasting Aeon, unending Light,
Spring of pity, accomplisher of valor
Through the sober lives of those who sing to God,
Christ Jesus! heavenly milk—your Wisdom's grace—
From a young bride's sweetest bosom. We tender babes
Drink with innocent lips as it is pressed forth,
Filled with the draught of the Spirit from a mystic
    breast.

Let us all sing together our chaste praise,
Our blameless hymns to Christ the King. Let us sing
Of the mead of his life's teaching. Let us sing
Of the mighty Son. Those born of Christ are a choir
Of peace, a prudent gathering. Let us all
Then sing together of the God of peace.

From the Paedagogus

1.6.41
–43
Stählin
The all-loving, beneficent Father rained down his
Word, and straightway did He become the spiritual
nourishment for the just. Ah, the marvelous mystery!
For one is the Father of all, one the Word of all, and
one is the Holy Spirit, one and the same everywhere.
And one is the virgin mother alone, and she is what I
like to call the Church. And this solitary mother had no
milk, for she alone was not woman, but she was at
once both virgin and mother—loving as a mother,
inviolate as a virgin—and gathering her babes, she
suckles them with her holy milk, that is, with the
Word of babes. . . . "Eat my flesh," He says, "and

drink my blood." Here the Lord offers us his own food, proffering his flesh and shedding his blood. The infants lack nothing that will help them grow. What a paradoxical mystery! We are told to put aside our fleshly corruption, as we would leave aside old food, and assume a new kind of diet, that is, Christ's, to store him up in our hearts as far as we can and to take unto us our Savior, in order that we might discipline the desires of the flesh. . . .

Exhortation to the Pagans*

The Word, therefore, the Christ, is not only the cause 1.7. of our coming into being long ago, seeing that He was in 1–3 God, but also of our well-being. The Word alone is God and man and the cause of all our good; appearing only recently in his own person to mankind, it is from Him we learn how to live correctly on earth and are thus brought to eternal life. For, in the words of the Lord's inspired apostle, the grace of God has appeared for the salvation of all men [Titus 2.11]. . . . Here is the new song, the shining epiphany among us of the Word existing in the beginning and before all. Only recently did our preexisting Savior appear on earth. He who exists in God (for the Word was with God) was made manifest as our teacher; the Word, by whom all things were made, came forth. And He who gave us life in the beginning, forming us as our creator, appeared as our instructor to teach us how to live rightly, in order that as God He might give us life everlasting hereafter.

Tapestries (Stromateis)

Now it is by faith alone that we can attain to the 2.4.14 principle of all the universe. Every science can be –15 taught; and all that is taught comes from prior knowl- Stählin edge. Now the Greeks did not know the cause of the universe, neither Thales, who held water to be the first cause, nor all the other physical philosophers who followed him. . . . Science is a process that advances by demonstration; but faith is a grace which makes us

---

* See the edition of C. Mondésert and A. Plassart, *Clément d'Alexandrie: Le Protreptique* (Sources Chrétiennes 2, Paris: Editions du Cerf, 1949), with an improved Greek text. There is an excellent analysis of the *Exhortation* on pp. 27 ff.

rise from things which are not demonstrable to a Being who is altogether simple, is not material, nor composed of matter, nor subject to matter. . . . Aristotle says that faith is the judgment which follows our knowledge of anything, affirming that this knowledge is true. So it is that faith is superior to knowledge, and is its criterion. . . .

7.10.57   Now faith is, so to speak, the comprehensive knowledge of all that is required. Knowledge is the firm, secure demonstration of all that is assumed by faith; it is built upon the faith by means of the Lord's teaching, thus leading to perfect and infallible certitude. In my view, the first movement towards salvation is that which pagans make by embracing the faith—as I have said earlier. The second movement is that from faith to knowledge, terminating in love, in which the knower and the known become as friends. And the life of such a one anticipates the life of the angels.

Who Is the Rich Man Who Is Saved?

[Clement explained Christ's severe words in verses 10 to 31 of Chapter 10 in Mark by claiming that the wealth He condemned was the abundance of passions—not money itself, but the excessive attachment to money. Rich men, in order to be saved, must learn to spend their money wisely, to give alms to help the poor, and to eradicate their sinful worldly attachments. The text may be an expansion of an actual sermon, for it corresponds with Clement's general doctrine with regard to worldly riches. Clement was at pains to show that wealthy pagans should not turn away from the Church because of the mistaken impression that it was the religion of the poor only. Then, Clement briefly depicted the life of the righteous Christian who obeys all the commandments.]

37   What else is necessary? Contemplate the mysteries of love, and then you will behold the bosom of the Father, whom alone the only-begotten God made manifest. Indeed, the essence of God is love, and it was through love that He became visible to us. Insofar as He is ineffable He is Father, and insofar as He loves us He is Mother. For the Father became a woman by his love; and a proof of this is the One He begot from himself, for the fruit that is born of love is love. This is the reason why the Son himself came to earth, put on humanity,

and willingly suffered the human condition. For, being restrained according to the infirmity of those whom He loved, He desired to measure us according to his own power. And when He was about to be poured out as a libation, and, offering himself up in redemption, He left us a new covenant: "I give you my love." What kind of love is this, and what is its dimension? For each of us He laid down a life that was worth the entire universe. And He demands in return that we lay down our lives for one another. . . .

17

ORIGEN OF ALEXANDRIA

Origen remains one of the most exciting and mysterious of all the theologians who wrote before the Peace of the Church. Born in Egypt, perhaps at Alexandria, about the year 185, he saw his father Leonidas martyred during the emperor Septimius Severus' reign, in the year 202. Eusebius, in his *Ecclesiastical History*,[1] wrote that Origen was appointed the head of the catechetical school at Alexandria by Bishop Demetrius, succeeding Clement of Alexandria, whose pupil he was. His very busy life may be divided into three periods: the "early period," beginning with his appointment at Alexandria (about 203) to the year 215; the "middle period," taking in his travels through Asia and Arabia (in 215) to his ordination, about the year 230; and, finally, his years of "retirement at Caesarea" in Palestine, which began in 231 until his death in 253/54 at Tyre. It was during the early period, according to Eusebius—who is our chief source—that Origen, in an overliteral application of the twelfth verse in Chapter 19 of Matthew, mutilated himself to become a eunuch for the kingdom of heaven. His early days at Alexandria he spent working on the great *Hexapla,* which arranged the Hebrew of the Old Testament and four Greek versions in six parallel columns, using critical and comparative symbols for the different variants. Around the same time he delivered many of his *Homilies* on the Old and New Testament, and the majority of them are now preserved in Latin. His second period was one of great movement. He visited Arabia, saw the mother of the

---

[1] Especially Book VI. For the general bibliography, see J. Quasten, *Patrology* (Westminster, Md.: Newman Press, 1953), II, pp. 37–101; and add the bibliography mentioned by H. Crouzel, *Origène et la Philosophie* (Paris: Aubier, 1962).

emperor Alexander Severus at Antioch, lectured at Caesarea and Jerusalem, and despite the complaints that were voiced at Alexandria at this impressive reception of the Church's great theologian, Origen allowed himself to be ordained a priest in Palestine. This act apparently cost him his Alexandrian post, for in 231 he retired to the school at Caesarea. Origen had completed his *First Principles* at Alexandria during his restless middle period, but the final security of Caesarea proved the setting for the creation of his greatest theological and exegetical works.

In this period, he completed his famous *Commentaries* on the Song of Songs, Matthew, Romans, John, and many other books of the Bible, but unfortunately these are extant only in fragments, fuller portions having been preserved by Rufinus and others in Latin versions. He also wrote his treatise *Against Celsus, On Prayer,* and the *Exhortation to Martyrdom;* of his wide correspondence little has been preserved, but the precious remains include a document called the *Letter to Gregory Thaumaturgus.* For it was in this period, too, that he met and converted Gregory Thaumaturgus, who would become bishop of Neocaesarea in Pontus and thus spread Origen's doctrines throughout Asia Minor. Then, in 254, he was officially called on to settle the doubts of Heraclides and a number of fellow bishops of Arabia. A stenographic report of the resulting debate was found in a papyrus codex near Cairo in 1941.

Origen was supposed to have been captured in the net that the emperor Decius spread throughout Palestine for those who refused to offer sacrifice before the imperial overseers. Eusebius described Origen's sufferings (*Eccl. Hist.* 6.39.2):

> Imprisonment and the rack, punishment inflicted on his body and during the time he lay chained in the darkness of his prison dungeon. After his feet had been stretched four spaces by the torture of the rack, he courageously endured threats of fire or anything else inflicted by our enemies.

About sixty-five years old at the time, the great Origen (or Adamantius, "the man of steel"—as Eusebius says he was called) never recovered from these indignities and died shortly afterwards at Tyre, around 253/54. His energy, vigor, and sheer courage have served as an example to Christians ever since.

When it comes to determining the nature of his achievement and the method to be used in evaluating his work, a theologian of Origen's stature necessarily provokes controversy.[2] Admittedly, the vast bulk of his works have been lost, many important treatises survive only in questionable Latin versions, and what remains is often difficult to interpret. Nevertheless, it is justly doubtful whether even Origen's preserved thought can ever be reduced to anything approaching a system.[3] The vastness of his achievement, his pioneering on many theological fronts at the same time, his absorption of many contemporary philosophical ideas, and his energetic imagination, all make it impossible today to organize his work into a consistent whole. Indeed, in our limited available space, only tiny, though typical, selections from his vast productivity can be offered. Whatever may be said of his debt to Platonic or even Gnostic thought, Origen was the first Greek theologian to produce any sort of clarity in the terminology of Trinitarian and Christological doctrine, and it was his contribution (despite his tendency to Subordinationism) that laid the foundation for the speculations of Athanasius and the Cappadocians in the fourth century.[4] He taught that the Logos issues from the Father (comparing their relationship to the one between man's will and intelligence), and that it is the Father's image from all eternity and shares in the same substance as the Father (*homoousios* —the precise term that the Council of Nicaea would adopt). Speaking of Christ, he was the first to use the expression God-Man, and showed that by an inseparable union the nature of the Logos and the human nature had been, through the divine economy, united into one being; thus the human nature of Christ could be given the predicates of divine dignity.

The purpose of the Incarnation, Origen wrote, was the union of all men with the Logos. This union would be definitive in Heaven, but could be glimpsed in this life through mystical experience, especially by the exercise of the spiritual senses. The ultimate reconciliation of all mankind with God—even those in hell, Origen believed, would finally be restored to Heaven—was achieved by the God-Man's life and death. "Christ was the great high priest," he wrote in his *Commentary on John* (1.40), "offering himself up as a sacrifice." This was a vicarious penalty imposed on Jesus,

---

[2] See my article, "The Recent Revival of Origen Studies," *Theological Studies* 24 (1963), 250–63, with the sources there cited.

[3] See especially the discussion of Crouzel, *op. cit.*, pp. 209 ff.

[4] See H. A. Wolfson, *The Philosophy of the Church Fathers* (Cambridge, Mass.: Harvard Univ. Press, 1956), I, 317–32.

in the spirit of the Servant Song of the prophet Isaiah (Ch. 53). His death was "voluntarily undertaken for the good of all" (*Against Celsus* 1.31); sinless himself, He reconciled us to God by the sacrifice of his blood (*Commentary on Romans* 4.8). Thus the altars of the Church are now consecrated with the precious blood of Christ; and Christ's propitiation is set forth in the mysteries of the memorial service, which give us the bread that comes down from Heaven (cf. *Homilies on Leviticus* 13.3).

Origen also conceived of Christ's death as a ransom paid to the Evil One, who had power over us until the ransom was given on our behalf. It was to be one life for many; and the ransom was paid, even though Jesus, by his rising from the dead, cheated the Devil, for "those who are with Jesus cannot be grasped by Death" (*Commentary on Matthew* 16.8). Indeed, Jesus' death was a kind of cosmic oblation, by which He reconciled all things, on earth as well as in Heaven, as He offered up his body in a spiritual sacrifice (*Homilies on Leviticus* 1.3).

But why did man have to be redeemed? Origen's general theory is that God's providence allows man's free acts of virtue to gain in glory because of the possibility of evil; in the end, good will emerge from evil and God's glory will prevail, even to the extent of destroying Satan's will to evil. But Origen's doctrine of the original Fall is unclear—and again we are somewhat at a loss, not having his original words, in many cases.[5] At times he detailed a preexistent state from which the human soul "fell" and was punished by being assigned to a body while at other times he referred to the sin of the first pair, Adam and Eve, whose guilt perdures mysteriously in their descendants, partly because of the inheritance of a defiled human nature, propagated by sexual intercourse, and partly because all men tend to imitate the sins of their parents. In any case, Origen clearly felt that the Church's baptism was needed to wash away the inherited

---

[5] Much of our text of Origen is extant only in a Latin version, and scholars naturally object to placing great weight upon any doctrine that we know only through such a version. The energetic Rufinus of Aquileia, who settled as a monk in Jerusalem about the year 378, made many translations of Origen's works (which he admitted he modified where he suspected heresy); he did the work *First Principles* and many homilies. Other versions of Origen were done by St. Jerome and also by an anonymous translator, and these are closer to the Greek. The point is a critical one, but where we have so little of the original, we can hardly neglect any versions in a study of our author. However, they must be used with caution, especially where the doctrine they expound seriously contradicts what is known from the Greek remains.

stain, even in the case of little children (*Homilies on Leviticus* 8.3; *Commentary on Romans* 5.9).

Origen not only made contributions in every area of theology, but also was influential in promoting the ideal of asceticism. An austere ascetic himself, with the habits of a hermit (if Eusebius and Gregory Thaumaturgus are to be believed), he viewed the life of personal self-sacrifice as, and elevated it to, a preparation for mystical vision and union with the Logos. The mystical kiss not only unites the Christian to Jesus but allows him to "see what is hidden, solve difficulties and understand the complex, explain riddles and parables, and the words of the philosophers along the right path" (*Commentary On the Song of Songs* 1). The Christian mystic who has knowledge of the Church's mysteries is then the perfect Christian (that is, short of martyrdom, which is the highest state), he it is who attains the "perfect likeness" to God, complementing the image which Adam received at creation.

In addition to his own textual work on the Scriptures, Origen evolved from the techniques of Philo and the Alexandrian grammarians the method of allegorical exegesis. He distinguished between the historical (or literal) meaning and the spiritual, which may be mystical or moral. To convey the spiritual meaning, and derive his various doctrines from a sometimes bare and unpromising text, he used every possible sort of metonymy, punning, and numerological device. Even so, his excesses can also be instructive.

Finally, Origen's eschatological doctrine, controverted though it was, had a lasting effect on the teachings of the early Fathers who came after him. It envisions that just as all men's souls came from Heaven (if the interpretation is correct) and were placed in bodies, so that their virtue might be tried and tested for God's glory, so all souls, both good and evil, will be restored in the end to the Father. Those who have sinned on earth will suffer purifying fire; but after a determined time, all will be restored, men will receive spiritual (apparently spherical) bodies, and God will be all in all. Indeed, Origen taught that at the end of the present world dispensation, there will be many others to take its place and renew the cycle of destruction and restoration (*First Principles* 3.5.3).

Although Origen was the first mystical theologian of the Church, as well as the first Christian philosopher, to assimilate and transcend the limited categories of Neoplatonism, and his vision of the Church had a profound influence upon the Cappadocian Fathers in the East and Augustine and his successors in the West, his theology was still in the throes of painful evolution. During this necessary process, the Church was emerging from the dark womb of the pre-Nicene period into the brilliant confidence of the fourth and fifth centuries.

First Principles*

[On Man's Free Will]

Let us inquire into the saying, "So it depends not upon 3.1. man's will or exertion, but upon God's mercy" [Rom. 18 9.16]. Our opponents may say: "In that case, our sal--19 vation is not at all our doing; it is either a question of the way we are made, and for this the Creator is responsible, or else it comes from the will of Him who shows mercy as He pleases. . . . We do not attain to perfection by doing nothing, and yet it is not achieved solely by our own activity: God plays the greater role in our attaining it . . . When a voyage is successful, only a small part is played by the skill of the pilot in comparison with the importance of the wind, the weather, the visible stars, for the safety of the travelers. Pilots as a rule do not dare to claim the credit for steering the ship safely by their intelligence; rather they attribute it all to God. It is not as though they had done nothing. But the divine providence was of infinitely more importance than their skill. So it is with our salvation . . ." Now we derive our existence as living animals and our rational existence from God—and hence our general power of motion and our general faculty of willing. Now even though we have the power of motion as animals from God, that is, of moving our hands or our feet, it would not be correct to say that any specific movement, such as striking a blow, destroying, robbing, is derived from Him. Though the generic faculty of motion comes from Him, it is we who use it for good or bad purposes. So, too, our faculty of willing and action comes from God, but it is we who use it for good or bad ends.

* For the text of these selections from Origen, see P. Koetschau, W. Preuschen, E. Klostermann, W. A. Baehrens, in the *Griechische christliche Schriftsteller* (Leipzig: Akademie-Verlag, 1899 ff.), unless otherwise stated. The first selection follows P. Koetschau (ed.), *op. cit.* (1913), p. 230.

On Prayer[*]

[Man's Will and God's Foreknowledge]

6.2   It is impossible to persuade a man that in human actions his will is not free. Does anyone believe that we cannot understand anything? Does anyone live on the presumption that we must have doubts about everything? Do we not punish a servant we catch doing something wrong? Do we not scold a child who does not properly respect its parents? And if a woman commits adultery, do we not blame and condemn her for committing a disgraceful act? No matter how numerous the opposite arguments may be, we are forced and compelled by truth itself to perform actions, and to express praise and blame: for we are convinced that our wills are free, and hence subject to praise or blame. . . .

6.3   God necessarily knew what our free choice would be like before it existed, together with all the other creatures that were to be from the creation and foundation of the world. In all the things that God has foreordained in accordance with his foreknowledge of our free actions, He arranged all in accord with each of our free choices, both that which was to be the result of his providence and that which was to take place in the natural order of things. At the same time, God's foreknowledge is not the cause of everything that will be, and indeed not of the results of our free actions following our own impulses. Even if God did not know what would happen, we would still be able to choose one thing or another; but because He does have foreknowledge, the free actions of every man are harmonious with the structure of the whole, and this is necessary for the existence of the world.

6.4   And so God knows and foresees the free will of every human being, and thus He can provide by his providence what is fitting, according to each one's merits. . . . And so He acts somewhat as follows, saying: I shall listen to this man's prayer, praying as he does with understanding, because of the prayer he will say; but I will not listen to the other, because he does not deserve to be heard, or

* P. Koetschau, *op. cit.* (1899), p. 312.

because he is praying for things that would not be good for him or right for Me to give. . . .

*Against Celsus**

[The Power of Christian Virtue]

Even men who are esteemed for naught because of their simplicity, men who are called slaves and fools, once they have embraced the doctrine of Jesus and put their trust in God, abstain from obscenity, impurity, and every kind of sexual abuse, and begin to lead the lives of perfect priests, many of them not only abstaining from intercourse but continuing to live in absolute purity. . . . For among the Christians you can see men who do not need hemlock [6] to serve God chastely, for the Logos is their hemlock, so that they may serve the Lord by their devotion, driving out every evil desire from their mind. Other alleged divinities have their virgins, rather small in number, some protected by men and others not (it is not my intention to discuss this here), and they apparently continue in purity out of respect for the god. But among the Christians they do not practice perfect chastity for the sake of human honor or silver or financial reward or even for glory. And as they saw fit to acknowledge God, God cherishes them in their upright mind and their performance of what is fitting, filled with all justice and goodness.

---

* Koetschau, *op. cit.* (1899), p. 199.

[6] The ancients believed that hemlock juice applied externally could calm sexual passion. See Dioscorides, *The Greek Herbal* (ed. by R. T. Gunther, New York: Hafner Publishing Company, 1959), IV.79, pp. 477–78. Others attributed the same effect to a brew made of the fruit of the agnus castus bush or chaste tree: see *ibid.*, I.135, pp. 73–74, and my version of *St. Methodius: The Symposium. A Treatise on Chastity* (New York: Newman Press, 1958), pp. 186–87, with the sources cited.

*Homilies on Leviticus**

[The Allegorical Interpretation of Scripture]

5   Now the Scriptures themselves consist, as it were, of a
visible body, a soul that we can perceive and comprehend, and a spirit formed according to the patterns and
shadow of heavenly things. Come, then, and let us in-
voke the One who made the Scriptures' body, soul, and
spirit: the body was for our forefathers, the soul was for
ourselves, and the spirit for those who will inherit everlasting life in the ages to come and the truth of the
Law. And so, let us search out not the letter, but rather
the soul of the text in the present case; then, if we are
able, we shall ascend even to the spirit in the account of
the sacrificial offerings of which we have just read.

First Principles †

4.   Now what intelligent person would believe that the
16 first, second, and third day took place without a sun,
moon, or stars—indeed, the first day, as it were, without
even a heaven? Who could be so childish as to think that
God was like a human gardener and planted a paradise
in Eden facing the east, and in it made a real visible tree,
so that one could acquire life by eating its fruit with real
teeth, or, again, could participate in good and evil by
eating what he took from the other tree?

And if the text says that God walked in the garden in
the evening, or Adam hid himself under the tree, I cannot think that anyone would dispute that these things
are said in a figurative sense, in an effort to reveal certain mysteries by means of an apparent historical tale
and not by something that actually took place. . . .

What need have we of further examples, when all who
are not completely unintelligent can bring forward innumerable instances of things which were written down
as though they happened, but did not take place in the
literal meaning of the term? Even the Gospels are full of

* W. A. Baehrens (ed.), *op. cit.*, 1920, VI, p. 334.
† Koetschau, *op. cit.* (1913), p. 323.

things of the same sort, as for example when the Devil took Jesus up into a high mountain, from there to show Him the kingdoms of the whole world and their glory. Now, who of all those who are not careless readers of these words would not condemn anyone who thought that the real bodily eye (which would require a height from which to be able to glimpse all that lay far below) could see the kingdoms of the Persians, the Scythians, the Indians, and the Parthians, and the glory all their rulers were given by men? An observant reader is able to detect innumerable cases like these, where things that literally took place are interwoven with accounts of others that did not actually happen.

Homilies on Numbers*

[Origen on the Atonement]

At the feast of Passover it is a lamb that purifies the 24 people, while at other feasts it is a bullock, at others a .1 goat, a ram, a nanny goat, or a heifer—such as you have learned in our reading today. The lamb, then, is one of the animals used to purify the people. And we know that this lamb is our Lord and Savior himself. This is what John, the greatest of the prophets, understood and expressed when he said, "Behold the lamb of God, behold him who takes away the sin of the world." Now if the lamb that has been offered for the purification of the people represents the person of our Lord and Savior, it would seem that the other animals appointed to the same sort of purifications should also refer to persons who, through the merits of Christ's blood, contribute in a certain way to the purification of the human race. Our Lord and Savior, led like a lamb to the slaughter and offered as a sacrifice on the altar, has obtained the remission of sins for the entire world; so also the blood of the other holy men and saints that has been shed. . . . If the Lord Jesus Christ is himself called a lamb,

* The text is preserved in Rufinus' bowdlerized Latin version, edited by W. A. Baehrens, *op. cit.*, Vol. 30 (1921). See the excellent French translation, introduction, and commentary by André Méhat, *Origène: Homélies sur les Nombres* (Sources Chrétiennes 29, Paris: Editions du Cerf, 1951), with the bibliography.

it is not because his appearance has been changed, that He has been transformed into a lamb; it is because He has willed in his goodness to reconcile the human race with God, and play the role of a lamb with respect to men, a spotless and innocent victim, through whom we believe God's wrath against men has been appeased. . . .

For so long as there are sins, we must find the victims to expiate them. Let us suppose that there had been no sin. If no sins were committed, then it would not have been necessary for the Son of God to become a lamb, and He would not have had to become man and be sacrificed. He would have remained what He was in the beginning, the Word of God. But sin entered into the world; the consequences of sin demanded an expiation, and expiation can only take place through a victim. Hence a victim had to be provided for sin. And seeing that there were different kinds of sin, sacrifices of different kinds of animals were commanded, corresponding to the various types of sin. . . .

Commentaries on the Song of Songs*

[The Love of the Mystic for Jesus]

1.2
-3   There is indeed a spiritual sort of embrace, and I pray that within me the embrace of the Spouse might more tightly hold the beloved, that I also might say the words that are written in this book: His left hand is under my head and his right hand will embrace me [Cant. 2.6].

And so, May he kiss me with the kisses of his mouth [Cant. 1.1]. . . . The beloved then perceives the Spouse: he comes dripping with perfumes; and, indeed, he could not come otherwise to his beloved, nor could the Father destine his Son in any other way for the marriage feast. He anointed Him with various perfumes and made Him the Christ. He comes breathing different perfumes and hears the words: For your breasts are better than wine [Cant. 1.1]. Very fittingly does

---

* The text, which is St. Jerome's version of Origen's Greek, has been edited by W. A. Baehrens, op. cit., Vol. 33 (1925); and see the edition of O. Rousseau (Sources Chrétiennes 37, Paris: Editions du Cerf, 1953).

the sacred word call the same thing by different names according to the context. . . .

Be in contact, as the bride was, with the feelings of the Spouse and you will know that such thoughts give a sense of joy and inebriation. Just as the chalice of the Lord with inebriates is exceeding good, so too the breasts of the Spouse are better than wine. . . . And if the Spouse deigns to approach my soul as his beloved, how beautiful should it be in order to attract Him to itself from heaven, to make Him come down to earth and visit his beloved? With what loveliness should it be adorned, with what love should it burn, that He might say to it the things He said to his perfect spouse, referring to her neck, her eyes, her cheeks, her hands, her belly, her shoulders, her feet? And in this connection, we shall discuss, if the Lord allows us, how it is that the different parts of the beloved are mentioned with a different praise for each. Then, after our explanation, we shall see how the same can be applied to our own soul.

Origen's Discussion with Heraclides and His Fellow Bishops on the Father, the Son, and the Soul*

The bishops in session raised the problem of the orthodoxy of bishop Heraclides, with the intention that he should make his profession of faith in their presence. After each one had expressed his views and asked some questions, bishop Heraclides spoke.

"I too believe what the Scriptures say, that In the beginning was the Word and the Word was with God and the Word was God. He was in the beginning with God.

* The first edition of the Dialogue was published by Jean Scherer, *Entretien d'Origène avec Héraclide et les Evêques ses Collègues sur le Père, le Fils, et l'Ame* (Cairo: l'Institut Français D'Archéologie Orientale, 1949), and republished with introduction and commentary in Sources Chrétiennes 67 (Paris: Editions du Cerf, 1960). Scherer places the discussion somewhere in Arabia about A.D. 244/49, probably in the church of bishop Heraclides, with the attendance of bishops Demetrius and Philip; Maximus and Dionysius may also be bishops as well. Our papyrus, now in the Cairo Egyptian Museum, was transcribed in the late sixth century; only the concluding section of Origen's great discussion is preserved. See the remarks of Scherer in 47 ff. of Sources Chrétiennes 67.

All things were made by Him, and without Him was made nothing [John 1.1–3]. You see, then, we agree in the same faith, and, further, believe that Christ was made man, was born, and that He ascended into Heaven in the flesh with which He rose from the dead, and that He sits at the right hand of the Father, from which He will come to judge the living and the dead, since He is at once God and man."

Origen said, "Now that the discussion is opened and we may speak on topics connected with the debate, this is what I have to say. The entire Church is our audience here. Different communities must not have differences in faith, for you cannot be a lying Church.

"My question is, Father Heraclides, do you agree that God is the all-powerful, unbegotten, supreme, who has made all things?"

"I agree," said Heraclides, "for this also has been my belief."

"Is it true," said Origen, "that Christ Jesus, being in the form of God, being distinct from God in the form in which He existed, was God before He became incarnate?"

"Yes," said Heraclides, "He was God before that."

Origen said, "He was God before He became man?" Heraclides said, "Yes."

Origen said, "And was He not distinct from that God in whose form He existed?"

"It is clear," said Heraclides, "that He was distinct from the other, and distinct from the Creator in whose form He existed."

Origen said, "Is it not true that the only begotten Son of God was God, the firstborn of every creature, and that we have no difficulty in asserting that there are, in one sense, two Gods, and, in another sense, only one?"

Heraclides said, "What you say is correct. And we declare that God is the almighty, without beginning and without end, who contains the universe and is contained by nothing, and that his Word is the Son of the living God, God and Man, by whom all things were made, man according to the spirit, and man insofar as He was born of Mary."

"I don't think you have answered my question," said Origen. "I may not have followed you. Speak clearly then: is the Father God?"

"Of course," said Heraclides.

Origen said, "Is the Son distinct from the Father?"

"Of course," said Heraclides; "how could he be the Son if He were also the Father?"

"Though distinct from the Father," said Origen, "is the Son also God?"

"Yes, He is also God," said Heraclides.

"And the two Gods," said Origen, "are one?"

"Yes," said Heraclides.

"Do we believe in two Gods?" said Origen.

"Yes," said Heraclides. "There is but one Power."

Said Origen, "Our brothers are amazed at the fact that there are two Gods, and hence we must treat the subject carefully, showing in what respect there are two and in what respect the two are but one God. . . ."

[Origen then enlarged upon the ways by which two things can be designated one: Adam and Eve were one, the just man and Christ are united in one spirit, but only Christ is simply called God. "I and the Father are one." This is the way we should speak, especially in our prayers to God.]

"Our oblation is always made to almighty God through Jesus Christ insofar as he communicates with the Father because of his divinity; hence the oblation is not made twice, but to God through God. . . ."

[Origen then went into the problem of Christ's death and resurrection, which was proof that He had a real body, showing that all those who believe will also rise. For bishop Maximus Origen explained that Christ had a truly human soul as well as a body; yet, admitting that he himself was not completely clear on what took place, Origen suggested that at Christ's death his *pneuma* was committed to the Father and remained with Him; the soul or *psychê* parted from the dead body and descended into Hades; and only the *psychê* was reunited with the body at the resurrection, the *pneuma* remaining with the Father. Origen then spoke of the importance of moral behavior in addition to orthodoxy of faith.]

"And so we have examined all the problems that have been troubling us. But we should realize that we will be judged at the divine tribunal not only on our faith but also on our lives, just as we shall not be examined on our lives alone apart from our belief. If both of these are as they should be, we shall be justified; if they are not, this will be the reason why we shall be punished for both.

But there are also some men who will be punished for deficiency not in both but in one alone. . . ."

[Origen enumerated the various sins that St. Paul counted among those that bring destruction, putting vices like drunkenness and calumny alongside more serious crimes such as pederasty, adultery, and fornication. Suddenly Origen dropped this subject and proceeded to a more general discussion.]

"If there is still anything left to discuss on the rule of faith, please make mention of it; we shall make further comments on the Scriptures."

Dionysius said, "Is the soul blood?"

Origen said, "I have heard (and I speak from knowledge) that some here, in this area, believe that the soul, after leaving this life, is deprived of all experience and remains in the grave with the body. I recall having been carried away with some violence against the other Heraclides and Celer, his predecessor; and I was so excited that I wanted to throw over the discussion and walk out. Nonetheless, for the sake of respect and also for the discussion, he summoned me back again; and I consented to the discussion. . . . Very logically does our beloved Dionysius put this question. I shall first cite all the passages which cause difficulty (without omitting any), and, God willing, I shall answer each of them according to your request. . . ."

[Origen replied that this problem of the soul as blood is part of a much larger problem, the relationship between the interior and the exterior man, and man as the image and likeness of the Creator; it follows that man's being is somehow "immaterial, superior to any material substance." But Origen was inspired by this discussion to make a general statement about his own difficulties in teaching and his own attitude towards the truth; this is perhaps the most valuable section of the entire dialogue.]

"These questions are rather subtle, and they require an audience of delicate perception. Hence I beg my listeners take care lest they cause me to be charged with casting holy things to the dogs or to malicious souls. For the currish barkers and those given to fornication and calumny do nothing but howl like dogs, and I must not throw holy things to such a crew. . . . Hence I beg you: you must change, you must be willing to learn that the power of transformation is in your hands, to put off the form of the pig, with impure soul, the form of the dog, as a person who howls and barks with abusive speech. One can even change from the shape of a serpent. . . .

"Now, then, since we have to speak about man and especially about the human soul in our inquiry whether it is blood, this brings us to the subject of the two men—and this is a subject of mystery. Hence I beg you not to have me charged with casting pearls before swine or holy things to the dogs, or things divine to serpents, or of giving the serpent a share in the tree of life. If you would not incur this charge, then transform yourselves: put off malice, strife, anger, quarrels, wrath, grief, and double-mindedness, that there may be no divisions among you, but be perfectly united together in the same mind and belief.

"It is torture for me to speak, and torture for me not to speak. But I shall speak for the sake of those who are worthy, lest I be blamed for depriving those of the Word who are able to listen. But I hesitate to speak because of those who are not worthy, as I said before, since I am afraid to throw sacred things to the dogs and cast pearls before swine. To Jesus alone belonged the knowledge, the ability to distinguish among his listeners those who were from within and those who were from without, so that He could speak to those from without in parables and explain the parables to those who had entered into his dwelling. Being outside and entering into the house has a mystical meaning. It is the true disciple of Jesus who enters into his house, and he enters in by thinking according to the Church and living with the Church. Inside and outside have a spiritual dimension. . . ."

[Thus, Origen explained that in all of us there is an exterior and interior man. Man was made in the image of God, hence immaterial and spiritual. In the soul, then, dwells that which is in accordance with the image; and so, if the soul were not freed from the body after death, if it did not go to paradise and the bosom of Abraham, Paul would have been wrong when he taught that after death the soul goes to be with Christ.]

"And so I am ready to die for the truth; therefore, in the face of what is called death, I despise it; therefore, bring on the beasts, the cross, the fire, the torture. For I know that, no sooner dead, then I shall depart from my body and take my rest with Christ. For this let us fight, for this let us struggle. Let us lament that we are in the body, convinced that in the grave we shall not be merely confined to our bodies, again, but we shall be released and shall exchange our body for a more spiritual one. How then shall we lament, in the body as we are, since we are going to be dissolved and be with Christ?"

Bishop Philip had just come in, and another bishop named Demetrius said, "Our brother Origen has been teaching that the soul is immortal."

Origen said, "What Father Demetrius has said involves us in another problem. He has quoted me as saying that the soul is immortal. To this I shall reply that the soul is both mortal and immortal. . . ."

[Origen distinguished three kinds of death: physical death, which the soul cannot suffer; dying to sin, which the vigilant soul should suffer; and, finally, death by serious sin, and this the soul can and should avoid. He then concluded with a fervent exhortation to the audience.]

"But if the soul is confirmed in blessedness so that death can never touch her, possessing eternal life, she is no longer mortal, but becomes immortal even under this aspect of the Word. How then can the Apostle say, speaking of God, 'who alone possess immortality' [I Tim. 6.16]? Investigating, I find that Christ Jesus died for all except God. And thus you understand that God alone possesses immortality.

"Let us then grasp eternal life and grasp it with all our force. God does not give it, He offers it to us. Behold I have set life before you. It is in our power to stretch forth our hand by good acts, grab hold of life and place it within the soul. Christ is this life, as He has said: I am the life. This is the life that is now present to the just in shadow, but then it will be face to face. . . . If this shadow of life brings us so many good things such as Moses had when he lived as a prophet; as Isaiah had when he saw the Lord of hosts seated high upon a throne and lifted up; as Jeremiah had when he heard the words: Before I formed you in the womb I knew you, and before you were born I consecrated you [Jer. 1.5]; as Ezekiel had when he saw the Cherubim, when he saw the wheels, those ineffable mysteries—how then shall our life be when we shall live no longer in the shadow of life but in its reality? For now our life is hidden with Christ, but when Christ our Life shall be made manifest, then shall we be manifested with Him in glory.

"This is the life we should hasten toward, weeping and mourning that we are in this tabernacle, that we inhabit the body. The more we inhabit the body the more we live apart from the Lord. It should be our desire to live apart from the body and dwell with the Lord, in order that, living with Him, we may be united with the God of all creation and that we may see his only begotten Son, finding complete beatitude and salvation in Christ Jesus, to whom be glory and power forever. Amen."

18

METHODIUS OF OLYMPUS

Methodius of Olympus is one of the obscurest figures of the pre-Constantinian Church. If St. Jerome was right, he composed a treatise against the Neoplatonic philosopher Porphyry, the disciple of Plotinus—which would place him at about A.D. 270—and if the tradition about his martyrdom is also correct, his death occurred some time before the peace of the Church. Despite the evidence of Eusebius in his *Ecclesiastical History* (6.13), Jerome's *On Famous Men,* and the attribution of the manuscripts, we are not certain that Methodius was a bishop or even a cleric. It is, however, clear from his work that he was an itinerant teacher, who worked in the famous centers of Lycia—Olympus and Patara —and in Termessus (not far from Gulluk in modern Turkey), that he was associated with a community of consecrated women (to whom the *Symposium* is dedicated), and, though deeply imbued with the writings of Plato, waged constant war upon the teachings of Origen and the Neoplatonists in his native Asia Minor.[1]

The Symposium or *A Treatise on Chastity,* which seems to come from about the year 290, is the only work of Methodius that is extant fully in the Greek. Of his other works we have merely Greek fragments or partial versions from Old Church Slavonic; they are *On the Freedom of the Will, Aglaophon* or *On the Resurrection of the Body,* and minor works such as *On Jewish Food, On Creatures, On the Leech.* In the treatise *On the Freedom of the Will* Methodius proposed the voluntarist theory of perfection; by Adam's sin man lost the perfect freedom of the will by which he was an image of

---

[1] For bibliography see H. Musurillo and V.-H. Debidour, *Méthode d'Olympe: Le Banquet* (Sources Chrétiennes 95, Paris: Editions du Cerf, 1963).

God, and hence the entire purpose of the Christian life is ultimately to restore man's control over his passions, and especially the capacity to be chaste. The same theme appears in the *Symposium*. In the treatise *On the Resurrection*, Methodius (calling himself Eubulius) attacked the Origenist interpretation of Adam's Fall and the resurrection of the body.

The *Symposium* contains Methodius' doctrines on the Church, the Incarnation, the Atonement, and the Last Things. It was composed in imitation of Plato's *Symposium*, except that instead of the Greek philosophers and intellectuals, there are ten consecrated maidens of Lycia who dine at the home of Aretê, who represents the Church; the Scriptures and the teaching of Mother Church replace the intricate arguments of Plato; and the Platonic love or *Eros* is supplanted by the mystical attraction to Jesus, the Arch-virgin and Bridegroom, and the heavenly meadows watered by supernatural streams. Employing a series of vivid, poetic images, Methodius exposed his doctrine of God's plan for the universe. Adam fell because of Satan's jealousy (men were created to fill the depleted ranks of the angels), and his Fall caused the loss of the complete control over his lower drives or passions. Hence, the entire story of the history of mankind has been one of God's attempt to raise man and restore to him His divine image, whereas, at the same time, Satan has striven to acquire more and more dominion. But just as Adam came from the womb of the virgin earth, so too Christ is God mingled with flesh in the womb of a virgin. By means of the Incarnation, God's Son—the first of archangels, the first of the Aeons, as Methodius calls Him—restored grace to the fallen flesh of men, because Christ was "fired" in the same mold from which Adam came. Christ's final act was the "sleep in the ecstasy of his Passion," during which He procreated through the virgin Mother Church all those who would be baptized in his blood. The Church's teaching and nourishment enable the faithful to imitate Jesus and to help restore the image of God, which was effaced by Adam. By adhesion to the teachings of the Church and the practice of virtue (especially chastity), men and women prepare for the final coming of Jesus, when, after the six days of the world's history, He will come to dwell with his faithful for a thousand years before beginning the eternal banquet of Heaven. Towards the end of the *Symposium*, one of the virgins, Thecla, leads a spiritual marriage hymn, to which the young girls accompany the Church, clad in bridal gown, to the marriage chamber of Heaven on the last day. The wicked are condemned to fire and torment, but on this point Methodius did not elaborate.

There have been many misapprehensions about Methodius' teaching, mostly resulting from the fact that the text of the *Symposium* comes from a tradition that has apparently been contaminated. On the one hand, the later Arians advanced their own text—which is something the patriarch Photius knew—and, on the other, a militant orthodox group apparently issued an edition (from which ours descends) with more precise qualifications on the nature of the Logos or the Son of God. Hence, the extant text has contradictions. It speaks of Christ as an Aeon and an archangel, but then it also describes him as being generated by the Father before time began, that is, being God equally with the Father. In my own view, Methodius, though far from being a semi-Arian, was a sub-ordinationist (much as Justin, Tatian, Origen, and others were), and the more precise texts are orthodox interpolations from the fourth century.

"Thecla's Hymn" from the Symposium *

Refrain: Chastely I live for You,
             And with lighted lamp in hand,
             My Spouse, I go forth to meet you.

1 From Heaven has come the sound of a voice, dear girls,
   That wakens the dead and bids us go and meet
   The Bridegroom in the east with speed, all dressed
   In white with lamps alight—awake before
   The King comes in within our gates!

                    (Refrain)

2 I have fled from mortal wealth that brings but wealth
   Of sorrow; I have fled from love and from the joys
   Of this life. I want You to shelter me
   In your life-giving arms and then forever
   Gaze on your matchless beauty, Blessed One.

                    (Refrain)

3 For You, my liege, I rejected mortal marriage,

---

* The text is from H. Musurillo (ed.), *Symposium*, Discourse 11, Sec. 284 ff. (Paris: Editions du Cerf, 1963), 311–32, with some parts omitted.

A household rich in gold; to You I've come
In spotless dress, that I may enter in
Your blessed bridal chamber, Lord, with You.

(Refrain)

I have escaped the Dragon's countless snares   4
Set to bewitch me, O my Blessed One.
Awaiting here your coming from above,
I have fought with fire and flame and ravenous beasts.

(Refrain)

In love with your grace, O Word, I forgot   5
My native city; I think not of the dances
Of my friends, the pride of mother and family.
You, O Christ, are all these things to me!

(Refrain)

Hail, O Christ, provider of life, Light   6
That knows no setting, receive my cry. The choir
Of virgins calls upon You, the perfect flower—
Love, Joy, Prudence, Wisdom, Word!

(Refrain)

O Queen, adorned in beauty, receive us too   7
Within your bridal bower, doors open wide.
Ah, bride of virginal body, glorious in triumph,
Breathing loveliness! At Jesus' side we stand
In gowns like yours, singing in unison,
O youthful maiden, of your blessed marriage.

(Refrain)

Outside the chamber doors girls are sobbing   8
Bitterly, and pitiful are their cries.
Their lamps have all gone out; they have come too late
To see the bridal chamber of happiness.

(Refrain)

These unhappy girls have turned aside   9
From virtue's ways: they forgot to take more oil
For life's contingencies. And so they sob
In spirit as they carry lightless lamps.

(Refrain)

10 Full bowls of nectar stand hard by. Come, drink!
   Virgins, it is a heavenly draught which He,
   The Groom, has set before just those of us
   Worthy to be invited to the wedding.

(Refrain)

[In stanzas 11–17, Methodius, following the Eastern
tradition, sang of Abel, the patriarch Joseph, Jephte, Judith,
Susanna, and John the Baptist, regarding them as forerunners
of the Christian model of self-sacrifice and chastity. The Old
Testament stories are utilized for instruction, in the manner
of the later poets Ephraem and Romanos.]

18 Even the virgin who bore You, Grace all pure,
   Carried You without stain within her womb,
   Still virginal, and yet was thought to have betrayed
   Her bed. Yet she, with child, sang (Blessed One):

(Refrain)

19 All the angels have been gathered here by You
   Their ruler, Blessed One, in haste to see
   Your wedding day. They have come with precious gifts
   For You, O Word, and clothed in shining robes.

(Refrain)

20 Stainless maid, God's blessed bride, we come,
   Your bridesmaids, to sing your praises: Church
   Of snow-white body, dark-tressed, chaste, all lovely!

(Refrain)

21 Disease is fled, with all its tearful pain,
   And all corruptibility. Now death
   Is captive, all weakness crushed, heart-melting grief
   Is past; God's lamp sheds joy on men once more.

(Refrain)

22 Heaven is no longer empty; once again

By God's renewed decree, he has returned
Who once was exiled by the Serpent's wiles.
Now he is blessed, immortal, free from fear.

(Refrain)

Singing a new refrain, our virgin choir   23
Escorts you, Queen, to Heaven, bathed in light.
And, garlanded with whitest lily cups,
We carry living lamps here in our hands.

(Refrain)

O Blessed One, who lives in heaven's seat   24
From all eternity and governs all
With everlasting sway, behold, we come!
Receive us also, O almighty Father,
With your Servant, within the gates of Life.

Chastely I live for You,
And with lighted lamp in hand
My Spouse, I go to meet You.

Epilogue

Eubulion: Thecla has deserved to win the first prize, Gregorion.

Gregorion: Yes, she has indeed.

Eubulion: And tell me, what of our friend from Termessus? Wasn't she listening at the keyhole? I would be very surprised if she did nothing when she heard about this banquet, and did not rather rush straightway to listen in to our discussion, like a bird in search of food.

Gregorion: No. The story is that she was with Methodius when he was asking Aretê about the affair. It is really a wonderful, blessed thing to have a teacher and guide like Aretê.

[The two ladies then embark on a discussion of the value of passion in the acquisition of virtue. Eubulion, who is the questioner, much like Socrates, attempts to show Gregorion that it is the greater virtue to practice chastity even though one is beset with temptation than not to experience any difficulty at all. Gregorion, however, acts as though she is hard to convince.]

Gregorion: Well, you can argue as much as you like, Eubulion, but I can show you to your satisfaction that a person who has no passion is better than one who has. And no one will be able to refute you.

Eubulion: My goodness, but I like to hear you speaking with such confidence; it shows how deeply versed you are in wisdom.

Gregorion: If I may say so, Eubulion, you are a talker.

Eubulion: What do you mean?

Gregorion: You talk this way merely to tease me instead of telling me the truth.

Eubulion: You mustn't talk that way, my dear. Really, I have the greatest admiration for your reputation for intelligence. But I said what I did because you not only claim you can understand a problem that many philosophers have often disputed among themselves, you even boast you can explain it to others.

Gregorion: Well, answer me then. Do you really find it hard to believe that those who have no passion are completely superior to those who practice chastity and still experience passion? Or are you simply joking with me?

Eubulion: How can I merely be teasing you when I say that I do not know? But come, you tell me, my lady philosopher, how it is that those who are chaste without passion are superior to those who experience passion and remain chaste? . . .

[Eubulion, like Socrates, succeeds in battering down his opponent's opposition. Ascetics who have kept chaste despite the struggle with passion are rather like successful pilots who have been tried by squalls, doctors who have had experience with disease, and athletes who have conquered after many contests. The victorious struggle is proof of the strength and fortitude of the soul. The discussion is not, for all its apparent tone, a plea for Stoic virtue, for Methodius had already taught that Christ won for all men the power to struggle with the Dragon, by adhering close to Mother Church and to her teaching. The dialogue concludes as the two ladies prepare to return to their normal activities.]

Eubulion: And is not this fortitude the very essence of virtue?

Gregorion: Yes, it is.

Eubulion: Well, then, if the force of virtue is perseverance, then the soul that perseveres against its passions despite violent struggle surely seems stronger, does it not, than the soul that is not so disturbed?

Gregorion: Yes.

Eubulion: And if it is stronger, is it not superior?

Gregorion: Yes, it is.

Eubulion: Then it is clear, from what we have admitted, that the soul that controls itself despite concupiscence is superior to the one that controls itself without passion?

Gregorion: Yes, it is true. And I should like to discuss this matter further with you. Hence, if you like, I shall return tomorrow and listen to these things once more. But now, as you see, it is time to leave and to give our attention to the outer man.

19

CYPRIAN AND THE DECIAN
PERSECUTION

St. Cyprian of Carthage

St. Jerome wrote that Cyprian was converted by a priest named Caecilius. Shortly afterwards (in 248) he was ordained a priest at Carthage, where he most probably was born, and soon was consecrated bishop despite the opposition of some of the local clergy, who resented the sudden rise of so recent a convert. Late in 249, the soldier-emperor Decius came to the throne of the Roman empire and began an intense persecution of the Christians, and early in the following year Bishop Cyprian took refuge in a secret hiding place, from which he attempted to administer his diocese. His *Epistle* 20 represents his attempt to soften the surprise of the clergy at his action; indeed they had written a complaint about him to Rome. When Cyprian returned in 251, a further split occurred within the ranks; some of the clergy, including Cyprian, were in favor of an immediate reconciliation with those who had lapsed during the persecution. Novatus, a member of the group that was against reconciliation, went to Rome to support Novatian in the quarrel with the new Pope Cornelius.

The problem of the lapsed was settled by the synod of Carthage, but a new crisis soon arose in connection with the validity of baptism when administered by heretics. Cyprian, and the local synods, refused to accept the validity of such sacraments, and even refused to yield when warned and contradicted by Pope Stephen (254–56) in Rome. Another persecution soon cast the quarrel aside. Stephen was executed in Rome, and Cyprian, after banishment for a year, was finally beheaded outside of Carthage on September 14, 258.[1]

In his short time as bishop of Carthage, Cyprian produced no less than thirteen treatises and some sixty-five letters; about thirteen more pieces have been attributed to him without good foundation, and sixteen letters dealing with local problems form part of the complete corpus. Though interesting from a doctrinal point of view, the entire collection is more important for the light it throws on the problems of the early Church in Africa, such as the ways in which the lapsed could be reconciled to the Church, the question of obedience to the Roman see, and the validity of baptism (and, implicitly, other sacraments) when administered by heretics. Most interesting to see, however, are the methods by which all sides arrived at their conclusions in the sometimes violent controversy. Appeal was made to Scripture and to the manner in which certain practices were handed down from the ancients—this being indeed a Roman legal principle that now was applied toward the understanding of Christ's revealed doctrines. Special problems have been raised about the famous fourth chapter of Cyprian's *On the Unity of the Church,* but these will be referred to below. A practical man, Cyprian wrote like a born administrator. What he lacked in imagination—his work has none of the charm of Tertullian or Minucius Felix—he made up for in clarity and precision.[2]

On the Unity of the Church*

[This short treatise on the authority of the ecclesiastical hierarchy, consisting of twenty-seven chapters, has aroused a good deal of controversy, primarily because of the two versions or recensions of the fourth chapter. One version (called PT or primacy text) mentions the "primacy given to Peter" in reference to the Roman see; the other (TR or textus receptus) omits this and stresses the power of the episcopal college. The TR was the only version accepted as authentic by W. Hartel in his edition of the work in the Vienna corpus

---

[1] See J. Quasten, *Patrology* (Westminster, Md.: Newman Press, 1953), II, 340–83, and for the manuscript problem, especially M. Bévenot, *The Tradition of Manuscripts: A Study in the Transmission of St. Cyprian's Treatises* (Oxford: Clarendon Press, 1961).

[2] M. Spanneut, *Le Stoïcisme des Pères de l'Eglise* (Paris: Editions du Seuil, 1957), index, *s. v.* "Cyprien," quotes a good number of passages from the bishop's works that stress his attitude towards contemporary philosophy.

* I have followed Bévenot, *op. cit.*

(CSEL III.1-3, Vienna, 1868-71); but in recent years opinion seems to be veering in the direction suggested by M. Bévenot in a number of works, namely that both versions go back ultimately to St. Cyprian himself.[3] Bévenot views the primacy text as coming from Cyprian's first publication of his treatise late in 251 after the Novatianist schism had begun; it was in this form that the text was sent to Rome. The modified text, with the primacy reference omitted, was presumably the one that Cyprian circulated in Africa about 255, when Cyprian was in disagreement with Pope Stephen with regard to the validity of heretical baptisms. Whatever view one might take, it would seem in any case that both texts are early and go back either to Cyprian himself or else to his entourage of clerics, who were in sympathy with his opposition to Stephen during the final days of his episcopate.]

1   The Lord warns us with the words, "You are the salt of the earth," and bids us be simple to the point of innocence and at the same time cautious in our simplicity. It surely then befits us, beloved brethren, to use foresight, to watch with constant heart and perceive the wiles of our cunning enemy and thus beware lest we, who have put on Christ, the Wisdom of the Father, should seem to fall short in wisdom in providing for our soul's salvation. For persecution is not the only thing we should be afraid of, nor all the things that approach by open attack to overwhelm and destroy God's servants. Caution is always easier where the danger is obvious; the mind is all ready for the conflict when the opponent shows himself openly. More to be feared and guarded against is the enemy that steals up in secret. . . .

---

[3] "St. Cyprian's *De Unitate*, 4, in the Light of the MSS," *Analecta Gregoriana* 11 (1937); *St. Cyprian: The Lapsed and the Unity of the Catholic Church* (Ancient Writers 25, Westminster, Md.: Newman Press, 1957); and, finally, *The Tradition of Manuscripts*, cited earlier. In the last-named work, Bévenot edited a critical edition of the *Unity* from a study of a hundred and sixty manuscripts and presented the evidence for his conclusions about the priority of the two recensions. The work is an excellent introduction to the complex problem of dealing with Latin patristic manuscripts. See also the note in Quasten, *op. cit.*, pp. 349-52; F. L. Cross, *The Early Christian Fathers* (London: Gerald Duckworth & Co., Ltd., 1960), pp. 151-52; and B. Altaner, *Patrology* (tr. by Hilda C. Graef, New York: Herder & Herder, Inc., 1960), pp. 196-98, with the literature.
    It is only fair to say that the idea of making both texts go back to Cyprian himself originated with the great Dom J. Chapman in the *Revue Bénédictine* 19 (1902), 246 ff. and subsequent works. Others, too, have adopted the same position, although there is disagreement on details. For the bibliography, see Quasten, *loc. cit.*

[Cyprian was speaking of the latent danger of schism within the Church itself; the "hidden adversary" is an implicit reference to Novatian and the presbyters who supported his position both in Carthage and in Rome. It is the fault of the Evil One, who has spawned disunity in order to try to destroy what Christ founded on a rock.]

Now there is no need for long discussion or argument, 4 if one would only consider and carefully examine what I have said. We can find an easy support for our belief in a short summary of the truth; as the Lord said to Peter: I say to you that you are Peter and upon this rock I shall build my church, and the gates of hell shall not prevail against it. I will give you the keys of the kingdom of Heaven, and whatever you bind on earth shall be bound in Heaven, and whatever you loose on earth shall be loosed in Heaven [Matt. 16.18–19].

[*Here follows in some manuscripts the "primacy text":*]
And similarly after his resurrection He says to him, 4a "Feed my sheep." Upon him He builds his Church; to him He gives his sheep to feed; and although He gives all apostles equal power, He sets up one throne and by His authority ordains but one source and principle of unity. Assuredly the other apostles were the same as Peter, but to Peter was the primacy given, and thus was shown one Church and one chair. All indeed are pastors, but the unity of the flock comes from their being fed by the apostles in unanimous consent. If a man does not hold this unity under Peter, can he believe that he has the faith? Whoever deserts the chair of Peter on whom the Church was founded, can he believe that he is in the Church?

[*Other manuscripts present a modified text:*]
It was upon one that He built his Church: indeed, after his 4b resurrection, He gave them equal authority, saying: As the Father has sent me, even so I send you. Receive the Holy Spirit. If you forgive the sins of any, they are forgiven; if you retain the sins of any, they are retained [John 20.21–23]. Yet, that He might make clear their unity, He arranged for a source of this unity by his authority, beginning from one man. Certainly the other apostles were the same as Peter, endowed with equal partnership of dignity and of power, but [the Church's] beginning proceeds from a unity, that the Church of Christ

might be shown to be one. The Holy Spirit also designates this one Church in the person of the Lord in the Song of Songs, saying: My dove, my perfect one, is one; she is the only one of her mother, chosen to her that bore her [Cant. 6.8 (9)].

Whoever does not adhere to this unity of the Church, can he say he has the faith? Can he who strives against the Church and resists her trust that he is in the Church, when the blessed apostle Paul teaches the same doctrine, setting forth the sacrament of unity, when he says: There is one body and one Spirit, one hope of your calling, one Lord, one faith, one baptism, one God [Eph. 4.4–6]?

5   Those of us who are bishops ought especially to hold to this unity and defend it, for we preside in the Church, in order that we may also demonstrate the episcopate itself to be one and undivided. No one should deceive our brothers by falsehood; no one should corrupt the truth of the faith by malicious lies.

[*The text then continues as follows in both versions:*]
The body of bishops is one, and each one who has a share in it possesses the whole. The Church is one, extended as it is far and wide among men by its increase in fruitfulness. . . . In her rich abundance she spreads her branches over the entire world; she pours forth abundant streams which flow far and wide, though her head and source is one, and she remains one mother, overflowing in the effects of her fecundity. Born from her womb, we are nursed by her milk, envigorated by her soul.

6   Christ's spouse cannot be defiled, for she is chaste and pure. She knows one home, and in holy purity she guards the sanctity of one couch. It is she that holds us safe for God, for she assigns to his kingdom the sons she has brought forth. Whoever is separated from the Church is wed to an adulteress and is separated from the promises made to the Church, whoever leaves Christ's Church will never attain to the rewards of Christ. . . .

[Cyprian pleaded for mutual understanding, peace, and harmony. At the same time he warned those who have fallen into schism to come back to the fold. He asked for kind words and peace, quoting Ps. 33:14–15, "Keep your tongue from evil. . . . Seek peace, and pursue it." He reminded them of the unity which prevailed among the apostles with the mother of the Lord in the earliest days of the Acts of the Apostles (1.14 and 4.32). He finally recalled the coming of the Lord on the Last Day.]

Let us arouse ourselves so far as we can, my dearest 27 brothers, and ending our former sleep of inertia, let us watch to observe and execute the precepts of the Lord. . . . We must have our loins girt, lest, when the day of our setting forth comes, He may find us hindered and entangled. Let our light shine in good works; let it glow, that He may lead us out of the night of this world to the light of his eternal brightness. Let us always be ready and on our guard for the sudden coming of the Lord, so that when he knocks, our faith may be awake, ready to receive the reward of vigilance from the Lord. If we observe these commandments and keep these counsels and precepts, we shall not be able to be deceived by the Devil and overcome in our sleep, but as watchful servants we shall reign with Christ in his kingdom.

A Document from the Decian Persecution (A.D. 250)

The emperor Decius had but a short reign (249–51), which he began while he was military commander in the Danubian campaign under Philip. He was born in Pannonia and served as a city prefect in Rome. Conservative by nature, he attempted to use various means to revive the State religion throughout the empire, and one of these was a vigorous persecution of the Christians. His decree, issued late in the year 249, not only made Christianity a crime against the State, but ordered all under his jurisdiction to offer sacrifice to the gods and obtain a certificate (called a *libellus*) to prove it.[4] All of the forty-odd *libelli* that we have today are written in Greek and come from Egypt, mostly from the village of Theadelphia; of these, at least one is for a pagan priestess, and hence most scholars assume that Decius' ordinance was not restricted merely to those suspected of Christianity. Cyprian in his treatise *On the Apostates* (*De lapsis*) mentioned Christians who bribed officials and thus obtained certificates without

---

[4] On Decius, see the article by Wittig in *Pauly Wissowa* 15 (1931), 1244–84, with the list of extant certificates. See also A. von Premerstein, "Libelli," *Pauly Wissowa* 13 (1926), 46–48, where the regular formula of the certificates is given. There is a good article with bibliography by L. De Regibus, "Decio," *Enciclopedia Italiana* 12 (1931), 461–62.

having had to perform the requisite sacrifices; such Christians he called *libellatici* ("certificate-takers") and put them in the same category as those who had apostatized and given up the faith. The documents only cover June to July of 250; in the spring of 251 Decius was killed in battle and the persecution, the first explicit harassment of Christianity as such, was over. The "execrable animal," as Lactantius would call him, was dead.

Certificate Attesting Pagan Sacrifice*

To those chosen to superintend the sacrifices, from Inaro Akis of the village of Theoxenis with her children Ajax and Hera, who dwell in the village of Theadelphia.

It has always been our custom to sacrifice to the gods, and now in your presence in accordance with the decrees we have offered sacrifice, made libation, and tasted of the offerings, and hereby request that you countersign the statement. May you have good fortune.

We, Aurelius Serenus and Hermas, witnessed your sacrifice.

In the first year of the emperor Caesar Gaius Messius Quintus Trajan Decius Pius Felix Augustus, the twenty-third day of the month Pauni [June 18, A.D. 250].

The Martyrdom of St. Cyprian*

[Cyprian, bishop of Carthage, had escaped the persecution of Decius by going into hiding. In A.D. 257, under the emperor Valerian, he was arrested and sent into exile in Numidia, as related in the *Acts of St. Cyprian*. But in July 258, Valerian ruled in an edict that all members of the recalcitrant Christian hierarchy be put to death, and this time Cyprian, refusing to escape, was arrested. The details of his final condemnation are given in the *Acts*. He was executed by beheading on September 14, 258.]

2.2   Cyprian, the holy martyr who had been chosen by God, had returned from the city of Curubis, which had been

---

* The text of our document, which comes from Theadelphia in Egypt, is taken from F. Preisigke and F. Bilabel, *Sammelbuch griechisher Urkunden aus Aegypten* (Strassburg: K. J. Trübner, 1915 ff.), 6824, reprinted by M. David and B. A. van Groningen, *Papyrological Primer* (Leiden: A. W. Sythoff 1952), no. 67.

* Text of the *Acts* in G. Hartel, *Cypriani Opera* (CSEL, Vienna: Gerold, 1871), III, CX-CXIV.

assigned him as his place of exile at the command of Aspasius, the proconsul at the time; he remained in his gardens according to the Lord's command, and he daily expected to be summoned from here, as it had been revealed to him.

While he was still there, on the thirteenth day of September in the consulship of Tuscus and Bassus, there suddenly came to him two high officials: one was an officer of the staff of proconsul Galerius Maximus, the other a member of the same staff, an official of the bodyguard. They carried him into a chariot and placed him between them and conducted him to the estate of Sextus, for it was here that the proconsul Galerius Maximus had withdrawn to convalesce.

At any rate, Galerius Maximus the proconsul ordered Cyprian to be held over until the following day. . . .

On the following day, the fourteenth of September, a huge crowd gathered in the morning at the estate of Sextus, as the proconsul Galerius Maximus had ordered. This was the day on which the proconsul Galerius Maximus had ordered Cyprian to be arraigned before him, privately, within the atrium which was called Sauciolum. When he was brought before him, the proconsul Galerius Maximus said to the bishop Cyprian, "Are you Thascius Cyprian?"

"I am," Bishop Cyprian replied.

Galerius Maximus, the proconsul, said, "Have you put yourself forward as the 'Pope' of these men who hold sacrilegious views?"

"Yes," said the bishop Cyprian.

Galerius Maximus the proconsul said, "You have been ordered by the most sacred emperors to perform the religious rites."

"I will not," said the bishop Cyprian.

"Take care," said the proconsul Galerius Maximus.

"You do as you are ordered," said Bishop Cyprian. "There is no need for deliberation in so clear-cut a case."

Galerius Maximus consulted with his staff of advisers, and, with much reluctance, spoke as follows, "You have long persisted in your sacrilegious views, and you have joined to yourself many other members in a vicious conspiracy; you have set yourself up as an enemy to the gods of Rome and to our religious rites, and the pious and most sacred emperors Valerian and Gallienus, the Augusti, and Valerian, the most noble of Caesars, have not been able to bring you back to the observance of their rites.

"You stand convicted as the instigator and leader in

crimes most atrocious, and therefore you shall be an example for all those whom you have drawn to yourself in your wickedness. The law shall be enforced by blood."

When he had said this, he read the following decree from a tablet: "It is decreed that Thascius Cyprian should die by the sword."

The bishop Cyprian said, "Thanks be to God!"

5   After the sentence, the multitude of the brethren said, "Let us also be beheaded with him."

The result was an uproar among the brethren, and he was followed by a great crowd. And Cyprian was led out onto Sextus' estate, and he took off his cloak, knelt on the ground, and bowed himself in prayer to the Lord. He then took off his dalmatic and handed it to his deacons and, clad only in his tunic, stood waiting for the executioner. The executioner came, then, and Cyprian told his friends to give him twenty-five golden pieces. The brethren began spreading cloths and napkins in front of him.

The blessed Cyprian then bound his own eyes. But when he could not tie the ends of the handkerchief, a priest named Julian and the deacon Julian fastened them for him.

And so the blessed Cyprian suffered, and his body was stretched out nearby to satisfy the curiosity of the brethren. At night it was moved from there and, accompanied by torches and candles, was conducted with prayers and great triumph to the cemetery of Macrobius Candidianus, the procurator. This lies near the fishponds along the Mappalian Way. And a few days later, the proconsul Galerius Maximus died.

6   Cyprian, the most blessed martyr, suffered on the fourteenth of September under the emperors Valerian and Gallienus in the reign of Jesus Christ our Lord, to whom belong honor and glory forever and ever. Amen.

20

ARNOBIUS: AGAINST THE PAGANS

Like Minucius Felix's *Octavius*, Tertullian's *Apology*, and other early works, Arnobius' treatise against the pagans was written in large part to refute the false charges that were being made against the Christians. St. Jerome wrote that Arnobius had been a pagan teacher of rhetoric at Sicca Veneria (mod. El Kef) in Africa and was finally won over to the new religion by a dream; the treatise was apparently written to convince the local bishop of his sincerity. If St. Jerome's dating is accurate, Arnobius was writing during the persecution of Diocletian and prior to A.D. 311. The sincerity of *Against the Pagans* need not be doubted, but the work's organization and orthodoxy leave much to be desired. Its great merit consists in the vast numbers of references to pagan Greek and Latin writers and the discussions of myths and cults. The Latin writer Varro, for example, is quoted fifteen times, and Plato fourteen, as well as others, including Cicero, Sophocles, Homer, Aristotle, and a host of writers whose work has been lost. The passionate indictment of pagan religion is the work's strong point. But the explanation of Christianity seems confused—something even St. Jerome pointed out. Arnobius was not clear when discussing the nature of the Christian God and the Trinity, and his teaching about the status of the pagan deities seems contradictory and indistinct. He did not believe in the creation of the human soul, and taught that its immortality is a free gift of God, conditional on the following of Christ's teaching. Indeed, many scholars believe that this doctrine—or rather Arnobius' distorted view of the Christian belief in immortality—was chiefly responsible for his turning away from paganism. He revealed surprisingly little knowledge of the origins of Christianity, of the Old Testament, or the Gospels.

All of this is most surprising in Africa Proconsularis, in the year 300 or 310. But clearly *Against the Pagans* is a hastily conceived and possibly incomplete work, written when Arnobius had not yet become fully conversant with Christianity. Despite its faults, it contains some very fervent, moving passages that reflect Arnobius' somewhat Platonic piety; and apart from the evidence it preserves of pagan practice, it remains an important document that depicts the varied and sometimes confused history of the Church during this early period.[1] The text, derived from the same eleventh or twelfth century manuscript as Minucius Felix's, still provokes much controversy (see p. 173).

Against the Pagans*

I.1   Some men have the greatest confidence in their own wisdom and rave madly as though they were inspired by some oracle: at any rate they claim, so I have been told, that once the Christian sect came to exist in this world, everything went to ruin, men became prey to many different forms of disease, and even the gods themselves were exiled from the earth as a result of a neglect of the ceremonial worship through which they had been accustomed to govern human affairs. Hence I decided, despite the limitations of my language and intelligence, to contradict this unjust reputation and refute the slanderous charges. Otherwise, these men would think they have made a very important statement when they have only circulated the rumors of the crowd, or that they have won their case when we restrain ourselves from engaging in such controversy, as though our side were inherently weak and not simply because of the silence of our defenders. . . .

[Arnobius began by refuting the charge that the Christians were responsible for many calamities which had begun to crush the Roman empire. The charge, he suggests, was invented by the pagan priests, who saw their income being diverted elsewhere (I.24). Arnobius stressed his own personal conviction of the truth of Christ's revelation about the nature

---

[1] For discussion and bibliography, see the translation and commentary by G. E. McCracken, *Arnobius of Sicca: The Case Against the Pagans* (Ancient Christian Writers 7 & 8, 2 vols. Westminster, Md.: Newman Press, 1949), I, 3 ff.; and J. Quasten, *Patrology* (Westminster, Md.: Newman Press, 1953), II, 383–92.

* C. Marchesi (Turin: Paravia, 1934).

of the Godhead; this had shown him suddenly how foolish he had been to worship images.]

Not long ago (ah, the blindness of it!) I, too, worshiped I. statues that came out of ovens, gods hammered out on 39 an anvil, gods in elephant tusks, in paintings, streamers on aged trees. If I saw a stone stained with olive oil, I would venerate it as though a divine power was present, I would address it and ask for favors although it were merely a block without any feeling. And the very gods whom I believed existed I actually treated with scorn, thinking as I did that they were merely wood, stone, or bone, or at least that they dwelt in such material.

But now that I have been instructed in the ways of truth, I am aware that all that I believe is worthy of the things I know are worthy; I insult no divine name, and whatever is in honor due to a person or authority I offer this without any confusion in rank or dignity.

Are we not then to believe that Christ is God and is he not to be honored with the highest imaginable worship? For we have received so many benefits from Him in this life, looking forward to more abundant ones on that final day.

[That Christ was a man and died on a gibbet, Arnobius protested, is no argument against his divinity. For the proof that "he was sent to us by the supreme King" is clear from a consideration of his many miracles (42–46); Arnobius herewith enumerated many of the miracles of the Gospels in detail, culminating with Christ's own resurrection from the dead. He did these to show us "that we might come to imagine what the true God is by a consideration of the beneficence of his actions" (I.47). In the final chapter of the book, he made a ringing appeal to pagans to cease their persecutions and to recognize in Jesus the healer and doctor of the age (65), "bringing the message of good health, with the good auspices of prosperity for all who believe."

[In Book II, Arnobius proceeded to attack the pagan philosophical idea of the soul, especially the theory of pre-existence, as held by the Platonists and some Christians of the Alexandrian school. Men as they exist in the world, Arnobius argued, are too vicious, too dirty, and foul to be the dwelling place of a soul that comes from Heaven—"to spend their lives imprisoned in these gloomy bodies, in blood and phlegm, in these sacks of ordure and foul latrines" (II.37). Arnobius here approached Juvenal's violent cynicism and ill-humored

attacks on mankind's follies. Indeed, he asked, what good are
men to the world?]

II.   For, to take first things first, what good are the great
38   kings to the world? Does it help to have these tyrants,
lords, and untold other magnificent magistrates? What
good are the generals with their experience in military
tactics, so clever at sacking cities, and the soldiers that
are inconquerable, so immovable whether in cavalry
clashes or on foot? What good are the orators, the grammarians, and the poets, the chroniclers, encyclopedists, and
musicians? Of what use are the pantomimes, the mimes,
actors, singers, trumpeters, flute players, and those who
blow on the pipes? And the sprinters, boxers, chariot
racers, bareback riders, acrobats, ropedancers, and jug-
glers? And what of the hawkers of pitch, salt dealers,
fish sellers, perfumers, goldsmiths, fowlers, and people
who weave baskets and winnows? And what of the fullers,
wool combers, embroiderers, cooks, candymakers, mule-
teers, slave dealers, butchers, and courtesans? We could
make a list of all the other kinds of tradesmen, teachers,
and craftsmen, but even a whole life would not be long
enough; but what do they all contribute to the meaning and
structure of this world, such that one should think that
without mankind it could not have been founded nor have
reached its perfection—that is, without the struggles of a
pathetic and superfluous animal?

[Arnobius admitted that he could not answer all questions; but one thing he would admit: nothing comes from God
that is not good, and that men have become evil by their
own free will and choice. Men can, then, receive immortality
from God if they follow his commands, and believe in Christ,
whom He has sent. Otherwise, there awaits for them a grim
death and the punishment of bitter torture (II.61–62).

[Arnobius continued his impassioned attack on the pagan
gods and their often absurd ceremonial worship in great detail. His passion and conviction were those of a former believer who had seen the light. Only rarely did he enlarge upon
the beliefs that forced him to change his life, i.e., the true
God cannot be dwelling in such absurd and even immoral
trappings. The final book, the seventh, comes to an end without a rounded peroration, and some editors have shifted the
order of the text to make the following paragraph occur last.

VII.
37   Since all this is so, and since there is such a wide

divergence between your beliefs and ours, how can you claim that you are religious and we are not? Surely the measure of piety and impiety should depend upon the sentiments of the parties involved. He is not to be thought religious who worships a statue of his own making or kills a harmless animal and sacrifices it on a holy altar. The essence of religion is belief, the true judgment about the gods, so that you do not believe that they have any desires beyond what is fitting to their dignity. All else that we offer them we see consumed before our eyes; hence the things that we ought to believe truly rise up to them are our beliefs, beliefs that are worthy of the gods and eminently appropriate to their name. These are the surest gifts, these are the authentic sacrifice. Gruel, incense, and flesh only feed the greedy flames and are only fit companions for the memorial service of the dead.

21

LACTANTIUS

Lucius Caecilius Firmianus Lactantius, to give him his full Roman name, was born in Africa, perhaps in the city of Cirta (mod. Constantine), and, according to St. Jerome, had been a student of Arnobius. Though the details of his life are scarce, the emperor Diocletian (284–304), again according to St. Jerome, appointed him to teach rhetoric in Nicomedia (mod. Izmit), the new capital city of Bithynia. He was not successful, however, and had also, in the course of events, become a Christian. Forced to leave because of the persecution, about A.D. 305/6, he was shortly afterwards summoned to Treves in Gaul by the emperor Constantine and asked to tutor his eldest son Crispus. At this time he was already advanced in years, but how or when he died is unknown.

Even Jerome recognized the classical style of this African rhetorician, whom later Renaissance scholars would call the Christian Cicero, but Jerome was among the first to admit that Lactantius' knowledge of Christian doctrine was neither profound nor accurate. He either did not know or else ignored the specific Christian teaching on the sacramental Church, the liturgy, and the redemption. Although he believed in the supremacy of God, he was confused about the Trinity and the Incarnation. He regarded the Trinity, for example, as being comprised of two persons, with the Son subordinate to the Father; a third person generated by the Father revolted from the divine authority and became the Evil One. He also taught that there would be the restoration of all things at the end of the world and that after six thousand years, the world would end, with a special reign of divine righteousness for the last period of the world (the seventh) for a thousand years; the periods of the world thus correspond to the seven days of creation. Although he was indebted to Stoic and Platonic philosophy for much of the moral doctrine that he presented as being Christian, Lactantius throughout his works engaged in a number of debates with pagan philosophers, and the exact basis of his disagreement is not always apparent. The treatise *On God's Handiwork* (about 303/4), addressed to a former pupil named Demetrianus, is the earliest of the works preserved; it adapts the Stoic view that man's body is a masterpiece of divine providence—quite a different view from Arnobius'—and is the finest of God's creation, endowed as it is with intelligence and reason. Hardly a Christian work, its main sources are Cicero and Varro. The *Divine Institutes* was begun shortly after the completion of the previous work and finished shortly after Constantine's edict of Milan in 313. Not long afterwards, Lactantius published a much abridged version, with some modifications, entitled *Epitome of the Divine Institutes*; the complete manuscript was discovered in the eighteenth century in Turin. The *Epitome* is perhaps the best brief guide to Lactantius' complex doctrines, but it has very little of the charm or style of the original work. Another smaller work from the same period is the treatise *On God's Anger*, which develops the thesis of God's hatred of the Evil One and attacks the pagan philosophical view of a God uninvolved in the deeds of mankind. Perhaps Lactantius' final work, and most important from a historical viewpoint, is the tract *On the Deaths of the Persecutors*, addressed to his friend Donatus and completed some time before A.D. 321. Extant in only one precious Paris manuscript (Paris. lat. 2627 of the ninth century), the account of how the various persecuting emperors died is extremely valuable for its eyewitness testimony of the persecution of Diocletian. Its attribution to Lactantius was once disputed, but all evidence seems to corroborate its authenticity. Finally, the Latin elegiac poem *The Phoenix*, composed of eighty-five distichs, was attributed to Lactantius by Gregory of Tours. It is a pompous, rhetorical poem on the death and symbolic resurrection of the phoenix bird, whose mythological existence was thought (both by pagan and Christian writers) to be a parable of the human soul. Only questionably a Christian piece of work, the best that can be said of this tedious poem is that if Lactantius did write it, it must have antedated his conversion to Christianity.

Undoubtedly, Lactantius' finest work is the *Divine Institutes,* composed in seven books. More extensive in scope than Minucius Felix or Arnobius' works, its purpose was substantially the same: both by positive explanation as well as deliberate counterattack "to overthrow once and for all everyone" who had attacked the Christians. For this Lactantius drew on his rhetorical background; he employed the technique of the personal, *ad hominem* argument, and demonstrated the contradictions in his opponents' position. Books I and II attack the pagans' false worship of gods; Lactantius concurred with Euhemerus' view that the gods were once simply human beings, who were venerated after death. Book III attacks pagan philosophy, especially eclectic Stoicism and Epicureanism, as a secondary source of religious error. Book IV discusses the coming of God's Son, who brought infallible wisdom to earth; the alleged evidence (again adduced in rhetorical fashion) is taken from the Old Testament, the *Sibylline Oracles,* and the secret *Hermetic Books*. Books V and VI are the core of the work and on them Lactantius lavished his best efforts; they explain the meaning of true worship of God in piety and in justice towards fellowmen. For it was this that Christ brought to men: a knowledge of the goodness of God the Father and the meaning of our union with Him. Finally, Book VII presents a description of the rewards in store for all believers, and at this point Lactantius embarked on a grim, almost prophetic picture of the final destruction of the world, the coming of Jesus in judgment, the damnation of the unbelievers, and the final reign of Christ for a thousand years before the inauguration of the eternal beatitude of Heaven. The conclusion of this work as well as that of the *Epitome* both give the classic view of millenarianism, or chiliasm, as it has been called—a view evident in the work of St. Methodius of Olympus, the *Epistle of Barnabas,* and other works of the third century. It is the inevitable scene, the final denouement—dear to the apologists' heart—in the world drama, in which the truth of Christ is vindicated by a triumphant reign upon an earth transformed for his final coming; the visible overthrow of the Evil One takes place and the realization of God's eternal providence over his elect. But this stirring eschatological vision, so influential in Lactantius' conversion to Christianity, would be shattered by the sharper theological analyses of the Fathers of the golden age.

The Divine Institutes*

Our subject for discussion, therefore, is religion and the I.1 things of God. Some of the greatest orators, when they had completed their days of pleading, veterans as it were of their vocation, gave themselves to the study of philosophy; and they felt this would be a deserved rest from their work, tormenting their minds in the quest of things that they could not discover—indeed, they seem to have sought rather more occupation than leisure, giving themselves far more trouble than they had in their former work. How much more fitting is it for me to take refuge in a most secure haven, the piety and truth of divine wisdom, where all things are ready to be uttered, good to hear, easy to understand, and worthy to be discussed. . . .

[After a eulogistic address to emperor Constantine, "the first of Roman princes to banish error," Lactantius embarked on a demonstration of the existence and providence of one God. He called upon the pagan philosophers and oracles; he used the argument of Euhemerus—as did Arnobius and Minucius, though only the latter is quoted—to show that the gods were simply men who had been dignified with worship after death. He attacked the absurdities of pagan mythology and cult. Book II continues the discussion, taking up Stoic and Epicurean beliefs, dreams, astrology, magic, and other connected topics. Book III, on false philosophies, shows how the pagan philosophers, for all their efforts, were the source of many errors among men before divine revelation. Book IV demonstrates the nature of true wisdom, as brought to earth by Christ. Lactantius referred to the prophecies which foretold the coming of Jesus and the miracles which testified to his divine mission. The final chapter 30 warns against heresy and schism.]

And so the Catholic Church alone retains the true IV.30. worship of God. She is the fountain of truth, the home 11–13 of the faith, the temple of God; whoever does not enter here, or whoever leaves, shall be removed from

* For the text I have used S. Brandt (CSEL, Vienna: Tempsky, 1890–97); see also the introduction and commentary of J. Moreau, *Lactance: De la Mort des Persécuteurs* (Sources Chrétiennes 39; 2 vols.; Paris: Editions du Cerf, 1954); for the bibliography, see J. Quasten, *Patrology* (Westminster, Md.: Newman Press, 1953), II, 383–92.

the hope of life and of salvation. Hence let no one flatter himself on his persistence in opposition, for it is a question of eternal life and salvation, which, without proper and diligent care, can be lost and extinguished. There are, however, individual groups of heretics that feel that they are the Catholic Church and they alone are Christians; hence, it should be known that the true Church is the one in which admission of sin and repentance still effectively heal the wounds and sins to which the weak flesh is heir.

[And so Book IV closes with an admonition on the subject of the true religion. Book V deals primarily with the hardships that all just men, and especially Christians, have had to endure at the hands of the wicked and concludes with the threat that the tormentors of the Christians will be punished by the divine anger (V.24). The true Church propounds the brotherhood and equality of all men: all have an equal share in the worship of the one, true God, the Father of all men. For "in his sight, no man is a slave, no man is master" (V.15). Book VI contains "the chief and greatest section of my work: how, by what sort of sacrifice, God is to be worshipped" (VI.1). Lactantius felt that he had already paved the way for the positive exposition of the essence of Christian worship in the five previous books. God denies Heaven to no one (VI.3), but the way of justice is "difficult and uphill, and full of piercing thorns" (VI.4). Lactantius' Christianity here suggests a kind of higher form of Stoicism revealed by Christ; he placed little stress upon the sacramental aspects of the life of the Church.

[In the final book, the seventh, the author devoted himself primarily to an exposition of the Last Things, and this section, though among the least orthodox of his discussions, is one of the most interesting for the modern reader (VII.20–26). He taught that there are two resurrections; the first one is for the just alone, and they will reign in their immortal bodies for a thousand years. At the end of this time, there will be a resurrection in which the wicked will be given bodies, to be tortured in fire forever, while the good will enjoy the sight of God and the angels in a transformed universe.]

VII.21.   The Scriptures teach us the nature of the punish-
3 ff.   ment that the wicked will have to undergo. They committed sins in their bodies; therefore will they be

clothed with flesh once more and pay their penalty in the body. But it will not be the flesh with which God clothed man, this earthly flesh, but rather indestructible and lasting forever, so as to withstand the torment of eternal fire. For this fire is again different from the fire we use for the necessities of life, which goes out if it has no fuel to feed it. . . .

The same divine fire with the same force and power will both consume the wicked and vivify them again, restoring as much as it consumes of their bodies, and shall supply forever its own sustenance—the same property, indeed, which the poets have given to the vulture that consumed Tityus. In like manner will this fire burn their bodies and inflict pain without destroying them as they constantly revive.

God will also examine the just by fire when they come for judgment. Those whose sins shall prove excessive either in number or gravity shall be singed and burned. Those who have been fully matured by justice and the ripeness of their virtue will not feel the fire. For they possess within them something divine that repels and rejects the force of the fire. Such is the power of innocence that the flame shrinks from it and cannot do harm, only having the power from God to burn the wicked and spare the just.[1]

However, let no one think that souls are judged immediately after death. Rather all of them are detained in a common prison until such time as the great Judge holds a hearing on their deserts. Then those whose innocence He approves of will receive the prize of immortality; but the others whose sins and crimes are uncovered will not rise but will be buried with the wicked in the same darkness, marked for certain punishment. . . .

Now I will tell you the rest. The Son of the most great and mighty God will come to judge the living and the dead. So the Sibyl tells us, saying:
VII. 24.1 ff.

Then will there be confusion on the earth
For men when God the almighty one shall come
To his tribunal, there to judge the souls

[1] Lactantius' theory of the test of fire for the just, perhaps a caricature of the doctrine of purgatory, and his other views on the final coming of the King to reign over the world, are peculiar to the Chiliast school and found little favor with the rest of the Church.

Of the dead, the living, and of all the world.

And when He shall complete his final judgment and shall wipe out iniquity and restore to life the good who have lived from the beginning of the world, He shall stay with men one thousand years and be their King in most righteous rule. . . . Those who will be alive at that time will not die, but for these thousand years will produce an infinite multitude, and their children will be holy and loved by God. Those, however, who will be brought back from the dead will rule over those living as judges. The various nations will not be entirely destroyed but some may be allowed to stay as a triumph for God, that they may serve the just as an occasion for victory, being subjected to everlasting slavery.

At the same time, the prince of devils who is the plotter of all evil, will be bound with chains and shall remain in prison for the duration of the thousand years of heavenly rule; for then goodness will so prevail in the world that he will not be able to plot any evil against God's folk. . . .

Then will the darkness that overspread and blackened the heavens be swept away; the moon will shine in the glow of the sun and will no longer wane. The sun will become seven times brighter than it is now. The earth will open its bounty and will bring forth quantities of fruit all by itself. The rocky mountains will drip with honey; there will be streams of wine flowing down, and rivers will flow with milk. The world, in fine, will be happy and all of nature will rejoice once it is redeemed and freed from the dominion of evil, wickedness, crime, and error. During that time the wild beasts will not feed on blood, birds will not seek prey, but everything will be calm and peaceful. Lions and calves will stand together at the feed trough, the wolf will not carry off the sheep, the hound will not hunt for his prey, hawks and eagles will do no harm, and the baby will be able to play with the serpents. In short, all the things that the poets spoke of as being achieved during the reign of Saturn will then come to pass. . . .

VII.   When the thousand years are completed, God shall
26.5 ff. renovate the universe: the heavens will be folded together, and the earth will be transformed. And God will change men into the image of angels, and they

will be white as snow; they will dwell constantly in the sight of the omnipotent, and, sacrificing to their Lord, they will serve Him forever. At the same time there will be the second public resurrection of everyone,[2] when the wicked shall be restored to suffer eternal torment. They are the ones who have worshipped what their own hands have made, who have ignored or denied Him who is the Lord and Father of the universe. . . .

On the Deaths of the Persecutors[*]

[Lactantius furnished a vivid description of emperor Galerius' sadism in this work. The period is some time before 311, when Galerius joined Constantine and Licinius in subscribing to the principle of toleration of the Christians.]

Arrived at the pinnacle of power, he had but one thought, to lord it over the world that he had subjected to himself. . . . First of all, he deprived his victims of their honors; he tortured not only municipal magistrates but also the highest persons within the cities, persons of upper-class and equestrian rank, and even in very trivial, civil matters. If they were judged worthy of death, the cross was prepared; for lesser crimes, there were fetters. Mothers of families who were Roman citizens and even the well-born were dragged off to factories. When men were to be flogged, he would have four posts fixed in the ground for them—even slaves had not been scourged this way before. 21. 1ff.

What shall I say of his own amphitheater and his sport? He used to keep bears (they resembled him in both size and viciousness) that he selected all through the course of his reign. Whenever he felt like being amused, he had one brought in by name. Then he would feed them a couple of men, to be devoured slowly. The emperor would roar with delight on seeing their bodies

---

[2] That is, of those who were not already raised for the enjoyment of the thousand years of Christ's final reign on earth. The just had either been alive at his coming or else were raised from the dead to live forever. Lactantius' doctrine of a double resurrection is peculiar to his system. See, in this connection, A. Vasilev, "Medieval Ideas of the End of the World, West and East," *Byzantion* 16 (1942–43), 463–502.

[*] For the text, see J. Moreau, *Lactance: De la Mort des Persécuteurs* (2 vols.; Sources Chrétiennes 39 Paris: Editions du Cerf, 1954).

being torn apart. He never dined without a bit of human blood.

The punishment of fire was only for those who had no standing. It was for the Christians that the emperor had first of all perfected this method of punishment, and he decreed that after being tortured they were to be burned by a slow fire. After they were tied to a stake, a light flame was applied to the soles of their feet, until the flesh, contracting under the heat of the flame, separated from the bones. Then torches, lit briefly and then extinguished, were applied to all parts of their bodies, so that no part was left intact. All the while they sprinkled the faces of the victims with cold water and moistened their mouths so that they wouldn't die too quickly with their throats parched with dryness. . . .

[After further descriptions of the Roman practices, Lactantius concluded his account with the story of Constantine's victory by means of the heavenly sign.]

44   Already civil war had broken out between Constantine and Maxentius. Although Maxentius remained at Rome—an oracle had predicted that he would die if he crossed the city gates—the war was conducted by his able commanders. His forces were superior to those of his adversary. For he not only had his father's army, which had deserted from Severus, but his own as well, which he had just collected from Mauritania and from the country of the Getulians. They clashed, and Maxentius' troops held the advantage, up until the time when Constantine, prepared either to win or to die, brought all his forces close to Rome and encamped near the Mulvian bridge. It was near the twenty-eighth of October, the anniversary of Maxentius' accession to the throne and the celebration of his completion of five years of reign.

During his sleep Constantine was directed that God's heavenly sign should be inscribed on the soldiers' shields before they should begin the battle. He did as he was commanded, and he had inscribed on the shields the name of Christ by means of an X that was crossed by an I curved over at the top.[3] Armed with this sign, his soldiers stood to arms. . . . And the hand of God was stretched over the fray.

[3] The text is somewhat corrupt here and I follow Grégoire's correction.

22

THE TRIUMPH OF CONSTANTINE

Constantine, inspired by his vision of the symbol of Christ, fought and defeated Maxentius at Saxa Rubra, to the north of Rome near the Mulvian Bridge, on October 28, 313. Eusebius, among others, recognized that this battle heralded the end of paganism and compared it to the destruction of the Egyptian Pharaoh by Moses in the book of Exodus. Along the Triumphal Way between the Caelian and Palatine Hills was erected the famous arch—the largest and best preserved in modern Rome—called the Arch of Constantine. Upon the attic the Senate had engraved the following inscription: *

To Emperor Caesar Flavius Constantine the Great, Pius, Felix Augustus, because inspired by the Godhead, by the greatness of his spirit, at one stroke avenged the State upon the tyrant and his entire faction by a just show of force together with his army, the Senate and the People of Rome have dedicated this arch in token of his triumph.

Elsewhere on the Arch appears: "Liberator of the City," "Founder of peace."

* There is a good picture of the arch and the inscription in F. van der Meer and C. Mohrmann, *Atlas of the Early Christian World* (London: Thomas Nelson & Sons, 1958), p. 59. In commenting on the inscription, H. Stuart Jones notes that "the Senate clung to the old religion, and could not bring itself to do more than record . . . that the vengeance exacted by Constantine from the 'tyrant' " (i.e. Maxentius) was "inspired by heaven"—*Classical Rome* (London: Grant Richards Ltd. [1910]). For the Latin text see Ernest Diehl, *Inscriptiones Latinae Christianae Veteres* (Berlin: Weidmann, 1961), I, 2, with the references.

23

ATHANASIUS OF ALEXANDRIA

Athanasius (*ca.* 295–373) was born in Egypt, probably in Alexandria. Early embracing an ecclesiastical career, he was ordained a deacon by the year 318 and achieved priesthood shortly afterwards, during the period in which Alexander was bishop of Alexandria (313–28). About the year 318, Arius, an ascetic priest of the diocese, was condemned by a local synod for his suspicious teaching with regard to the Trinity. Arius taught that the second person, the Logos or Son, was born from the Father in time and that his divinity was derivative; it was with this Logos that the man Jesus was united at birth. But the union did not make Jesus God, and there was no substantial union between the Logos and the man whom Mary bore.[1] Despite condemnation, Arius persisted in teaching his doctrines, and, under the pressure of the bishops, the emperor Constantine convoked the first general ("ecumenical") Council of the Church at Nicaea in 325. Athanasius accompanied bishop Alexander as private secretary, and although the records of the Council have not been preserved we can glean much information from Eusebius, Socrates, and Theodoret. Arius and his party were con-

---

[1] See the discussion in H. A. Wolfson, *The Philosophy of the Church Fathers* (Cambridge, Mass.: Harvard Univ. Press, 1956), I, 218 f., 306 f., 585–87, 593–94. Wolfson contends that Arius' doctrine of the Logos is dependent upon the teaching of the Jewish first-century writer, Philo of Alexandria. See also J. Quasten, *Patrology* (Westminster, Md.: Newman Press, 1960), III, pp. 6 ff. Arius studied at Antioch under Lucian, whom bishop Alexander once referred to as the father of Arianism; but Lucian's connection with Arius' teaching is still controverted, especially since none of his writings are extant.

demned and the famous Creed of Nicaea was drawn up and signed by the majority of attending bishops: [2]

> We believe in one God, the Father almighty, creator of all things visible and invisible. And in one Lord, Jesus Christ, the Son of God, the only-begotten of the Father and from the Father's substance (*ousia*): God of God, light of light, true God of true God, begotten and not made, consubstantial (*homoousios*) with the Father, and through Him all things in heaven and on earth have been made. For us mortals, for our salvation, He came down, became incarnate, became man, suffered, rose from the dead on the third day, ascended into heaven, and He will come to judge the living and the dead. And in the Holy Spirit.

> And to all those who assert: There was a time when He was not, before He was begotten He was not, He was made out of nothing, or from a different substance (*hypostasis*) or essence (*ousia*), the Son of God is created, changeable, mutable—all such ones the universal Church declares anathema.

Such was the triumph of Nicaea. Athanasius succeeded bishop Alexander at the latter's death in 328, inaugurating one of the stormiest eras in the history of the Church. His struggle against the Meletian heretics within his own jurisdiction, as well as his efforts to win back the various splinter groups of Semi-Arians by a reinterpretation of the Trinitarian formulas, showed Athanasius to be a courageous and diplomatic patriarch. Exiled from his see on five separate occasions, he encouraged the monastic movement within the Egyptian desert and spread the *Life of Antony* throughout the Latin West. Emperor Valens recalled him from his fifth exile in 366, and he was allowed to remain in Alexandria, where he died on May 2, 373.

A small, energetic man—Julian the Apostate called him "this troublesome bit of a man"—he was shrewd, brilliant, but perhaps uncompromising. At heart a monk, he attempted to spread the ascetic ideals of the Egyptian desert (with the *Life of Antony,* the *Life of St. Syncletica,* and the treatise *On Virginity*), coupled with a rigid orthodoxy and unswerving devotion to ecclesiastical superiors. His teaching on the

---

[2] See my article, "Athanasius," *Encyclopedia Britannica* 2 (Chicago: Encyclopedia Britannica, Inc., 1964) 664–67.

Incarnation and Atonement of Jesus derives from Origen, but without Origen's mysticism or subordinationism; he saw the restoration of the divine image in man being accomplished through the gesture of Christ, "the substantial image of the Father"; we partake of the fruit of Christ's work through the mysteries which the Church celebrates, and especially through "the bread and wine, which, though before were ordinary food and drink, become the body and blood of the Lord."

His enormous output can be divided into four classes: (1) the letters, to his flock, as well as to individuals on dogmatic matters; (2) the controversial works written primarily against the Arians, as, for instance, the *History of the Arians*; (3) a considerable exegetical corpus, of which little remains today; and (4) the ascetical writings, such as the *Life of St. Syncletica* (which is included among the authentic pieces, but is not from the saint's hand), the *Life of Antony,* and a treatise *On Virginity,* whose authenticity is debated. There are fragments of other treatises in Coptic, Syriac, and Armenian translations. In addition, there are a number of works in Latin that have been attached, though erroneously, to Athanasius' name; these include, for example, the twelve books *On the Trinity,* which most likely originated in northern Italy or Africa, and the famous *Athanasian Creed,* consisting of forty rhythmic Latin clauses and used as a confession of faith, which probably originated in northern Italy or southern Gaul in the middle or late fifth century. The textual transmission of Athanasius' works has been highly complicated mainly because of the rival editions which were published by the Athanasian party on the one hand and his enemies on the other.[3]

On the Incarnation of the Word[*]

4   In speaking of the coming of the Savior, it is necessary also that we speak of man's origins, that you may under-

[3] Though the edition of J.-P. Migne, vols. 25 to 28, is sadly in need of revision, it is the most available source for the text of many of Athanasius' works. The new critical edition in the Berlin series has been in progress since 1934 under H. G. Opitz, W. Schneemelcher, and others. For the bibliography, see Quasten, *op. cit.,* III, 23 ff.

[*] For the Greek of this beautiful treatise, I have used F. L. Cross, *Athanasius: De Incarnatione: An Edition of the Greek Text* (Texts for Students 50, London: S.P.C.K. House, 1957), which has been taken basically from the Paris manuscript, Coislinianus Graecus 45.

stand that it was our sin that was the cause of his descent, our transgression called forth the loving kindness of the Logos, that He might come to us and manifest himself as Lord among men. We then were the occasion for his incarnation; it was for our salvation that He so showed his love for men as to be born a man and to be revealed in a body.

God made man in immortality and it was his wish that man could remain in this state. But men made little of the knowledge of God and turned away from it, planning and plotting evil for themselves, and (as we said earlier) brought on the threatened condemnation of death and from then on no longer remained as they had been created, but became corrupted as they had planned, and Death reigned as their king. For the sin against God's precept turned them back to their natural state; thus, having come into being out of nonexistence, they logically suffered the disintegration into nonexistence in the course of time. . . .

For God not only created us out of nothing; He also 5 gave us a divine life by the grace of his Word. But mankind turned away from things eternal and, taking the devil's advice, turned to the things of corruption, becoming responsible for their own corruption and death. For by nature they were subject, as I said before, to corruption, but they would have escaped their natural condition by participation in the Word, provided they remained good. Because of the indwelling of the Logos the natural corruption of their natures did not affect them. . . . But after [the Fall] men began to die, and then destruction grew strong in them, and indeed had greater power over all of mankind than it had by nature; for, because men had sinned against the commandment, it was reinforced by the punishment of God. . . .

And so with the greater power of Death, corruption 6 abided among men and the human race was being destroyed. Man, a creature with intelligence and made in God's image, was fading away, and God's work had begun to perish. For Death, as I said, held legal sway over us, and it was impossible to escape this law, for it was being carried out by God because of the transgression. The situation was indeed both unseemly and paradoxical. For it was paradoxical for God to go back upon his word: He had warned that man would die if he sinned; He would be denying his own word if man now did not die after the sin was committed. God would not have been truth-

ful if man did not die after God had said that he would.
And it would have been unseemly if men who had been
created as rational beings and had participated in his
Word should die and should return to nonbeing through
corruption. It would be unworthy of God's benevolence if
what He had created should perish, especially since mankind had been deceived by the Devil. . . . If, then, such
works, God's rational creatures, were to be destroyed, why
should God have made them and found them good?
Should he allow destruction to have power over them
and death to have its sway? What was the good of caus-
ing them to be in the first place? It would surely be better
not to be, rather than after coming into existence to
perish through abandonment. . . .

7   What was God to do in this situation, and what action
must He take? Ought He demand that men repent of
their sins? This, you would say, would be worthy of God;
just as men had gone to destruction by sin, they would
come to immortality by repentance. But no, such repentance would not safeguard God's glory, for He would
still remain inconsistent, if men were still not subject to
death. Nor could repentance recall men from what was
their natural condition; it could merely make them cease
from sin. . . . Surely there was need of nothing else but
the very Word of God to restore man to his primitive
grace, the Word, who had created the universe out of
nothing from the beginning. It was to be his task to
bring back man from corruption to immortality and to
safeguard the infallible glory of the Father. For the Logos
was of the Father and yet above all creatures, and,
hence, He alone would be able to restore all things, to
suffer for all men, and He alone would be worthy to be
men's legate before the Father.

8   This was the reason why the incorporeal, spiritual, and
immortal Word of God comes to our dwelling—though He
was not far from it before. For no part of creation had
been abandoned by Him, seeing that He has filled all
things completely while remaining with his Father. But
He comes down to live with us, because He loves us and
would manifest himself. He saw the human race perishing,
and death holding dominion over them by corruption.
. . . He had pity for our race and sympathy for our infirmity . . . and so took unto himself a body no different from our own. . . . Being himself the mighty
Demiurge of the universe, He prepared a body as his
temple in the body of the Virgin, and appropriated it to

himself as his instrument, that He might live and be known in it . . . .

The Word, then, realizing that mankind's destruction 9 could be ended in no other way save by true death, and, since it was impossible for the Word to die (immortal as He was and the Son of the Father), for this reason took to himself a body that had the possibility of death; again this body, by partaking in the Word, who is above all things, might be able to face death on behalf of all men and remain immortal through the power of the indwelling Word, that henceforth destruction should be banished from mankind by the grace of the resurrection. Thus He offered unto death the body that He had assumed as an offering and a sacrifice free from all blemish, and in this way He forthwith destroyed death for all those who are like Him by offering himself as a substitute. For being above all men in his quality of Word of God, it was reasonable that He should offer the instrument and the temple of his own body as a redemption price for all and thus pay by his death the debt that was owed. Immortal, as the Son of God, He dwelt with all men in virtue of his similarity to them; and thus it was reasonable that He should clothe them all with immortality by a guarantee of bodily resurrection. For the disintegration of death no longer holds sway, because of the indwelling of the Word in them through the one body. When a great king enters into a mighty city and lives in one of its dwellings, the city counts it as an absolutely high honor, and no enemy or brigand ever attacks it because the king has taken one of its houses and so it was worthy of all the more consideration. So it is in the case of the King of the universe.

Excerpts from On Virginity*

Ah, virginity, image of immortality and tree of life!
Virginity . . . face of God immortal!
Virginity, crown of glory and scepter of the kingdom. . . .

---

* A fragment from one of Athanasius' homilies on virginity, as cited among the works of Schenoudi in Coptic; see the edition by L.-Th. Lefort, *S. Athanase: Lettres festales et pastorales en copte* (Scriptores Coptici 19–20, Corpus Scriptorum Christianorum Orientalium, Louvain: Impr. Orientaliste L. Durbecq, 1955), pp. 19, 106–8 (Coptic text), and 20, 85–86 (French version). The litany-like style is typical of many of the passages of Athanasius' writings.

Ah, virginity, you who carry off the victory and dance
with the great kings.
Virginity, valiant gift for Heaven, and secure dowry.
Virginity, O light incomprehensible shining on every man
who loves.
Virginity, close to God but despised by men.
Virginity, unfettered light, life of the immortal one.
Virginity, God's temple and the dwelling of the great
King. . . .
Virginity, fruitful tree, and sweetness without regret.
Virginity, paradise and house of the Pantocrator. . . .
Virginity, firm pedestal supporting the King. . . .
Virginity, glorious in blessedness, because you have
received the holy commandments.

The Life of Antony

The year 270 marks the beginning of the anchoretic movement; about this time the great Antony went into the desert
and drew flocks of pilgrims and ascetics in his train. Antony
is the first great ascetic whom we know by name. St. Jerome, in his largely fictional *Life of Paul the First Hermit*,
attempted to place a man in the desert before Antony, but
his work was suspect even in his lifetime. The *Life of
Antony* bears all the marks of authenticity and was composed
about the year 356 by Athanasius, bishop of Alexandria
(328–73), or by a member of the bishop's circle and under
his direction.

Antonios, as he was called, came from a well-to-do Coptic
family and was born about 250 in Middle Egypt in a little
town not far from the banks of the Nile. The historian
Sozomen calls the town Coma, but this is perhaps a vague
reference to one of the many hamlets called Kom, not far
from Aphroditopolis (Atfih; mod. Kom. Ishqaw). When his
parents died, he placed his sister in the keeping of some
pious women, distributed his goods to the poor, and began a
life of asceticism outside of his native village, living occasionally in the cavernlike tombs in the area. Some fifteen
years later he moved to the so-called Outer Mountain at
Pispir on the east bank of the Nile, about fifty miles south
of Memphis. Here he lived in a deserted fortress. The period
at Pispir, the *Life* indicates, lasted about twenty years and
during this time monks began to surround the great master of
the spiritual life. He is said to have led a delegation of

monks to Alexandria during the persecution of Maximinus Daia. At length, he departed from Pispir and headed across the desert towards the Red Sea. He finally settled at the foot of Mt. Colzim, about seventy-five miles east of the Nile River, where the foundation of the building still exists today, despite the ravages of time and the Moslem invaders of the fifteenth century. The monastery, called Dêr Mar Antonios, houses ikons that go back to the tenth century and is the oldest religious convent in Egypt; today, the cavern where Antony prayed is still pointed out to the passing pilgrim. By the time of his death, in 356, at the age of one hundred and five, monasticism had become an established phenomenon throughout the Christian world.

The Anthanasian *Life,* however, is more than mere biography. It is a eulogy of the entire Egyptian anchoretic movement—with which Athanasius was in deep sympathy —and a plea for a return to the primitive ideals of the gospel, together with a militant reaction against paganism and Arianism. Translated into Latin in the third quarter of the fourth century, it presented to the West the romantic archetype of Egyptian monachism: the ascetic who died by a daily martyrdom, confuted the heretics, and routed the malign demons of the desert. This blueprint for future centuries was supported and abetted by volumes of legendary tales and ascetical collections of sayings.

The heart of the *Life* consists of Chapter 16 to 43, wherein Antony instructs his disciples on the importance of the ascetical struggle within and without. The section represents —apart from random remarks in the writings of Clement of Alexandria and Origen—the first ascetical treatise in the history of the Church and shows the direction which Anthanasius' reform movement was taking before his death. The attack upon the Arians in Chapters 69 and 70 further reflects the atmosphere out of which the work grew.[4]

Within a decade after the Greek text was published there were two Latin versions, a polished paraphrase by Jerome's friend, Evagrius of Antioch, and a more literal, older anonymous version published earlier. This old Latin version, which

4 For a discussion and bibliography, see J. Quasten, *op. cit.,* pp. 39–45. On Athanasius, see also H. Nordberg, *Athanasius and the Emperor* (Commentationes Humaniorum litterarum, 30.3, Helsinki: S.P.C.K. House, 1963), with bibliography on pp. 67–69.

5 Codex A2 of the Chapter Library of St. Peter's, Rome, now in the Vatican Library; it dates from the tenth or eleventh century. For bibliography and discussion, see H. Hoppenbrouwers, *La plus ancienne version latine de la Vie de S. Antoine par S. Anthanase* (Nijmegen: Dekker & Van de Vogt, 1960).

reflects a tradition much earlier than our extant Greek manuscripts, was discovered by A. Wilmart and first published by G. Garitte in 1939.[5] I have chosen this Latin version as the basis of my translation of the *Life* in the following passages.

The Life of Antony*

Prologue

You have begun an excellent rivalry with the monks in Egypt in a desire to equal or even if possible surpass them in the practice of your virtues. For you, too, have your monks, and the name is common among you. Hence, one may justly praise your good resolution, and God will reward your prayers. But you have also decided to ask of me, wishing to become familiar with the life of Antony of blessed memory, how he began to practice his devotion to God, what he was like before he undertook this asceticism, and what was the nature of his death, and whether everything that is said about him was true. Your motive was, that inspired by his zeal, you might imitate his example. And so I have acceded to your request with great promptness and willingness; for there is a great advantage for me merely to recall the memory of Antony. And I feel that when you have heard the story you will be able to admire the man and to emulate his resolve. His is an ideal example for monks in the pursuit of asceticism. . . .

1   Antony was an Egyptian by birth, born of well-to-do parents whom the Greeks would call noble. His parents possessed as much property as they needed and, being Christian, had their son educated as a Christian. So long as he was a child he was taken care of by his parents, and he knew no one but them and their household. When he grew up and became mature, he would not study literature, as he did not wish to consort with other children. His one desire was to lead a simple life at home, just as the Scriptures speak of Jacob. He did, however, attend the liturgy with his parents; as a child he was not distracted, as a young man he did not make light of it.

* A. Wilmart (Paris: G. Garitte, 1939).

But, ever obedient to his parents and attentive to the divine readings, he derived great fruit from them. Nor did he, as boys often do, annoy his parents to give him richer food than they themselves had, nor had he cravings for special dishes. He was content with what was set before him and asked for nothing more. . . .

[Antony settles his property, places his sister with some consecrated virgins, and joins a group of ascetics who live outside of his native town. He gets the name of "the friend of God" (2–4). But the Evil One sets out to tempt him—in a passage which would become the source of many similar phenomena in the lives of later saints.]

The Devil, however, who is wont to hate what is good, 5 was envious and could not endure seeing such good resolves in this youth; hence, he made bold to do against Antony what he usually does. First of all, he tried to make him give up the life he led, recalling to him his property, the care of his sister, the love of home and family. He also tempted him with the desire for money, fame, the pleasures of eating, and many of the other vanities of this life. Finally, he put into his mind the difficulty of a life of virtue, all the labor it requires, and made him consider his weakness of body and the length of time involved. . . . He would put filthy thoughts in his mind, and Antony would reject them by prayer. He would then try to tempt his will to lust; but Antony with a sense of shame, as it were, would put a fortress around his body by means of faith and fasting.

The vicious Devil even dared to transform himself into a woman at night and act like one in every way so as to seduce Antony. But he thought of Christ, and bearing in mind the nobility of soul that we have because of Him, and its spirituality, he put out the fires of that passion and temptation. . . .

[The Devil now appears to Antony as a slave, speaking in a cringing, whining tone.]

"I've seduced a lot of men, very many have I over- 6 thrown, and I've done a good deal of other things. But now, attacking you and your ascetical works, as I have others, I've been shown to be weak."

"Who are you," Antony asked, "to talk to me this way?"

The other quickly replied in a whining voice, "I like

fornication. My job is to attack young men. I'm called the spirit of fornication. You would be surprised how many I've seduced who wanted to be chaste! I've persuaded them, tempting them with all sorts of tricks. It is on my account that the Prophet, reproaching the fallen, says: You were deceived by the spirit of fornication [Osee 4.12]. It was through me that they were tripped up. It is I who gave you trouble so often and was conquered by you so many times."

[The Devil flees, but Antony determines to avoid temptation by bringing his body into subjection.]

7   He watched at night with such fervor that very often he would pass the entire night without sleep, and this not once only but many times, to the admiration of all. Then he would eat only once a day after sunset, and sometimes he did not taste food for two or frequently for four days. His food was bread and salt; he drank only water. I need hardly discuss wine or meat, for this was not the practice even with others who were inferior to him in virtue. He slept only on the ground; and he refused to anoint himself with oil, saying, "It is better that young men practice asceticism in real earnest and not seek things which relax the body; they should rather accustom it to work, bearing in mind the Apostle's saying, When I am weak then am I strong [2 Cor. 12.10]."

In those days Antony used to say that the power of the mind is strong when the body's drives are weak; and he also held this remarkable conviction: the way of virtue, he thought, should not be measured by the amount of time passed, nor by the fact that he had withdrawn from the world; but he used to say that the proof of deifying virtue lay in a good will and desire. . . .

[At night the Evil One comes with "a great multitude of demons" and so beats the monk that he lies speechless on the ground. Another night the Devil sends in shapes of lions, bears, leopards, serpents, and other animals. Despite pain and anguish, Antony is still unmoved, and the Devil and his hordes leave in defeat (8–9). Afterwards, a beam of light comes through his roof, and he feels well again.]

10   And he asked the vision which appeared to him,

"Where were you? Why weren't you here at the beginning to stop my pain?"

And a voice came to him saying, "Antony, I was here, but I waited to see your struggle; and because you held fast and were not conquered, I shall be your assistance forever, and I shall make your name known everywhere."

Hearing this, he got up and prayed, and he was so comforted that he felt he had more strength in his body than he had had before. And he was about thirty-five years old.

[On the other side of the Nile, Antony found a deserted fort which had been abandoned and was now infested with reptiles. The reptiles left, Antony laid in a six-months' supply of bread, and then, blocking up the entrance, retired within. This was at the so-called Outer Mountain near Pispir, east of Atfih, but its exact site has not been located. But on occasion the great ascetic would emerge and visit his fellow monks, in order to instruct them. One such talk, which he gave in Coptic (16–43), could be entitled "Against the Demons." The following is an excerpt from it.]

"Hence we ought not inquire, labor, or make an effort 34 to have knowledge of the future, but simply to please the Lord. And let us make a prayer to the Lord, not that He should give us this knowledge, not that we wish a reward for the labor of our asceticism, but simply that He should be our collaborator against the Devil. . . .

"Hence, when they come to you at nighttime and wish to tell you future things, or say, 'We are angels,' do not pay attention to them, for they are lying. And if they praise your asceticism and call you blessed, do not answer them or pay attention to them. Instead, make the sign over yourselves and your dwelling and pray, and you will see they will not appear, for they are afraid, very afraid. They are afraid of the sign of the Lord's cross, because by it the Savior stripped and defeated them. And if they stand before you impertinently, either dancing or making any other appearances, do not tremble or give way, nor pay them any attention as though they were good. With God's help it is possible to understand the difference between the presence of good or evil spirits. When they are holy spirits, there is no disturbance about their coming or their appearance. For it is written that he shall not contend nor cry out, neither shall any man hear his voice [Matt. 12.19]. But the coming of such spirits is with calm and quiet, such that there is an immediate feeling of joy, hope, and exultation in the soul. For with them is the Lord who is our joy, and the Son who is the power of the Father. And the thoughts begin without disturbance and continue unruffled. . . .

36   "On the other hand, the attack of the evil spirits and their appearance is disturbed by confused sounds, shouts and tumult, like the movements of robbers or the games of undisciplined children. Thus, there immediately occur terror of mind, disturbance, confused thoughts, sadness, hatred for those who are engaged in asceticism, dryness, memories of one's kin, fear of death; from there we have a desire for sin, weakness with regard to virtue, and instability of good habits. And so if you have a vision and are afraid of something, if then the fear is removed and in its place you find an ineffable joy, if there is lightness of heart with hope, recovery of strength, orderly thoughts and all the other things I mentioned, and courage and love of God—then have faith and pray. For the soul's state of peace and joy reflects the sanctity of Him who is present. . . .

[Antony left the mountain to go to Alexandria during the persecution of Maximinus Daia and apparently courted martyrdom, but the authorities would have nothing to do with the monks. Antony stayed and ministered to those who were condemned (46) and when the crisis passed, he went back to his monastic fortress. But the concept of martyrdom left a lasting impression on him, associated as it was with the daily life of the ascetic. Thus the new concept was that the ascetic's self-discipline and persecution of the passions forms a kind of martyrdom for all those who wish to be perfect.]

47   The persecution was over at last. Bishop Peter of blessed memory had pronounced his confession of faith. And so he returned to his solitary dwelling, and there he daily practiced the martyrdom of his conscience, fighting the battles of the faith. He practiced an even more rigorous asceticism, for he fasted all the time, he wore clothing that had hair on the inside and skin on the outside, and observed this regime to his last day. He never washed himself, not even his feet, nor did he ever touch them to water without need. And no one ever saw Antony without clothes, except when they buried him after death.

[Desiring still more solitude, Antony then sets out for a new place to live. And after three days' journey with some Arab bedouins, he comes to a very high mountain, and at its base there are date palms and a spring of crystal-clear water. The chronicler tells us that it was almost by divine inspiration and that Antony "loved the place" (50). Here he lives on the offerings of pious people; he also tills a garden for vegetables and makes his own bread. Here many animals come, but, warned by the saint, they leave, never to trouble him again. There are more visitations from demons, and the importunities of monks that he visit them and give them spiritual comfort. There are pilgrims who come to be healed of loathsome diseases (56–64). He is favored with visions of divine things, with spiritual messages, and locutions (65–66); he honors all clerics, bishops, priests, and deacons above himself (67); he avoids the Meletian heretics and the Manichees (68); he confutes the Arians (68–70); he is kindly to pagans as well as Christians (70–71), and the author—presumably Athanasius—mentioned a miracle he performs on leaving Alexandria for his monastery on the Red Sea. He disputes learnedly, through an interpreter, with Greek pagan philosophers (72–80). The emperor Constantine and his sons write to Antony, and the good monk writes back, urging them to practice Christian virtue (81). A few more stories are told (82–88), and the author gave an account of his passing (89–93).]

It is right for me to tell you how the close of his 89 life took place, since you so desire to hear. For in this, too, he was worthy of emulation. He was visiting some monks, as was his custom, who lived here on the mountain near the Nile. He had known about his passing from God, and he spoke to his brothers as follows, "This is my last visit to you. I should be surprised if we saw each other again in this life; for it is now the time for me to die."

They, however, began to weep when they heard this, and, clinging to him, kissed him. And he said, "I am about one hundred and five years old."

But he kept talking to them joyfully and confidently, as though he were going home from a foreign city. He told them not to grow slack in their labors or torpid in their divine asceticism, but practice the diligence of the saints, to live as though they were daily dying, as I have said before. "And don't go near the Meletians, for they're schismatics and you know their wickedness and unholy malice. And have nothing to do with the Arians, for their impiety is clear to everyone. . . .

90 The brethren were urging him to stay and end his life there, but he would not give in for many reasons that he indicated without saying anything, but especially because of something the Egyptians do. For they have the custom of carefully wrapping with linens the bodies of the dead and of all the dear martyrs who have died holy in the Lord; but they do not bury them in the earth, but rather keep them in their homes on couches. In such wise they think they do honor to the dead or to those who have been martyred. . . .

91 He knew this and was afraid they would do the same thing to his body; and so, forcing himself to say good-bye to the monks, he proceeded to the Inner Mountain, where he was used to laboring for the Lord. And some months later, he fell ill and called those who were with him—there were only two who had remained, practicing piety according to the Lord for fifteen years there and ministering to Antony because of his advanced years.

Antony said to them, "As the Scripture says, I am going the way of my fathers; for I see that I am being called by the Lord. And so be heedful and do not lose the long asceticism which you have lived for the Lord, but straightway endeavor to keep your will ready just as though you were just beginning. You know the demons that lie in ambush: you have seen how violent they are and yet how powerless. So do not be afraid of them, but always breathe Christ, believe in Him, and live as though dying daily, taking heed of yourselves, and remember how much I have counseled you. . . .

"So bury my body and hide it below the earth, and abide by my word, so that no one will know where my body is or where it has been laid except you alone. For I shall receive it back incorrupt from the Savior in the resurrection of the dead. But divide my garments and give to bishop Athanasius the one sheepskin and blanket on which I used to sleep. It was he who gave it to me and I have worn it by my use. Give the other sheepskin to bishop Serapion. You may keep the hairshirt. And so good-bye now, my children. For Antony is on his way and will be no longer with you."

92 He finished, and they kissed him, and he drew up his feet. Then as though he were gazing on friends who had come to see him, and joyful because of them with a smile on his face, he passed away and was gathered to his

fathers. And afterwards, following the orders he had given them, they wrapped his body and buried it in the earth, and no one knows where it is hidden except they alone. . . .

24

CHRISTIAN EPITAPHS

The Abercius Inscription

One of the most fascinating early Christian epitaphs is the one composed by a certain Abercius (or Avircius), bishop of Hieropolis in Phrygia, which he composed for his own tomb in the latter part of the second century, in the seventy-second year of his life. The content of the inscription had long been known from a late life of Abercius attributed to Metaphrastes, but some doubt had been cast on its authenticity. In 1882 Sir W. M. Ramsay, on an expedition in Phrygia, discovered an inscription that seemed to be an imitation of the one given in the *Life of Abercius*; and, finally, in the following year he discovered in the area of Sinnada, in Phrygia, a fragment of the original Abercius inscription inserted into the wall of an ancient bath. Written in highly symbolic language, the epitaph relates how Abercius had in the course of his travels to Rome and Nisibis (mod. Nusaybin) in Syria found the same Christian belief everywhere. There are references to the chaste Shepherd (Christ), and the unsullied virgin (the Church or the Virgin), and the Eucharist under the figure of the Fish. Subsequently, the ruling sultan of Turkey, Abdul Hamit II (1876–1909), graciously gave the fragmentary inscription to Pope Leo XIII, and it now reposes in the Lateran Museum in Rome. The days are long past when scholars suggested that the epitaph, written in twenty-two Greek hexameters, was not Christian, and the work of Cumont, Dölger, Abel, and others has established its authenticity beyond any doubt.

The Abercius Inscription*

Side A [now lost; supplied from the *Life of Abercius*]:

Citizen of a famous city, I erected this
In my lifetime, that I might have one day
A resting-place for my body. My name is Abercius,
And I am a disciple of the chaste Shepherd
Who feeds the flocks of his sheep upon the
     mountains
And in the plains, and has great eyes that see
Everywhere.[1] He taught me the faithful
     writings. . . .[2]

Side B [from the stone in the Lateran Museum, with words supplied from the *Life*]:

He it was who sent me to Rome to contemplate
Its majesty, to see the Queen adorned
In golden raiment, and with sandals of gold.
There I saw a people who wore a shining
Seal.[3] I also saw the Syrian plain
And all the cities, and Nisibis, [4] crossing
The Euphrates. And everywhere I found
My colleagues. Having Paul [5] for my companion,
The faith led me everywhere; everywhere
It offered me as food a Fish from the spring,
Large and pure, caught by an immaculate Virgin.[6]
And she gives it constantly to her own dear ones
To eat; she also has an excellent wine
To drink, which she offers with the bread.

Side C [now lost; supplied from the *Life*]:

I, Abercius, dictated all of this
In person at the age of seventy-two.
Let any brother who understands these lines
Pray for Abercius. Let no man place
Another tomb above this one. If he does,
He shall pay the Roman treasury two thousand
     pieces
And a thousand for my beloved Hieropolis.[7]

* See O. Marucchi, *Guida del museo Lateranense profano e cristiano* (Rome: Vatican Press, 1922), pp. 171–74, and his *Christian Epigraphy* (tr. by J. A. Willis, London: Cambridge University Press, 1912), pp. 126–35, with a plate (viii.1), which shows the only face (the second) still extant of an original three-sided marking stone. For the recent literature, see J. Quasten, *Initiation aux Pères de l'Eglise* (tr. by J. Laporte, Paris: Newman Press, 1955), pp. 193–96. It is very likely that Abercius is the same person as Avircius Marcellus, mentioned by Eusebius (*Eccles. Hist.* 5.16.3).

NOTES

1. A reference to early portraits of Christ.

2. A few words are lost here.

3. The imagery is ambiguous, referring partly (it would seem) to the majesty of Christian Rome and partly to Christians there who bear the "seal" of baptism.

4. Nisibis, a major city under the Seleucids, and later an important Christian center of Mesopotamia. Since A.D. 363 it was under the domination of the Persians, after which it became a source of Syrian Nestorianism. Indeed, the famous abbess Egeria, in her pilgrimage to the ancient Christian sites about the year 400, was prevented from entering this area because of the presence of the Persians.

5. The text seems corrupt here, but the reference would appear to be to St. Paul the apostle, that is, to the faith reflected in his epistles.

6. The imagery seems to refer both to Mother Church and to Christ's own mother, the Virgin. The intermingling of the two figures is common in the literature of the early Church (cf. Rev. 12.1 ff.). The reference to Christ as the great Fish, given as food under the form of bread and wine, seems clear.

7. Hieropolis, not to be confused with the more famous Hierapolis, was apparently situated near the modern Turkish village of Suhut; at any rate, it was in this area that the tombstone was found.

The Epitaph of Pectorius

This mysterious epitaph was found in seven marble fragments in an ancient Christian cemetery not far from the village of Autun, France, in 1839 and was first published by Cardinal J. P. Pitra. The style of the letters has caused scholars to date the inscription as late as the fifth or even the sixth century A.D.; but the content of the epitaph indicates that it must be a copy (or an imitation) of a second-century original, for it is reminiscent both of the doctrine of Irenaeus and of the well-known epitaph of Abercius. The eleven lines are divided into two parts. Lines 1 to 6 are in Greek elegiac verse, and the first five lines form an acrostic in Greek of the word Fish; these lines urge all Christians, the race of the heavenly Fish, washed in the fountain of divine water, to partake of the Savior's sweet food. Part 2, lines 7 to 11, are in hexameters and seem to be added on; here Pectorius, son of Aschandius, prays that his departed parents may remember him in Heaven, but the text of these last lines is doubtful and controverted.

The Epitaph of Pectorius*

O race divine of the celestial Fish,
Guard your heart pure among men, for you have received
An immortal source of wondrous water. And so,
My friend, warm your soul in the everlasting waters
Of copious Wisdom. Take the honey-sweet food
That the Savior give his holy ones. Sate
Your hunger, holding the Fish in your hands.[1]

Lord and Savior, feed us then, I beg, [2]
With this Fish. We beg you, Light of the deceased,
May my mother sleep in peace. O father, Aschandius, [3]
Beloved of my heart, together with my [sweet mother]
And my brethren, do you remember
Pectorius [sleeping in the peace of the Fish].

A Christian Curse-Inscription from Tanagra*

Discovered in 1936 by Dr. N. Paton of Heraklion, in Crete, this curious burial stone has been placed at about A.D. 400, but it seems to embody ideas from an early period both pagan and Christian. The stone was found in the

* See Quasten, *op. cit.*, pp. 196–97; for a plate, see F. van der Meer and C. Mohrmann, *Atlas of the Early Christian World* (London: Thomas Nelson & Sons, 1959), 55, p. 43. For the town of Autun, see their index, *s.v.* Augustodunum, p. 187.

[1] Referring to the ancient manner of receiving the Eucharist in the palm of the hand. The words recall the doctrine of Irenaeus of Lyons, especially as expressed in *Against Heresies* (4.18.5).

[2] The text is corrupt here and the reading somewhat conjectural.

[3] The name suggests Syrian ancestry; there were Syrian Christian colonies in the area of Lyons and Vienne in Gaul. The name Pectorius may perhaps be equivalent to Victorius (Victor).

* For a discussion and full bibliography, see my article "A Christian Sepulchral Stele from Tanagra," *Theological Studies* 11 (1950), pp. 567–69.

wall of a medieval tower at Tanagra and is now in the
Tanagra Museum. Philomenes, or whatever the author's
name was, leaves directions in forty Homeric hexameter lines
for the care of a shrine on his property and also of the
graves of members of his family.

[Philo] menes orders these instructions fulfilled
By mortals yet to come. If any man
Not of our race, from a far-off land, is made
Lord of this place, he should perform the rites
That are proper, first by singing a hymn to God
The mighty, next by bringing to the precinct
Sacred to the Trinity that rules all things
Gifts pleasing unto Christ our God on the sixth
Day, on behalf of brothers, sisters, parents,
Children, husbands, wives, and in-laws of old
Deceased, twelve round loaves and goodly wine,
Like the rays of the sun or flakes of snow.
One must accomplish this with readiness
And perform the ritual pleasing to the dead.
Look after all these graves of the departed
Lest the whitened bones of those beneath,
Of those who have passed away, come to harm
By reason of the torrent of winter's rain.
Have respect for them, and with your eye
Upon the woe to come, protect their homes
Secure, unharmed. Grant them the favor of a light
At night, for this is the merit of the dead.
And, drawing from your present means, donate
Enough to the poor, for this too is their due.
Watch and guard the tall-leaved trees, lest time
By its attrition bring the edifice
To ruin with the revolving years, by reason
Of the dour frosts and sickly gales the while
The raindrops fall stealthily upon the house.
Holily perform these duties: pass
Your life in piety, for to the wise
And well-disposed man comes many a blessing
After toil, and his fame shall be forever.

But if now or in future a lord of the land
Full of idle speech should go astray
In purpose through his overweening pride
Or in his folly try to circumvent
Our orders, then may his life be never secure,
May he reap woe on woe. Worn in spirit

By sorrow and death-dealing battles, he
Shall be taken into slavery by brutal force.
And besides the many evils God has fashioned
For man by fate, may he never go beneath
The earth who does not heed the rights of the dead.
May he beg on both sides of the grave, though eager
To fill himself with food and drink. May dogs
Tear him utterly, flesh and bone, and so
May he meet his cruel destruction. And after
Suffering an ignoble death, may he
Pay the final bitter penalty,
He and his family, before the eternal King.

SELECTED BIBLIOGRAPHY

For the English reader who would wish to go on in the study of the Fathers of the early Church, there are the "Translations of Christian Literature" (London: S.P.C.K.); "Ancient Christian Writers," edited by J. Quasten, J. C. Plumpe, and W. Burghardt (Westminster, Md.: Newman Press); "The Fathers of the Church" series, published in New York (now Catholic University Press), and the "Library of Christian Classics," published by the Westminster Press, Philadelphia. For a more precise guide to the individual Fathers, one should consult:

B. Altaner, *Patrology* (tr. by Hilda C. Graef, New York: Herder and Co., 1960)

F. L. Cross, *The Early Christian Fathers* ("Student Christian Movement" [London: Gerald Duckworth & Co., Ltd., 1960])

J. Quasten, *Patrology* (4 vols.; Westminster, Md.: Newman Press, 1950 ff.)

E. J. Goodspeed, *A History of Early Christian Literature* (Chicago: University of Chicago Press, 1942)

H. Bettenson, *The Early Christian Fathers* (London: Oxford Univ. Press, 1956).

For an introduction to some of the more complicated problems relating to the early Fathers, see:

H. von Campenhausen, *The Fathers of the Greek Church* (tr. by Stanley Godman, New York: Pantheon Books, Inc., 1959); and *Men Who Shaped the Western Church* (tr. by M. Hoffman, New York: Harper and Row, 1964).

Virginia Corwin, *St. Ignatius and Christianity in Antioch* (New Haven, Conn.: Yale University Press, 1960)

Robert M. Grant (ed.), *Gnosticism* (New York: Harper & Row, Publishers, 1961)

R. P. C. Hanson, *Origen's Doctrine of Tradition* (London; S.P.C.K., 1954)

R. A. Norris, *Manhood and Christ* (Oxford: Clarendon Press, 1963)

E. F. Osborn, *The Philosophy of Clement of Alexandria* (London: Cambridge University Press, 1957)

H. A. Wolfson, *The Philosophy of the Church Fathers* (Cambridge: Harvard Univ. Press, 1956), I.

This is only a small selection of the books that are available on this early period; others will be found in the bibliographies supplied by Altaner, Cross, Quasten, Goodspeed, and Bettenson.

INDEX

Abercius, 261

Acts of the Apostles, 11

Aeons, 23

African Church, 150-172
  Acts of the Scillitan Martyrs, 150-152
  Tertullian, 152-161
  theology of, 41-43

Africanus, Sextus Julius, 25

Ambrose of Milan, 24

Antoninus, Marcus Aurelius, 20, 117, 142

Antony, asceticism of, 25, 28-29, 250-259

Apocalypse, 17

Apollonius, 154

Apologists, 22, 117-141

Apostolic Fathers, 22

Apostolic kerygma, 12-18

Arianism, 251

Aristides, 117

Aristo of Pella, 117

Aristotle, 229

Arius, 24

Arnobius, 43-44, 229-234
  Against the Pagans, 173-174, 229-233

Asceticism, 27-28, 245, 250-259

Athanasius of Alexandria, 40-41, 45, 244-259
  achievements, 245-246
  The Life of Antony, 25, 28-29, 250-259
  On the Incarnation of the Word, 246-249

Athenagoras, 22, 117-118

Bardaisan, 23

Barnabas, Epistle of, 63-66

Basilides, 23, 118-119

Beatty, Chester, 142

Bévenot, M., 222

Bibliography, 266-267

Bithynia, province of, 103-104, 234

Bonner, Campbell, 142

Bryennios, Philotheos, 57

Bultmann, Rudolf, 15

Burkitt, F. C., 125

Caecilius Natalis, 176-178

Carrington, Philip, 21

Catacombs, 111-116
  arts of, 112
  inscriptions, 111-116

Celsus, 117

Cerinthus, 118

Chalcedon, Council of, 153

Christians, persecution of, 20

Christology, Athanasius, 40-41
  nature of Jesus, 39-40

Church, 24-26
  further developments, 24-26
  and Hellenism, 29-31
  Roman opposition, 19-21
  spread of Christianity, 18
  worship and practice, 16-17

Cicero, 229, 235

Clemens, Titus Flavius, 21, 50, 188

Clement of Alexandria, 63, 188-194, 251
  Exhortation to the Pagans, 191
  Hymn to the Savior, 189-190
  Paedagogus, 24, 189-193
  Tapestries (Stromateis), 191-192
  Who Is the Rich Man Who Is Saved? 192-193

Clement of Rome, 22, 49-56
    First Epistle, 50-56
    Second Epistle, 67-71
Constantine, Emperor, 43-47, 235, 241-243
    Arch of Constantine, 243
    triumph of, 243
Coptic manuscripts, 23-24, 119-120
Coptic Museum, Cairo, 119-120
Council of Jerusalem, 14
Cross, F. L., 143
Cyprian of Carthage, 27, 200-228
    and the Decian Persecution, 225-228
    martyrdom of, 25, 226-228
    On the Unity of the Church, 221-225

Dead Sea Scrolls, 13, 119, 125
Decius, Roman Emperor, 20, 195
    persecution of, 173, 225-228
de Jerphanion, Père G., S.J., 115
Demetrius, Bishop, 194
De Rossi, John Baptist, 113
Dessau, H., 173
Dibelius, Martin, 15
Didache, 57-62
Diocletian, 229
Diognetus, epistle or apologia to, 146-149
Dionysius, Bishop of Corinth, 20, 27
Domitilla, 21

Ebionite sect, 120
Ephesians, epistles to, 74
Ephraem of Nisibis, 24
Epistle of Barnabas, 63-66
Epistles, 16
Epitaphs, Christian, 260-265
Eschatology, primitive Christian, 31-32
Essenism, 13, 27, 119
Estienne, Henri, 146
Eusebius, 20, 25-26, 80, 142, 212

Ecclesiastical History, 25, 194
    on Origen, 27, 195-196

Fronto, Marcus Cornelius, 117

Galen, 20, 27
Galerium, emperor, 241
Garitte, G., 252
Gibbon, Edward, 22, 25
Gnostic codices, 23
Gnosticism, 23-24
    apologists, 117-141
    "Light Serene," 131-132
    Odes of Solomon, 125-129
    origins, 119
Gospel of the Egyptians, 67
Gospel of Thomas, 120-122
Gospel of the Truth, 23, 119, 129-131
Gospels, 12-18
    analytic approach, 16
    form-critical approach, 15
    literary forms, 15-16
    Synoptic, 12
Graffito, Palatine, 102-103
Gregory of Tours, 136, 235
Grenfell, B. P., 120
Grosser, F., 114

Harnack, A. von, 29, 67
Harris, James R., 67, 125
Hartel, W., 221
Hellenism and the Church, 29-31
Heracleon, 118
Heraclides, Bishop, 195, 205-210
Hermas, 20, 88-101
    The Shepherd, 22, 90-101
Hippolytus of Rome, 23-24, 183-187
    Apostolic Tradition, 183-187
History, religious, 25, 34-36
Homer, 229
Hunt, Arthur S., 120
Hymn of the Naassenes, A, 12
Hymns and songs, 23-24

Ianuarius, Octavius, 173
Ignatius of Antioch, 22, 72-87, 120

to Bishop Polycarp, 77-78
to the Ephesians, 74
epistles, 72-74
Martyrdom of Bishop Polycarp, 80-87
to the Romans, 75-76
to the Smyrnaeans, 76-77
to the Trallians, 75
Inscriptions, 111-116
Abercius, 260-262
magic squares, 114-116
Pectorius, 262-263
Roman catacombs, 111-116
Iranaeus of Lyons, 20, 23, 118, 120, 136-141, 154, 183
Against Heresies, 137-141

Jesus, nature of, 39-40
John, *The Secret Book of John*, 122-125
Jung Foundation, 119, 129
Justin the Martyr, 20, 22, 117, 183

Kahle, P., 143
Kenyon, F. G., 142

Lactantius, 44, 234-242
Divine Institutes, 235-241
On the Deaths of the Persecutors, 241-242
Lateran Museum, Rome, 113, 183, 260
"Light Serene," 24, 131-132
Lightfoot, J. B., 67
Liturgy, early, 24, 32-33
Lives of saints, 25
Lucian of Samosata, 107-110
story of Peregrinus, 109-110

Magic squares, 114-116
Malinine, M., 129
Manichaeism, 23
Marchi, Fr. Giuseppe, 113
Marcion of Sinope, 20, 23, 80, 120
Marcus Aurelius, 20, 117, 142
Martyrs, Christian, 21-22
acts of, 25
The Acts of the Scillitan Martyrs, 150-152

Cyprian and Decian persecution, 225-228
Passion of Saints Perpetua and Felicitas, 161-172
Maxentius, defeat of, 243
Meletian heretics, 245
Methodius of Olympus, 23, 63, 137, 143, 183, 212-219
Symposium on Chastity, 24, 212-219
Militiades, 117
Milito, Bishop of Sardis, 118, 142-145
On the Pasch, 142-145
Minucius Felix, 173-182
Octavius, 174-182
Monachism, 251
Monasticism, 13, 26-29
St. Antony of Egypt, 28-29, 250-259
Montanist controversy, 25, 120, 136, 152-154, 161
Montanus, 152
Muratorian Canon, 88

Nag Hammadi Gnostic manuscripts, 23, 119, 121, 123, 129
Nautin, P., 143
Neoplatonists, 118
Nero, Emperor, 20, 102-103
Nicaea, Council of, 45, 244-245
Nicomedia, 234
Novatianist schism, 222
Novatus, 220

Octavius (Minucius Felix), 174-182
Odes of Solomon, The, 125-129
Ophite sect, 118
Origen of Alexandria, 27, 63, 183, 189, 194-210, 251
achievements, 195-198
Against Celsus, 201
Commentaries on the Song of Songs, 204-205
Discussion with Heraclides and His Fellow Bishops, 205-210
First Principles, 199-203
Homilies on Leviticus, 202

insight of, 38-39
On Man's Free Will, 199
On Prayer, 200
Oxyrhynchus papyrus, 24

Pagans, 102-112
  end of paganism, 243
  Lucian of Samosata, 107-110
  Pliny's letter, 105-107
Paradosis, 29-30
Passion of Saints Perpetua and Felicitas, 161-172
Paton, Dr. N., 263
Peace of the Church, 43-47, 212
Peregrinus, 109-110
Philo of Alexandria, 15
Phrygia, 154
Pitra, J. P., 262
Plato, 188, 229
Pliny the Younger, 103-107
  on Christians at Bithynia, 103-104
  letter to Trajan, 105-107
Plotinus, 212
Polycarp, Bishop, 20, 77-78, 136
  Martyrdom of, 25, 80-87
  to the Philippians, 78-79
Pope Anicetus, 80
Pope Callistus, 183
Pope Clement, 67
Pope Cornelius, 220
Pope Leo XIII, 260
Pope Pius IX, 113
Pope Stephen, 220-222
Pope Victor, 142
Porphyry, 212
Ptolemy, 118, 120
Puech, H.-C., 129

Quadratus the Asiatic, 117
Quispel, G., 129
Qumram, Essenian community, 13

Ramsay, Sir W. M., 260
Rome, catacombs, 111-116
  opposition to Church, 19-21

Sabaeus, Faustus, 173

St. Ambrose, 184
St. Antony, 28-29, 250-259
St. Cyprian of Carthage, 220-228
St. Ignatius, 154
St. Jerome, 173, 212, 220, 234
  Life of Paul the Hermit, 25
St. Justin, 132-135
St. Paul, 11
Saturninus of Antioch, 118, 120
Schisms, 44-45, 49
Secret Book of John, The, 122-125
Septimus Severus, Emperor, 188, 194
Shepherd, The (Hermas), 88-101
Simon the Magician, 118
Sophocles, 229
Stoicism, 188
Streeter, B. H., 67

Tacitus, 103
Tanagra, 263-265
Tarphon, Rabbi, 132
Tatian, a Syrian, 22, 117, 120
Tertullian, 43, 152-161
  Against Praxeas, 157-158
  Apologia for Christianity, 159-161
  On Flight in Time of Persecution, 155-157
  On the Prayer, 158
Thaumaturgus, Gregory, 195, 198
Theophilus of Antioch, 118
Till, Walter C., 123
Trajan, Emperor, 104, 105-107
Trinitarian theology, 37-38
Trypho, 134
Two Ways, doctrine of, 63

Valens, Emperor, 245
Valentinus, Gnostic, 20, 23, 118-119, 120
Varro, Latin writer, 229, 235

Whittaker, M., 89, 98
Wilmart, A., 252